THE BEST GUIDE
TO BUSINESS
SHAREWARE

The Best Guide to Business Shareware

**Judy Heim, John Heim,
and Mike Callahan**

Osborne **McGraw-Hill**

Berkeley New York St. Louis San Francisco
Auckland Bogotá Hamburg London Madrid Mexico City
Milan Montreal New Delhi Panama City
Paris São Paulo Singapore Sydney Tokyo Toronto

Osborne **McGraw-Hill**
2600 Tenth Street
Berkeley, California 94710
U.S.A.

For information on software, translations, or book distributors outside of
the U.S.A., please write to Osborne **McGraw-Hill** at the above address.

The Best Guide to Business Shareware

1234567890 DOC 9987654

ISBN 0-07-882076-6

Publisher
Lawrence Levitsky

Acquisitions Editor
Scott Rogers

Project Editor
Claire Splan

Computer Designer
Peter F. Hancik

Illustrator and Series Designer
Lance Ravella

Quality Control Specialist
Joe Scuderi

Cover Designer
Ted Mader Associates

This book is dedicated to all the tireless shareware entrepreneurs who program the night away so that we can enjoy state-of-the-art software at low cost. This book is also dedicated to Rufus Heim who was with us every step of the way.

Contents at a Glance

Table of Contents

Part One: What You Need To Know About Shareware

——1——

——2——

Part Two: Documents and Data

3

Word Processing with Panache 37

4

Graphics and Presentation Software to Make the World Sit Up and Take Notice

5

Printing Software That Brings Out the Best in Your Reports

——— 6 ———

Database Software That Keeps Your
World in Order 87

7

Spreadsheets and Accessories 105

8

Software to Make Desktop Publishing
Projects Shine 119

——9——

Communications Software for
Navigating the Information Highway . . 143

━━ *10* ━━

Software That Makes Windows and DOS
Easier to Live With 175

━━ *11* ━━

Tools and Toys 191

Part Three: Finance and Accounting

12

Software for Making Business Plans

13

General Ledger and Bookkeeping Software to Ease Your Accounting Headaches

14

Software to Track Budgets, Expenses, and Bank Accounts

Part 5: Administration and General Management

26

Security, Anti-Virus, and Backup Tools to Keep Your PC Safe from Intruders and Disaster **359**

27

PC Help Tools for When the Going Gets Rough **371**

Part Seven: Appendix

A

Computer Bulletin Boards and Online Services **383**

About the Software That Accompanies This Book

Acknowledgments

We'd like to thank the many kind people who so generously offered their insights, suggestions, and good humor to this project. Our special thanks go to Don Watkins, living legend, mensch, and sysop extraordinaire of the IBM forums on CompuServe, for suggestions on shareware that no one can live without; Greg Ryan of Exec-PC for hackerish insights into the best of shareware computer games; and Byron Go for snapping a mountain of screen shots in such a short period of time that it left us all astonished. Bill Pollock provided the initial outline and focus for the book, and suffered its worst moments. We'll always stand in awe of Bill's instincts as an editor. Judy Ziajka wrote the profiles of companies using shareware, providing color to the book, as well as taking a great burden off its overworked writers. Cindy Brown and Scott Rogers navigated this project through more perilous waters than those weathered by the S.S. Minnow in a three-day storm. Without their patience and sensibilities, none of us would have emerged with our canoes intact. Claire Splan and her crew of talented copyeditors and proofreaders, including Carl Wikander and Pat Mannion, transformed our rumpled prose virtually overnight into elegance, erudition, and complete sentences. We'd also like to thank book designers Peter Hancik and Lance Ravella for attending to all the minutia, like putting the icons on the right pages and making sure the screen shots didn't come out looking like squashed bubble gum cards. We also owe our gratitude to the gang on PC World's CCMAIL system—especially George Campbell, Robert Luhn, Eric Knorr, and Brett Glass—for e-mail solace, software suggestions, hand-holding, and reminders to aspire to lofty things; and Darcy Veach for grocery shopping, cat stories, and an inimical way of glowering at a PC that can get any software to run. Finally, we'd like to thank Debra Young and Scott Gerber of

CompuServe for providing access to the service and assistance in researching this book.

Introduction

This book is a survey of the best shareware programs for general and industry-specific business use. We compare shareware products with traditional shrink-wrapped products in terms of quality, performance, support, and cost and offer tips on where to find the best shareware. In an effort to show how shareware can offer a successful and cost-efficient alternative to commercial software, we interviewed people who depend on shareware in their day-to-day operations. These interviews, featured in the "Shareware in Action" profiles, provide real-world examples of how shareware works for both large and small companies. If it works for them, it may work for your company, too. We encourage you to give shareware a try!

How This Book Is Organized

Part One, "What You Need to Know About Shareware," provides a introduction to the philosphy of shareware and describes how shareware can help you and your business. You'll learn how to use Telix to download shareware from online services and get tips on where to find the best shareware.

Part Two, "Documents and Data," provides reviews and recommendations of free and low-cost programs in major general application areas: word processing, graphics and presentation, database, spreadsheets, communication, and desktop publishing. We also take a look at a few products that make working with Windows and DOS easier (and more fun). For some diversion, we've included a few of our favorite toys on the PC.

Part Three, "Finance and Accounting," reviews packages that make your business accounting more efficient, covering areas such as book-keeping, budgeting, payroll, and invoicing.

Part Four, "Sales and Marketing," covers programs that every retailer (as well as other business people) should know about to operate an efficient business. We look at all aspects of sales and marketing, from point of sale to inventory control to mailing.

Part Five, "Administration and General Management," reviews products that will make your day-to-day office routines more orderly. We cover time mangement programs, form generators, and software to track personnel and facilities.

Part Six, "Computer and Network Operations," deals with security utilities and anti-virus packages, as well as a few other tools to keep your PCs and networks up and running.

Part Seven, "Appendix," is a compendium of the most popular computer bulletin boards and online services.

A Word About the Nature of Shareware

Due to the fact that shareware is created by individuals rather than large software corporations, information such as addresses, phone numbers, filenames, and product version numbers tend to change frequently. While the authors and the publisher made every effort to provide accurate and up-to-date information on the products surveyed, it is likely that information will continue to change after this book goes to press. In cases where online filenames included version numbers which might be changing soon, we used "x" to indicate a variable in the filename. We encourage you to turn to the online services and BBSs covered throughout this book and listed in the appendix for the most current shareware filenames and addresses.

note

Shareware is the property of the shareware author. It is a unique concept by which you can acquire software via any means—from an online service, from a computer user group, from an assosicate's hard disk or floppy, or from the disk that accompanies this book—and use if for free for a period of time. When that time's up, if you decide to keep it, you must pay a registration fee to the author. We urge you to act responsibly and pay your authors!

WHAT YOU NEED TO KNOW ABOUT SHAREWARE

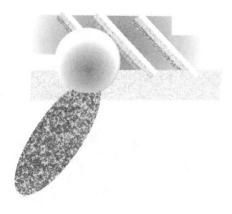

CHAPTER 1

WHAT IS SHAREWARE AND WHY DOES YOUR BUSINESS NEED IT?

world of high-quality, low-cost software tools is
available from online services, but most business
computer users are unaware of it.

"Is this legal?" a disbelieving office manager asked after listening to an explanation of shareware. *Shareware* is a special kind of computer software. It is not sold in retail stores. Instead, authors distribute it freely via online services, computer user clubs, and disks. They ask you to pay for it only if you like it. Exotic as the concept might seem, shareware is every bit as legitimate a product as that of any small business.

The shareware approach may seem like a ludicrous way to run a sales campaign, but it has spawned an industry. Many leading software publishers—Datastorm of Procomm Plus fame is just one example—can trace their roots to the pay-if-you-like-it concept. There are currently hundreds of thousands of shareware entrepreneurs filling the Information Highway with terrific software. Many of them have grown rich doing it, lots more have carved out decent livings. What this means for you and your business is that there's a universe of first-rate, low-cost software out there that's tailored to meet virtually any need your office might have—and, of course, it has the added attraction that you have to pay for it only if you like it.

A Gold Mine Fortune 500s Have Tapped for Years

Shareware was born over a decade ago when *PC World* magazine's founding editor Andrew Fluegelman wrote one of the first communications programs for PCs. He posted it on computer networks with a note—written as an afterthought to see what might happen—asking users to send him $25 if they liked it. He needed to hire three employees just to open the envelopes full of checks that flooded in.

Other entrepreneurs quickly jumped on the shareware concept, offering shareware word processors, spreadsheet programs, and even accounting software. The software was distributed through PC user's groups, computer bulletin boards, and online information services like CompuServe. Computer users were free to download and try it out for a trial period; if they liked it, they were either asked or required to send in the requested donation. In return they would get a license to use the software, just as with a commercial product, and sometimes—though not always—technical support. The manual for the product was contained in a text file that came along with the program. The user could get a printed manual in some cases by sending in an extra donation.

Before long, it wasn't just computer hobbyists who were mailing in the checks. PC-savvy Fortune 500 companies like Coca-Cola Foods and General Motors began site-licensing shareware products by the score. They discovered in this quirkishly distributed software an often astounding technical virtuosity, as well as cottage businesses anxious to cater to their whims in ways that big software houses often could not. Sure, a lot of big corporations were skeptical of shareware at first. Many worried that once they licensed a product, the author might vanish and they wouldn't get the tech support they needed. Some feared that employees would bring in shareware to work, run it on their PCs without sending in the required registration, and, since shareware was copyrighted just like commercial software, management would be hit by suits from shareware authors claiming theft of their products—a fear that turned out to be unwarranted. But by the late '80s, such fears were pretty much allayed in corporate suites, and corporate America began licensing software downloaded from computer bulletin boards with a bargain-hunter's frenzy. Shareware suddenly went mainstream. In fact, using it became techno-chic.

The explosion in shareware's popularity had both good and bad consequences for this genre of software. In an attempt to spruce up shareware's hobbyist image, shareware authors founded their own professional organization, called the Association of Shareware Professionals. The ASP set strict quality standards for products and a code of professionalism requiring that authors acknowledge all shareware registrations within 30 days of receipt, provide prompt technical support, plus fix any bugs that customers found in their products or else refund their money (a concept that would cause big commercial software houses to scream in horror should anyone suggest that they do it). The ASP also hired an ombudsman to mediate disputes between shareware authors and their customers. (You'll find more information about the ASP at the end of this chapter.) Within a year of the organization's energetic founding, shareware's reputation was quite literally transformed from one of futsy, half-hearted rec room programming efforts to blue-suit and shrink-wrapped-box respectability. Many shareware programs even found their way onto retail shelves in the aforementioned shrink-wrapped box, albeit with price tags rather than requests to send money.

Suddenly, every computer trade paper was full of shareware success stories—from multi-million dollar software companies that had sprung up overnight thanks to corporate site licenses to college kids who were earning $25K a year distributing former high school computer class projects. Many software companies found that it made good marketing sense to straddle both shareware and commercial worlds—distributing a full-featured shareware version of their product on online services as well as selling a shrink-wrapped version in stores. They found that they could double their customer base through the kind of product exposure the online world offered. It didn't take long for almost every programmer in America to decide they wanted to be a shareware author. Online services and BBSs (bulletin board services) found themselves flooded with products in the gold rush. Everywhere you looked there were screen savers and spreadsheet printers tagged with a request that the user send the author $5. Corporate America's enthusiasm for shareware began to wane as few PC managers had time to sort through all this stuff. Once again, it had become easier just to open up an Egghead Software catalog, send in a company purchase order, and hope for the best. That's where the idea for this book came from.

The Best Shareware to Search for

We've searched through hundreds of software libraries on computer online services and BBSs for the very best shareware for business PC users. We've downloaded the software, tested it out, and compared it with commercial products on the market whenever possible. You'll find in these chapters only the products that we consider to be the crème de la crème of shareware titles in each of the major business software categories. Be warned: We are opinionated. What we consider the best, others may view less favorably. But we are confident that the software we describe in these pages is tops at doing what you need to get done.

What we haven't been able to do, unfortunately, is evaluate the products on the basis of their vendors' reliability. We can't tell you if the authors of these programs will get back to you in a timely fashion if you phone or write them. We don't know anything about their technical support, although many shareware authors do provide conscientious tech support through telephone, online service forums, and BBSs. We don't know their product upgrade policies. We can't even tell you if their phone numbers will still be connected by the time you read this book. Shareware is a very mutable commodity. Often, some of the more obscure shareware authors can be downright hard to find. Sometimes they can be impossible to find.

Whenever possible, we've included the street address, voice, fax, and BBS numbers, plus e-mail addresses for the shareware companies we list. Remember, shareware authors change their addresses and phone numbers as regularly as normal people do. Many of the addresses (and even company names) changed as we wrote this book. For many of the free products we list, no street address was given.

The price that we list is merely the registration price—that is, the price you need to mail in if you download the software yourself, find it useful, and want to keep it. (Remember, unless noted otherwise, this stuff is *not* free, so please pay for it!) Most shareware companies will be glad to ship you disks containing their software for a small fee. Many will also be glad to send you a printed manual for an extra fee. Before you send a shareware author any money for disks or a manual, please contact him or her to verify the price. Shareware authors also often add shipping to their prices. We have included any additional costs for disks, manuals, and shipping in the product listings whenever that information was available to us.

We've worked to make sure that all the software we recommend can be found on most major computer online services. Still, there may be times when you have a hard time finding a particular program you're looking for. The major online services update and reorganize their software libraries monthly. Often while writing this book, we found that software that we had downloaded from a particular online service one week was gone the next. (See the end of this chapter for more tips on searching for shareware online.) We've also included two disks with this book, packed with great shareware. These are the programs that we've found to be the most useful, wonderful, or unique.

Before cruising store aisles for software, prudent software shoppers *always* check to see if what they're looking for is available as shareware. If it is, it will probably cost them about 50 to 75 percent less than what's available in the store, plus they can test drive it before buying.

You won't find every software package you need sold as shareware. And there's a lot out there that, frankly, looks like it was whipped up in a weekend. While you can find excellent shareware word processors and spreadsheet programs, such full-blown application software tends to be far more austere than what you'd get in the store. The reason is simple: A single shareware author (and most shareware companies are one-person shops) cannot replicate what a big software publisher requires 50 programmers to write.

Thus, your shareware finds will probably be richest in the area of utilities—those indispensable little programs that let you do simple things like print mailing labels or maintain disk catalogs. There are lots of businesses that can benefit from terrific shareware—just look through the table of contents for a sampling of the types of products available.

Best Places to Go for Shareware

Looking for good shareware to download is like looking for bargains at a garage sale. Some days you'll hunt and find nothing; other days you'll collect more than you can drag home. There are two general areas where you'll find shareware: commercial online services like CompuServe and America Online, and computer bulletin boards in your own backyard. We prefer computer bulletin boards. They're cheap (if not free) to call, their shareware collections are often as good (if not better) than those on big commercial online services, and they're easier to search and faster to download from than are the monolithic information services.

If you're looking for a type of software not covered in this book, the best way to start your search is to ask other computer users for recommendations. Ask around on either computer online services or computer user clubs. Most computer clubs keep a library of shareware, as well as free software that members can copy for free.

If you have a modem (and you should), commercial online services and computer bulletin boards are great places for finding shareware. CompuServe (614/457-8600, voice) offers the widest selection of shareware. Unfortunately, copying software from CompuServe to your computer—or *downloading*—can be expensive (it currently runs from $4.80 to $9.60 an hour, depending upon the connect speed). CompuServe can also be hard to search since its software libraries are many and its main software directory is poor. Still, CompuServe is going to be one of the first places you'll want to look for shareware.

General Electric's GEnie (800/638-9636, voice) and America Online (800/827-6364, voice) also offer shareware, and their hourly connect rates are slightly cheaper than CompuServe's—GEnie's rate is currently $3 an hour and America Online's is $3.50—but searching them can try one's patience and downloading can be slow. More and more shareware is appearing on the Internet, that formerly academic and military network that has become the world's de facto "information super-highway," but the Internet can be a pain to search. Most business computer users find searching for things on the Internet to be a time-eater and prefer reliable information services like CompuServe.

Our favorite shareware hunting grounds are computer bulletin boards. Bulletin boards are like mini-CompuServes, often run on a single computer in the basement of a really geeky hobbyist. Most are free to call, although some charge a subscription fee. The super-big ones, like Bob Mahoney's Executive Personal Computer Service in Milwaukee (414/789-4210—that's a number your modem can call, not you) offer file collections that rival in size what you'll find on CompuServe. Plus, they're easier to search and infinitely faster to download from than the big online services. Not surprisingly, many of these shareware-stocked BBSs have themselves evolved into successful businesses.

Almost any local computer store or computer club can provide you with a list of BBS phone numbers in your city. In fact, your local computer user group probably runs a very good BBS of its own where you can get all the hottest shareware. Check Appendix A, "Computer Bulletin Boards and Online Services," for a list of BBSs around the country. If you want to dial a BBS outside your city, but blanch at long-distance bills, several inexpensive long-distance modem services are available that let you dial a selected number of BBSs or area codes for either a flat monthly fee or low hourly rates. Two such services are Sprint's PC-Pursuit (800/736-1130, voice, $30 per month) and Global Access (800/377-3282, voice, $4 per hour). MCI Mail also offers a program called PC Connect that's similar to its Friends & Family promotion and that lets you dial selected BBSs for low rates (800/444-6245, voice).

If you've never downloaded software before, start by getting yourself a modem (go ahead, spring for a 14.4K bps modem—they're cheap enough that no one buys 2400 bps modems anymore). Then, get a list of local BBS numbers, available at any local computer store or from your PC user's club, and sign up for one of the commercial online services, if only to be well-rounded. In your new modem box you'll probably find sign-up packets for all sorts of online services. These are good deals because they usually give you some free time to play around on the service. If they don't, toss them out.

For shareware, CompuServe is our favorite. GEnie has a big file collection, but it's ugly to search, and downloading from it is slower than ordering pizza from Tibet. America Online is fun to use with its Macintosh-like user-interface, but its software collection is limited. (See Appendix A for the phone numbers of these services.)

You'll need communications software, too. You'll probably find some packed in your new modem box, but chances are that it will be the sort of thing that could only be given away free in boxes of cheap electronics. Dabble with it, but if it's not Crosstalk Communicator, spring for decent software like Procomm Plus for Windows or download one of the packages we recommend in Chapter 9, "Communications Software for Navigating the Information Highway." A copy of the popular Telix communications program is included on the disks in this book, and we'll walk you through using it in Chapter 2, "Dialing Online Services and BBSs and Downloading Shareware."

Should You Worry About Computer Viruses?

The chances of your computer contracting a virus—malicious computer code that passes from computer to computer and creates havoc—is no greater from using shareware than from buying retail software. (In fact, many viruses have been passed to unassuming consumers through shrink-wrapped software boxes. We don't know of any that have been passed through shareware.)

Similarly, your chances of contracting a virus by downloading software from an online service or BBS are equally low. In fact, no virus has ever been passed through a commercial online service. In the past, there have been scares that software on BBSs and online services would be attacked by *Trojan horses* (predecessors of viruses that are equally nasty, although not self-replicating).

To avoid running into any kind of prankish software, it's a good idea to practice "safe downloading." That means downloading software only from BBSs that you know are reputable, where you know the operator screens software regularly for viruses, and, ideally, ones where you know the operator personally. You should also wait for software to "age" on the system. Download it only after its posting date is a few weeks past. Let other people who run it first be the guinea pigs.

Keep in mind that most viruses stick to large corporate or university computer networks, where they're shuttled around when a disk from one computer is inserted in another. Calling online services and downloading shareware is not a likely way to contract a virus. Remember, too, that you cannot contract any type of virus or Trojan horse simply by scrolling through menus or reading messages on an online service or BBS.

We've included on one of the the disks that comes with this book the popular virus-scanner Viruscan by John McAfee. For peace of mind, use it to scan for viruses on files that you download as well as on your entire hard disk. No virus scanner can detect every virus, but Viruscan can find most of them.

Do Shareware Companies Offer Technical Support?

Many businesses are concerned that if they license shareware, the author will not provide as much support for the product as conventional shareware publishers do. This concern is unfounded. Shareware authors have a good track record for supporting their products. Many, in fact, go out of their way to provide customers with bug fixes and requested product enhancements.

The Association of Shareware Professionals sets high standards for tech support and requires that its members follow them. It also reviews products for quality and provides an ombudsman for mediating customer complaints with shareware companies. You can contact the ASP to find out if the author of a shareware package you plan to license adheres to ASP guidelines by calling 616/788-5131 (voice) or 616/788-2765 (fax) or by writing the Association of Shareware Professionals, 545 Grover Road, Muskegon, MI 49442-9427. You can also reach the ASP on CompuServe by typing **GO ASPFORUM** and pressing ENTER at any prompt.

CHAPTER 2

DIALING ONLINE SERVICES AND BBSs AND DOWNLOADING SHAREWARE

ost communications software will work with your modem right out of the box. The only things you'll need to do once you install it on your disk are to tell it which communications port your modem is plugged into and type in the phone number to dial. When you hear your modem pick up the phone and dial the number, you know you're home free. Once you hear the "whooosh!" of another modem picking up the phone on the other end (if you hear a woman crying "Hello? Hello?" you know you dialed a wrong number), hit ENTER to elicit a prompt from the other system. Remember: whenever your PC's screen goes blank and you start to wonder if you're still connected, hit ENTER to get a prompt.

The communications program Telix is included on the disks that come with this book, and we'll tell you in this chapter how to use it the first time to dial an online service or BBS and download software. To set up Telix to dial online services, begin by finding the disks with the files TLX322-1.ZIP, TLX322-2.ZIP, TLX322-3.ZIP, and TLX322-4.ZIP. Create a directory for Telix on your hard disk. Copy the files there by moving to the disk drive where the Telix files are located and typing **PKUNZIP TLX*.* C:\TELIX** and pressing ENTER. (In place of **C:\TELIX**, type the name of the hard disk directory that you have created for Telix.)

Turn on your modem (make a final check to make sure it's plugged into your computer, if it's an external one, and that the appropriate phone cords are plugged into its jacks). Move to the hard disk directory where Telix is now located and type **TELIX** and press ENTER. Telix will prompt you for the number of your communications port. You'll need to look it up in your PC's documentation or ask your computer dealer if you don't know. If you use a mouse, the modem is probably located on communications port 2.

You'll know that everything is working correctly if you see the screen in Figure 2-1. The "AT" commands are the instructions that Telix has sent to the modem and the "O.K.s" are the modem's signal that it's paying attention and following the commands.

To bring up Telix's dialing directory, press ALT-D. A blue screen will pop up. To add a phone number to the directory, press E. Telix will prompt you for a name for the BBS or online service—enter **Exec-PC, Milwaukee**. Press ENTER, and Telix will ask you for a number. Type **1-414-789-4210**. (This could be a long-distance number for you. If you don't want to pay the long-distance toll to call it, you'll need to find a BBS in your area to call and enter that number instead.) For "baud rate" select 2400 from the choice box. *Bits per second (bps)* or *baud rate* is the speed at which the modem will connect to the online service or BBS. When I call a BBS for the first time I always call at 2400 bps. A lot of incompatibilities exist among modems at speeds higher than 2400 bps, and sometimes it takes some tweaking of your modem and software settings to forge a high-speed link. So, to make sure that there is a BBS at the number I'm calling and that it will connect with my PC, I call at the low speed first. When I log on to the BBS, I then head to the Bulletins menu, which sometimes lists alternate phone numbers for the board. Some BBSs have several phone

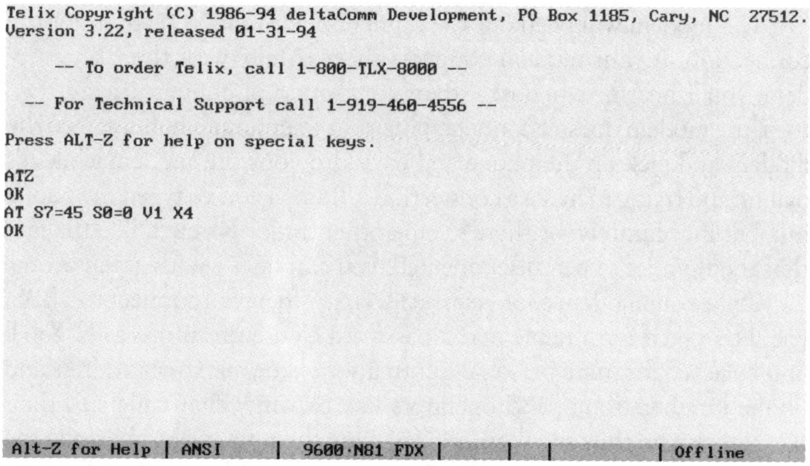

```
Telix Copyright (C) 1986-94 deltaComm Development, PO Box 1185, Cary, NC  27512.
Version 3.22, released 01-31-94

      -- To order Telix, call 1-800-TLX-8000 --

   -- For Technical Support call 1-919-460-4556 --

Press ALT-Z for help on special keys.

ATZ
OK
AT S7=45 S0=0 V1 X4
OK




Alt-Z for Help | ANSI      |  9600·N81 FDX |          |         |           | Offline
```

Figure 2-1   If your communications software and your modem
                   are talking to each other, you'll see a screen like this
                   one in Telix

numbers with different brands of high-speed modems answering the
phone. If your modem is the temperamental type that only connects with
certain brands, you'll want to try the board's alternate numbers.

Toggle through the rest of the entries in the dialing directory entry
setup screen by pressing ENTER. All the other communications parameters on that menu are set to their proper settings for dialing BBSs and
online services. At the prompt "Save this Entry?" select Yes.

You'll want to make one more setting. Press ALT-O to get to the setup
screen. Press M for the modem dialing setup menu. Now press K to change
the dial time. This is how long the modem waits for a connection, after
dialing a phone number, before hanging up and trying again. New modem
users often call a BBS again and again and are unable to connect; they
never suspect that the reason is that their communications software is
not waiting long enough for the modems to finish making the connection.
Change this setting from 30 to 50. Press ENTER, then W to save the new
setup to disk.

Head back to the dialing directory by pressing ALT-D. Once you're
back at the bright blue screen, dial the BBS by toggling the highlight bar
with the arrow keys to the BBS entry, and press D.

The modem will beep out the number, then wait 50 seconds for the connection. If your modem connects succcessfully with the BBS's modem, you'll hear a "whooosh," then a glissando of chimes. If, after two tries, the modem doesn't connect, plug your telephone's handset into the modem and pick up the phone and eavesdrop on your modem while it's dialing and trying to make a connection. Often, if you've typed the phone number inaccurately, or there's some other minor problem like the fact that the number's been disconnected, you can hear what's going wrong.

Once your modem connects, hit ENTER. When you connect to a BBS, you'll be asked for a name and a password to use on future calls. You'll also be asked for some personal information, like your street address and phone number. Some BBS operators like to verify that callers to their boards are who they say they are by calling them up, or by checking the area code of phone numbers against the street address. Should you be concerned about typing personal information into a BBS? If you know that the board is respectable (Exec-PC is) you should have no qualms. If it's the first time you're calling and you're uncertain of who runs the board, it's sometimes wise to enter something other than your real name and address. Some BBS owners may not appreciate our advising this, but it's a precaution that's certainly justified.

Tricks for Easy Searching

When you get through with the rigmarole of logging on to the board and familiarizing yourself with it, head to the file library section. It's usually a choice presented on the BBS's main menu. (Most BBSs will not give you full access to their software libraries until the board's operator verifies that you are who you say you are. They may however provide a mini-software library that callers can download software from in the meantime. Searching BBSs for shareware is generally easier than searching big commercial online services because all the software will usually be stored in a central library that you can search quickly by keywords or filenames. On big online services, once you find your way to the applicable forum where software you're looking for is housed (and believe me, that can take a while), you may still need to search several different libraries to find what you're looking for. Whether you search on a BBS or CompuServe, searching for a specific shareware program can sometimes be frustrating. Here are some tips to get you through it.

All BBSs and online services have different searching commands. The trick is to use wildcard characters when you specify filenames to search for, in case the file has been posted on the system with a slightly different name than what you expect, or its version number has recently changed. To search for a file called DESK83.ZIP, for instance, you might type at the search prompt **DESK??.ZIP** or even **DESK??.***. Or, the file may be called something different than what you expect. Say you're looking for the mailer Pony Express. It's listed in this book as PONY20.ZIP. If you can't find a file by that name, try some possible variations like PONYX.* or PONYEX.*.

Sometimes you can also search by "keywords," which are a few well-chosen words that describe the software. For instance, to search for the shareware package Banking Buddy you might search for the keywords "banking," "buddy," "checking," "budget," "budgeting," "finance," or the company name "Free Soul." The important thing to remember is, if your first search comes up dry, try again with all the different possible filenames or keywords you can think of.

As you search, the service will display lists of files that look something like this:

RICH.TXT	Get rich quick with this pyramid scheme!
TICKER.EXE	Create your own ticker tape parade
REMEDY.ZIP	Are you losing your mind? Read this!
SALE.LZH	Turn your screen blanker into This Space for Sale sign
ALIEN.ARC	Fun way to find out what your batch files are doing
GIVENS.GIF	Flattering picture of financial proselytizer Charles Givens

The filename extension—those three letters at the very end of a filename following the period—tell you what the file format is. Files that contain plain old text that you'll be able to read with any word processor or editor usually have a .TXT extension.

note

Pyramid scheme text files are the bane of the business online world. They are everywhere. Although they are illegal, people keep uploading them to online services, much to the distress of the services' owners. Don't be one of those troublesome modem users. Keep your pyramid schemes to yourself.

When a filename has any extension other than .TXT, it's usually a binary file. That means it's made up of 0s and 1s, and you won't be able to read it on your screen or print it out. If a filename has an .EXE extension, it's an executable file. You'll be able to run it as you would any piece of software by typing the beginning of its name—**TICKER** for TICKER.EXE, for example—at your PC's DOS prompt.

Many filenames with .EXE extensions that you'll find on online services are compressed and self-extracting. That means that the program has been squeezed down in size with compression software so that it takes less disk storage space on the online service, and also cuts your transfer time at least in half. The air has been let out of the file, in other words. Since the compressed file is self-extracting, the air will automatically be let back into the software when you type its name at the PC prompt. You don't have to do anything else to the file. If a file has a .ZIP, .LZH, or .ARC tag on the end of its name you'll have to download file compression software and uncompress the file yourself. Doing that isn't hard and will be discussed later in this chapter.

Some of the other filename extensions you'll spot online are .GIF, .PCX, and .TIF. These are picture files. You display them on your screen with a graphics viewing program. GIF is the picture format that's standard on CompuServe, while .PCX and .TIF are common in graphics software.

Getting the Software from Their Hard Disk to Yours

Once you find a file to download, you need to type the applicable commands to the BBS or online service to get the download started. These will vary and are often as simple as choosing the file download command from the file menu on the service, then typing in the name of the software to download. After that you must instruct the online service which file protocol you plan to use (see discussion on file protocols below), and then you must instruct your communications software to begin the transfer. You do this through its pull-down menus, clicking its download icon if you're using Windows, or pressing the PGDN key, as you do with Telix.

Picking a File Transfer Protocol

When you tell your communications software to begin a download, the software will usually give you a list of download protocols that you can pick from. A file transfer protocol, in its most basic sense, is a language that your PC and the remote system on the other end agree upon in order to facilitate the transfer of binary data. But most file protocols do more than just that. They also provide a way for checking the data as it's sent to ensure that it arrives at your PC accurately. Some file transfer protocols also compress data as they send it, in order to transfer files faster. There are dozens of file protocols, from Xmodem to Ymodem to Zmodem. Each is designed to work best in certain situations. Some check the file for errors as they send it; some, for speed's sake, do not. Some are designed to be fast, while others work best on noisy phone lines.

Which one should you use? On CompuServe, always use CompuServe B+. That protocol is the fastest when transferring files from that service. On GEnie, try speed-demon Zmodem first, then Ymodem. Only use Xmodem if nothing else works because Xmodem is as slow as it gets. You may find that you have to lower your connection speed on GEnie to 1200 bps to make the initial connection, because many GEnie modems are temperamental. America Online uses its own protocol, so you don't have to make any choices. See Table 2-1 for a quick look at the features of the different protocols.

FILE TRANSFER PROTOCOL	ADVANTAGES	DISADVANTAGES	WHEN TO USE
Xmodem (checksum)	Can be found everywhere; often transfers files when other protocols bomb out	Very, very slow; won't pick up all errors; won't work on networks like Tymnet or Telenet with built-in time delays	When you have scratchy phone lines; when absolutely nothing else works
Xmodem-CRC	Will pick up more errors than checksum Xmodem	Slow	When you have noisy phone lines; when nothing else works

Table 2-1   Which file transfer protocol to use

FILE TRANSFER PROTOCOL	ADVANTAGES	DISADVANTAGES	WHEN TO USE
Xmodem-1K (sometimes referred to erroneously as single-file transfer Ymodem)	Much faster than other Xmodems, better at picking up errors than checksum Xmodem	Slows down lots on bad phone lines	When you have good to moderate phone lines; if you don't have an error-correcting modem
WXmodem (windowed)	Designed to tolerate time delays of networks like Tymnet or Telenet	Slow	On Tymnet or Telenet
Ymodem Batch	The fastest member of the Xmodem protocol family	Slows down on bad phone lines	When you have good to fair phone lines with or without error-correcting modem
Ymodem-G	Super-fast when used with error-correcting modem	No error-checking; it will abort transfer on the first error	Good phone lines with error-checking modem
Kermit	One of the fastest protocols when properly implemented, but it is usually not; can tolerate telephone line noise better than any other protocol; works in mainframe and networking environments where other protocols won't	Badly implemented in most communications software packages, so it is consequently very slow in most uses	When nothing else works; or when you and receiving computer are both using Columbia University version, like that found in communications program MS-Kermit
Zmodem	A speed-demon that can adjust error-checking to line noise conditions; crash recovery will restart transfer where it left off if transfer ended due to line noise	Will be as slow as frozen honey if the phone line gets noisy	Use with an error-checking modem; if characters-per-second rate drops because of line noise, switch to Ymodem

Table 2-1   Which file transfer protocol to use (*continued*)

FILE TRANSFER PROTOCOL	ADVANTAGES	DISADVANTAGES	WHEN TO USE
CompuServe B+	Best thing to use on CompuServe	Don't use it anywhere else but on CompuServe because it will be slow	When downloading from CompuServe
Imodem	Fast, streaming protocol for use with high-speed modems	No error-checking	Use with high-speed, error-correcting modems on good phone lines
H/S or High-Speed Link	Supersonic fast! Lets you upload and download files, or "CB" online all at the same time	Not yet found in many communications programs; you need to buy it and install it yourself, but it's worth it	Will be a great speed performer under any conditions
Telink	Lets you send multiple files, plus add file size and creation data to program header	It's a form of Xmodem; and usually found only on FIDO BBSs	Any conditions, any modem
ASCII	Easy to use	Not an error-checking protocol, it just spits text out over phone line; won't send binary files like program or compressed files; won't send word processing files with formatting codes	On clean phone lines, when uploading text into e-mail messages

Table 2-1   Which file transfer protocol to use (*continued*)

When connected to a BBS, try Zmodem first. If you see your software tally lots of errors during the transfer, or if the transfer seems slow as you watch the characters-per-second box, telephone line noise may be slowing Zmodem. Switch to Ymodem instead. If for some reason you have a hard time getting a file transfer going—maybe there's a lot of telephone line noise, or the transfer keeps self-aborting—try Kermit. This workhorse protocol by Columbia University will work when everything else fails. The trick is to get the file transfer going as fast as possible to save you money in connect charges.

tip

Choosing the right file transfer protocol for the job is an art. Phone line quality, modem features, and type of file all make a difference. HS/Link, Zmodem, Ymodem-G, and Kermit (in good implementations) are the speed demons, all clocking comparably fast speeds under ideal conditions. On fuzzy phone lines, try Ymodem or Xmodem-1K. Kermit is also a good choice.

Once you've chosen a protocol, your datacomm software will display a box of statistics on how the transfer is progressing, as shown in Figure 2-2. Any errors that are encountered in transmission and corrected are noted at the bottom of the status box. (The "error" message shown in Figure 2-2 is nothing to worry about; the software is handling everything.)

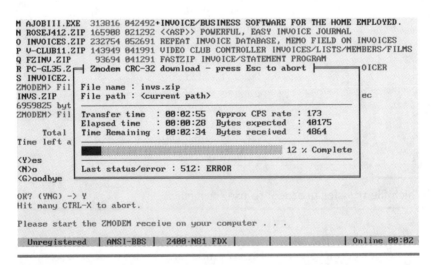

```
M AJOBIII.EXE  313816 042492+INVOICE/BUSINESS SOFTWARE FOR THE HOME EMPLOYED.
N ROSEJ412.ZIP 165908 821292 <<ASP>> POWERFUL, EASY INVOICE JOURNAL
O INVOICES.ZIP 232754 052691 REPEAT INVOICE DATABASE, MEMO FIELD ON INVOICES
P U-CLUB11.ZIP 143949 041991 VIDEO CLUB CONTROLLER INVOICES/LISTS/MEMBERS/FILMS
Q FZINV.ZIP     93694 041291 FASTZIP INVOICE/STATEMENT PROGRAM
R PC-GL35.Z┌┤ Zmodem CRC-32 download - press Esc to abort ├──────┤OICER
S INVOICE2.│
ZMODEM> Fil│ File name : invs.zip
INVS.ZIP   │ File path : <current path>                              │ec
6959825 byt│
ZMODEM> Fil│ Transfer time   : 00:02:55  Approx CPS rate : 173
           │ Elapsed time    : 00:00:28  Bytes expected   : 40175
     Total │ Time Remaining  : 00:02:34  Bytes received   : 4864
Time left a│
           │ ████▒▒▒▒▒▒▒▒▒▒▒▒▒▒▒▒▒▒▒▒▒▒▒▒▒▒▒  12 % Complete
<Y>es      │
<N>o       │ Last status/error : 512: ERROR
<G>oodbye  └────────────────────────────────────────────────────┘

OK? (YNG) -> Y
Hit many CTRL-X to abort.

Please start the ZMODEM receive on your computer . . .

 Unregistered | ANSI-BBS | 2400·N81 FDX |    |    |         | Online 00:02
```

Figure 2-2   While Telix is downloading software, it informs you of its progress

Once the file transfer is done, the software will beep or display a message signaling its completion. To hang up your modem, press ALT-H. To exit Telix press ALT-X. Some people prefer to download software to a floppy disk, then run it through a virus checker to protect themselves against viruses. We've included McAfee's popular Viruscan on the disks included with this book so that you can scan your downloads for viruses prior to running them. (See Chapter 26, "Security, Anti-Virus, and Backup Tools to Keep Your PC Safe from Intruders and Disaster" for more information on shareware virus checkers.) Some of us, however, prefer to live life dangerously and rarely do this.

BBSs are super spots to experiment with your communications software's download capabilities. But remember, when connected to a BBS, comport yourself as if you're in someone's family room, because that's where most BBSs are located. Be polite, follow the rules, and, if the board's operator requests software uploads (in other words, asks that you upload some shareware in exchange for having downloaded some), be sure to upload some after you've finished downloading. Not only is that the proper thing to do, but it will let you practice uploading software.

Decompressing the Software

After you log off from the BBS or online service, you'll need to unpack or decompress the software you've just downloaded before you run it for the first time.

If a filename has a .ZIP extension, you'll need to use the popular shareware compression program PKZIP to unpack it. You'll find a copy of it on the disks included with this book, but you'll also find it on virtually every online service and BBS, because most software you find online is stored with it. (Remember to mail in your registration for PKZIP because it's also shareware. For more information on it, head to Chapter 11, "Tools and Toys." We've also included PKZIP on one of the disks with this book, as well as Drag and Zip, which will make unZipping programs easier under Windows.)

Other popular compression programs are LZH by Haruyasu Yoshizaki and ARC-E by Vern Buerg and Wayne Chin. These are also shareware and are available from most online services. Files compressed with LZH have an .LZH extension to their filename, and those stored with ARC-E have an .ARC extension. There are other compression formats, such as ARJ and PAK, but you'll run into these less often.

Once the software is uncompressed, it's ready to test drive. If it's a DOS program, load it by typing the beginning of its name—**TICKER** for TICKER.EXE—at any prompt. If it's for Windows, load it by clicking on File in the Program Manager, then Run, then typing or selecting the filename.

You'll probably want to read the software's documentation before installing it. Look for the file with the .DOC or .TXT extension. Load it in your word processor or read it with Vern Buerg's indispensable text reading program List Plus. (See Chapter 11, "Tools and Toys," for information on List Plus.)

Finding Your Way to Shareware Libraries on Commercial Information Services

Finding your way to fertile shareware libraries on big commercial online services like CompuServe and America Online is much harder than on BBSs because the libraries are many and scattered. Online services are organized into forums. Each forum caters to a special interest, such as PCs, current events, or investing. Forums consist of a public message "bulletin board," which may contain thousands of messages, and one or more software libraries, which users can search and download programs from. The libraries will be arranged by topic. One library may hold shareware, for instance, while another may contain information files on special subjects.

You'll find lots of business shareware in the *PC Magazine* Ziffnet forum on CompuServe (type **GO ZNT** and press ENTER at any prompt). Microsoft's Windows Shareware forum is also a good hunting spot (type **GO WINSHARE** and press ENTER). Other forums to check are the Small Business Forum (type **GO ENTMAGAZINE** and press ENTER), the PR & Marketing Forum (type **GO PRSIG** and press ENTER), and the Legal Forum (type **GO LAWSIG** and press ENTER). There is a central software directory on CompuServe (type **GO IBMFF** and press ENTER), but it will search only the key libraries on CompuServe.

On General Electric's GEnie, check out the IBM PC forum (type **IBMPC** and press ENTER at any prompt) and the Home Office and Small

Business forum (type **HOSB** and press ENTER). On America Online, click on the Computing & Software icon to get to the file
libraries. On the Exec-PC BBS, select the Mahoney Collection
from the file menu.

Keeping Track of Your Shareware

You'll probably find yourself accumulating a hard disk full of shareware after just a short time of hunting. Before you know it, your directories
will be brimming with printer utilities, text viewers, Windows enhancers,
and God knows what else. It will be the biggest mess you've ever seen.
Before your hard disk starts to look like chaos upended, download one of
these snappy utilities and transform the mounting disarray into a sem-
blance of order.

WinCat

WinCat lets you catalog just about every medium you've ever wanted
to catalog—floppy disks, hard disks, CD-ROMs, even network drives.
Since it supports all the major compression formats—ZIP, LZH, ARJ,
ZOO, PAK, and ARC—you can quickly find and extract files stored by
these methods. You can write descriptions of the archive files' contents
with WinCat's editing features and clipboard, and you can export the file
into a dBASE database. You can also print reports that include details of
the contents of your archives and volume summaries. Figure 2-3 shows
a WinCat display.

Mark Heubel
De Heugden 161
6411 DR Heerlen
The Netherlands
Price: $15
Online filename: WINCATxx.ZIP

Volume-ID	Free	#F		Group	Description
AFTERDARK-1	79K	38		Windows	AfterDark - Enterprise version
AFTERDARK-2	81K	24		Windows	AfterDark - Enterprise version
BOOT	25K	77		DOS	Bootable disk (DOS,Stacker)
CICA_792	0K	1327	A	CD-Rom	CICA Windows Applications July 92
COMPUSERVE	419K	7	A	Install	CompuServe Information Manager
EURO_CD	0K	596		CD-Rom	Windows/NT Developer Resource Kit
LOTUSORG-1	58K	3	A		Lotus Organizer
MHE001	644K	5	A	Games	Games
MHE002	785K	1	A	Games	Games
MHE003	44K	22	A	Windows	Windows Utilities
MHE004	456K	13	A	Windows	Larry 2, Windows Utilities
MHE005	2K	3	A	Games	Larry 2
MHE006	45K	2	A	Graphics	XXX-rated pictures
MHE007	200K	12	A	Graphics	Computer Graphics
MHE008	140K	10	A	DOS	DanCad 3D, Twintalk, Telix
MHE009	321K	47	A	Windows	WinCat sources
MHE010	16K	34	A	Windows	Windows Utilities
MHE011	279K	20	A	Windows	Windows Utilities
MHE012	4K	20	A	Windows	Windows Utilities
MHE013	74K	3	A	Games	Larry 3, Modplay
MHE014	5K	23	A	Windows	Windows Utilities
MHE015	19K	2	A	Games	Larry 3, Stacker
MHE016	17K	4	A	Games	Larry 3
MHE017	401K	11	A	Windows	HyperDisk, Windows Utilities
MHE018	29K	23	A	Windows	Windows Utilities and Games
MHE019	130K	4	A	DOS	SuperProject, Imagescanner
MHE020	287K	25	A	Windows	Windows Utilities
MHE021	49K	10	A	DOS	Flight Simulator
MHE022	53K	11	A	Windows	FrontDoor, Windows Utilities
MHE023	38K	12	A	Windows	Windows 3.1 unused stuff
MHE024	70K	17	A	Windows	Windows Utilities

C:\TST3\SAMPLE.CAT   WinCat/PRO 3.2.0 - Unregistered evaluation copy

Figure 2-3   A catalog of disks in WinCat

CatDisk

DOS

CatDisk has been a shareware favorite for eons. It lets you maintain multiple catalogs so that, for example, you can list all your disks with shareware spreadsheet add-ons in one file, and all your disks with shareware databases in another. You can write a description for each disk, and a description for each file. Because you can import text files into CatDisk, you can use it to store and search online service library listings (thereby speeding up your search time online). You can print reports on disk capacity, file size, and archive descriptions. Its only flaw is that you can't search the insides of compressed archives (ZOO, ZIP, PAC, et al.).

Rick Hillier
98 Toynbee Crescent
Kitchener, Ontario
Canada N2N 1R9
Phone: 519/570-3523

Fax: 519/884-4887
BBS: 519/570-4132
Price: $40
Online filename: CDISKxx.ZIP

Power User Tricks

Once you feel comfortable with your communications software and downloading software, it's time to get adventurous. Try these tricks for speeding up your downloads, automating your file searches, and, in general, getting the most speed out of your modem and PC while you're online.

Front-End Software to Automate File Searching

Software is available for both CompuServe and General Electric's GEnie to automate searching of the software libraries. Typically, you first specify a forum and tell the front-end software the keyword or filename that it should search for; the software then dials up the service, heads to the forum, searches the libraries, downloads for you, and logs off. The advantage is that the front-end software can conduct the search and download much faster than you can.

Numerous shareware front-end programs are available for automating file and message retrieval from CompuServe. Our favorites for file-searching are TapCIS and OzCIS. You can read more about them in Chapter 9, "Communications Software for Navigating the Information Highway." We highly recommend that you try these programs. They'll save you time and money.

Tips for Downloading with High-Speed Modems

Whether your modem is a poky 2400 bps one or a zippy 14.4K bps, you can nearly double the speed at which it transmits data simply by setting it up and using it properly. There's a lot of black magic involved in getting top speeds out of a modem, just as there is with a high-perform-ance car. Here are some tips.

Watch Your Chips!

Get a 16550A UART. UART stands for Universal Asynchronous Receiver-Transmitter. It's a chip inside your PC or on your PC's serial card that handles the flow of data in and out of the PC. Many PCs have UARTs that are old, slow, and lack the buffering ability necessary for the PC to handle high-speed file transfers. Symptoms of an old UART are PC lock-ups during fast file transfers, especially while using Windows, and file transfers self-aborting after too many errors. New UARTs are cheap ($15) and easy to install (simply pop them into the socket of your old UART on the PC's motherboard—that's that big flat board with all the chips on it that looks like a small industrial nation on the bottom of your PC—assuming the old UART is not soldered in).

Don't feel like dinking around with a chip puller or you've discovered from the manufacturer that the UART is soldered in? Consider buying one of those special serial cards—they run $150 to $200—that include a 16550A UART. Our favorite is Hayes Microcomputer's Enhanced Serial Port, a souped-up muscle board with lots of extras for the modem jock who demands high-performance, like direct memory access transfers between the card's buffer and the microprocessor to lessen demands on the PC during multitasking.

Many high-speed internal modems already have UARTs built into them, so you won't need to buy one for your PC if you have one of these. Just make sure that your internal modem's UART is a real chip, not some glitchy faux-UART kludged together with firmware. When you buy the modem ask, "Is this modem's UART a real National Semiconductor NS16550A?" Do not accept impostors.

Get Good Communications Software

Use communications software that is 16550-aware and can make use of this chip's data buffering abilities (most major communications software is and can). That includes Procomm Plus and Procomm for Windows, Qmodem, and all the DCA products. Lower-end pro-grams—the kind you find packed in your modem's box—usually are not. Another advantage to quality communications software is that its error-correction protocols like Zmodem will be well-implemented, and designed to run fast.

Set the PC's Serial Port Speed High If You Have a Modem with Data Compression

This holds true whether your modem offers V.42bis, MNP 5, or both. Head to your communications software's dialing directory (that's where the phone numbers are stored and, one hopes, the communications parameters to call them). Set all the bps or baud entries to 57.6K bps. Then, deactivate autobaud detect (the setting for this will probably be found on one of the software's modem setup screens).

You and any online service or BBS you call will still be talking to each other at your modems' top speed of either 9600 bps or 14.4K bps, but your PC and your modem will be communicating at the faster rate of 57.6K bps. In other words, you've just locked your PC's serial port speed to 57.6K bps.

For your modem's V.42bis data compression to work efficiently, the PC's port speed must be locked to at least four times the speed of the communication on the phone line. This will prevent data from getting choked up—kind of like in a traffic jam—in its transit from the phone line into your PC. If your modem has just MNP 5 compression, the port speed should be locked to a lower speed of just 2 to 3 times the connect speed.

Set Flow-Control

Head to your communications software's setup screens and find the entries for flow-control. *Flow-control* is how the PC regulates the flow of data between the modem and the communications port. There are two kinds of flow-control: *software flow-control* (also called XON/XOFF), which is controlled by your communications software, and *hardware flow-control* (also called RTS/CTS), which is controlled by electrical signals between the PC and the modem.

If you have a data-compressing modem, you will need to deactivate software flow-control and turn on hardware flow-control. Again, you need to do this so that high-speed transfers do not overflow the port. When modem users have problems getting a high-speed connection to work, it is usually because they do not have the flow-control set properly.

You will also need to activate hardware flow-control in your modem by adding the appropriate modem commands to your communications software. Modem commands are called AT commands because they all begin with "AT." The commands to turn on hardware flow-control vary with the brand of modem, so you'll need to look in your modem's manual for the proper command to do this. It may look something like this: &K3.

Now head to the setup screen in your communications software where you can find various strings that begin with "AT" and look like Russian code. There will be a short one called the *dialing string* (usually "ATDT" or some variation). This is what the datacomm software sends to the modem to dial the phone. There will be a shorter one called the *hang-up string* ("ATH0"). Then there will be a long one that looks like a code to arm a nuclear weapon. It's called the *modem initialization string* and is what the software sends to configure it to its needs when it's first loaded. It may look something like:

ATE10V1X4&C1&D2 S7=60 S11=50 S0=0^M

You need to insert your "&K3" command (or whatever the command to activate your modem's hardware flow-control) in this string. The safest place is right before ^M, which is the ENTER character.

Figure 2-4 shows the modem setup screen in Procomm Plus for Windows. It isn't easy to find. Press ALT-S, then click on Connection, then Advanced!, then Modem Setup. You can just make out segments of the AT modem strings.

Turn Off MNP 5 Data Compression in Your Modem

This seems like a contradiction in concepts. Data compression is supposed to make data transmission go faster. And it does, but in the case of MNP 5, it will actually slow down a file transfer if the file is already compressed with a program like PKZIP or LZH, because it will add extra characters to the transmission.

V.42bis compression, also found in your modem, is smart enough to tell when a file being transferred is already compressed and to comport itself accordingly. Again, you'll have to look in your modem's manual for

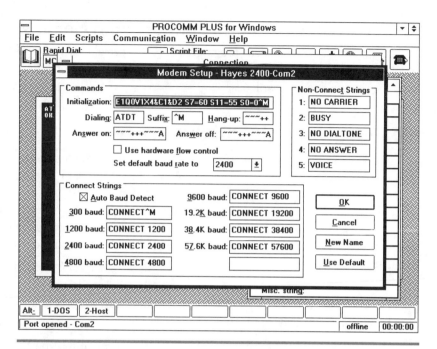

Figure 2-4 The modem setup screen of Procomm Plus for
Windows

the command to turn off MNP 5. As with the command to activate
hardware flow-control, add it to your modem's initialization string.

If your modem lacks V.42bis, you can always turn MNP 5 back on by
typing the command on the screen prior to calls in which you'll only be
reading e-mail. You can also insert it into a function key in your communications software so that whenever you want to turn MNP compression
back on, you just press the function key to activate it prior to going online.

Use the Best File Transfer Protocol for the Job

BBS denizens like to argue about which file protocol is fastest—
Zmodem, Ymodem-G, or HS/Link. The fact is, at high speeds the differences
between these three are minuscule. Refer to Table 2-1, which appears earlier
in this chapter, to determine the best protocol for the situation.

Remove Memory-Resident Software from Memory

Terminate-and-stay-resident programs (TSRs), especially cachers and spoolers, slow down file transfers. If you don't need TSRs in memory, don't keep them there during downloads.

Downloading Under Windows

Windows is one of the worst things to ever happen to modem users. When you download a file while running Windows, all the data coming into your PC through the serial port is forced to follow a circuitous route through Windows and its poky communications driver. That slows things down a lot. What's more, if your modem is a fast one, your transfer may lose lots of characters, error-out, or even lock up Windows. Here are some defensive actions.

▶ Be *sure* to get a 16550A UART. Most communications problems in Windows are solved by a new UART.

▶ Adjust flow-control. Turn on hardware flow-control, and turn off software flow-control as detailed above.

▶ Consider running all your high-speed files transfers in a DOS window. Run the communications software full-screen. The file transfers will work more efficiently that way.

▶ Whenever you run a communications program under Windows—even a DOS one—make sure to run it from a Windows PIF file with the proper settings. If transfers error out, boost the value of the foreground and background priorities in the PIF settings. To prevent Windows from swapping communications software out of memory while characters are arriving over the serial port, check the box "Lock application in memory."

▶ Cut down the number of memory-resident programs that your PC is loading at boot-up.

▶ Get a current copy of Windows. Windows versions prior to 3.1 do not support 16550A UARTs.

▶ Give Windows a new communications driver. Windows' communications driver, COMM.DRV, found in Windows' main directory, is slow. Worse, it will not permit communications software that you run in a DOS window to take advantage of a 16550A UART. It lets only Windows software take advantage of this chip.

A popular COMM.DRV replacement is TurboComm, available for $47.50 from Pacific CommWare, 180 Beacon Hill Lane, Ashland, OR 97520, 503/482-2744, 503/482-2627 (fax). Or download a copy of the shareware program CHCOMB.EXE from Compu-Serve or any of the major online services; you can also order it for $10 from Cherry Hill Software at 518/786-3153, or 518/786-3158 (fax). Both of these drivers will also speed up your file transfers. They come with good directions for installing them.

So that your DOS datacomm software can talk to the 16550A chip even better, add the following line to Windows' SYSTEM.INI file, found in its main directory:

    COMxBuf=0

In place of the *x* add the number of the communications port that the software is using.

If you're running Windows in 386 Enhanced mode, edit Win-dows' SYSTEM.INI further to add the line **COMxFIFO=1** to the [386Enh] section. Instead of the *x*, type the number of the com-munications port. If the line already exists, change it appropriately.

If you're running Windows in Standard mode, remove the line DOS=HIGH from your CONFIG.SYS file. Load Windows' SYS-TEM.INI in a text editor, find the [standard] section and add the line **FasterModeSwitch=1**, or edit it if it already exists.

Disable SmartDrive's delayed write caching. It disables all inter-rupts when it writes to disk and this can interrupt a file transfer. Load AUTOEXEC.BAT in a text editor and edit the SMARTDRV entry to include the drive letter of each hard disk volume on your system. The entry for a system with C and D drives might read: D:\WINDOWS\SMARTDRV C D 1024 512.

If your high-speed modem is an internal modem, and you're still losing characters during Windows transfers, the only remedy may be to lower the connection speed. What a bummer, hey?

DOCUMENTS AND DATA

2

CHAPTER 3

WORD PROCESSING WITH PANACHE

ffice PCs spend more time word processing than any other chore. That's not surprising. Where would your business be without effective communication? One of the first successful shareware programs back in the early '80s was a marvel of an editor called PC-Write by shareware pioneer Bob Wallace. It was the word processor of choice for many PC hobbyists. Businesses meanwhile flocked to commercial word processors like Microsoft Word and WordPerfect. These programs offered sophisticated capabilities, like built-in spell-checkers, that simple editors like PC-Write lacked.

Word and WordPerfect remain the leading PC word processors, having grown more feature-packed through the years. The shareware world stands behind in the dust when it comes to full-blown word processing software with all the beeps and icons. (What shareware author, working alone, can compete with a product that has taken scores of Microsoft or WordPerfect wizzes years to twiddle to perfection?) If your word processing needs are simple (say you don't need to import bit-mapped graphics into documents), or you're low on hard disk space, or you simply don't wish to pay a premium to load a word processor on every PC in your office, you may find that there's a shareware editor out there that will keep you happy for years to come. Simple shareware editors also come in handy for composing e-mail that you plan to whiz onto some online service in basic ASCII characters; big word processors like Word require extra steps to compose text in an ASCII format that an e-mail system can swallow.

Many of these "simple" shareware editors offer features beyond the simple. For example, if you want built-in document faxing, you'll find it in a shareware product that we'll discuss here. You'll not only get built-in faxing with this product but a spell-checker as well. We'll tell you about a straightforward text editor that includes mouse support and the ability to edit multiple documents at once. Both of these products cost only about $50 to $90 to register, and they take up no more than a few megabytes on your machine when they're installed. Compare that to WordPerfect 6.0, which can take over 30MB when completely installed and can slow your machine to a crawl.

Beyond word processors, the shareware world is rife with little utilities that endow even entry-level clerical workers with the ability to manipulate words with the finesse of a publishing house. You'll find spell-checkers that correct your spelling as you type, word processing document organizers, and a style-checker that will help you compete with Hemingway.

You'll also find, among the shareware libraries, lots of indispensable add-ons and macros for WordPerfect and Microsoft Word. There are macros that let you whiz faxes from documents in these word processors to your fax software with the press of a key. There are add-on utilities that give Word essential but otherwise forgotten features, like the ability to browse documents easily, and then erase them if you want. We've included many shareware add-ons and macros for these word processors, but we can't even begin to chronicle all the ones out there that we think you'll find useful. For that reason we urge you—beg you, bid you—to head to the public forums for WordPerfect and Word on the major online services. You'll find so many terrific shareware and freeware add-ons in these conferences that your head will spin.

Full-Fledged Word Processors

In the computer world, the difference between having a "full-fledged word processor" and what's known as a "text editor" is like the difference between having a little dog and a big hairy buffalo. We will ignore that difference for the moment. The products described next span the word processing evolutionary tree, from itty-bitty dog to economy-sized buffalo. What they have in common is that you can use them to write and manipulate text. For simplicity's sake, we will call them all *word processors*. You figure out how much buffalo you need.

StarWriter

DOS

Here is a shareware word processor (super economy-sized buffalo) with star quality. If you live and breathe by pi symbols, you'll love StarWriter's built-in scientific calculator of 500 symbols. For the less calculating, there's a graphical interface that mimics the Windows one with radio buttons, pull-down menus, and dialog boxes. Although Star-Writer is not a Windows program per se, it works well in a DOS window under Windows.

You can edit multiple documents in StarWriter, cut and paste between them, and use StarWriter's macro ability to automate common word processing tasks. Its built-in spell-checker and thesaurus are every bit as good as those found in commercial word processors. It uses between 4 and 14 megabytes of hard disk space, depending on how you install it, so you know how big its dictionary is. StarWriter even offers dictionaries in German, French, and Mexican Spanish.

Other virtues include mail-merge ability, easy document faxing direct from the screen (even over networks), and the ability to import documents from other leading word processors including WordPerfect and Microsoft Word. StarWriter also lets you import data from dBASE-compatible databases to manipulate on the screen. It offers over 40 different scalable fonts, and support for 300-plus printers. A toned-down version called StarWriter Lite offers most everything that its big brother does except the spell-checker and thesaurus.

Star Division LTD.
The Rutland Center
56 Halford St.
Leicester LEI ITQ
Price: $99
Online filename: SWE_LITE.ZIP

BOXER

Many of the chapters for this book were written in this wonderful little text editor before being transferred into Word 6.0 for Windows for final formatting. A *text editor* is distinguished from a word processor by its simplicity. A text editor is for writing and editing text. That's all. A *word processor* lets you do much more to text than just writing it, such as running mail merges and spell-checkers. Text editors also create text in plain text—or ASCII symbols—while more sophisticated word processors store text in their own convoluted formats. Text editors come in handy for writing electronic mail (which is in plain text format), reading software documentation files off the disk, and other little text-related chores for which a full-blown word processor would be overkill.

One of BOXER's virtues is that it's easy to learn. It supports a mouse, plus it lets you edit multiple files in different windows and cut and paste between them. It also offers a whopping 26 clipboards to help you with your editing. Admittedly, few people need 26 clipboards, but if you're cutting and pasting lots of snippets of text between multiple files, knowing that you have more than one clipboard at your disposal can be reassuring. Commands can be issued from the keyboard or from any of the pull-down menus. You can choose to make BOXER's editing key combinations emulate those of any of a number of popular word processors, including Microsoft Word, WordPerfect, WordStar, and for techies, Epsilon. It's a highly configurable program, with 26 definable macros and keyboard customization capability. With either keyboard commands or the pull-down menus you can mark and move blocks, conduct textual searches, and perform global replacements as you can see in Figure 3-1. You can use BOXER to locate lost files on your disk and, with its drawing mode, create boxes and frames. Formatting commands allow you to set the format for columns, pagination, and headers and footers. In other words, you could use this program to write a company report.

The plain vanilla version of BOXER will edit files of up to 250K (don't worry, that's the size of a slim paperback). If you need to edit larger files you'll need BOXER/TKO which will handle files of several megabytes in length. An OS/2 version is also available. BOXER supports Epson, HP Laserjet, ProPrinter, Okidata, Panasonic, and Quiet Writer printers.

David R. Hamel
P.O. Box 3230
Peterborough, NH 03458
Phone: 603/924-6602 or 800/98-BOXER (orders only)
Fax: 603/924-4471
BBS: 603/924-3859
Price: $50; $89—BOXER/TKO; $89—BOXER OS/2
Online Filename: BOXERxx.ZIP

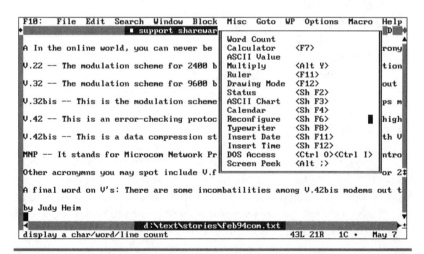

Figure 3-1   You can use keyboard commands or pull-down menus to edit files with BOXER, which comes with extras like a built-in calendar and calculator

Breeze

Breeze is more than a text editor, but less than a full-blown word processor. Use it to edit with block commands, conduct search-and-re-places, add boxes and tables to your text, or calculate a column of numbers with spreadsheet commands. A spell-checker and mail merge capability offer extra power. Pull-down menus and mouse support make it easy to use. Other pluses include the ability to print text in multiple-column format and a pop-up calculator. On the negative side, it lacks fonts and the ability to include special formatting in the text.

The feature that makes Breeze special is its ability to take a document and convert it to an executable file. What this means is that, when the reader wants to read the file, he or she need only type the beginning of the filename at the DOS prompt, just as when loading software, and the file executes by displaying itself on the screen. This is a good way to distribute text files on floppy disks to people who might not be PC literate enough to know how to display the files.

Kevin Solway
P.O. Box 207
University of Queensland
St. Lucia 4067 Australia
Price: $35
Online filename: BREEZE.ZIP

Grammar Checkers

Your fourth-grade teacher would have loved them. Grammar checkers sift through the tortured syntax of your prose and come up with advice on how to make things better. Get rid of all those clauses, a checker might say, or change those passive verbs into active ones to make you sound more confident. The major word processors include grammar checkers, but often they leave something to be desired. These puckish pop-up pedants prove themselves indispensable to the most polished poetaster. (Now get rid of that silly alliteration, our own style checker cries.)

PC-Proof

PC-Proof would have found a way to improve Shakespeare. This invincible grammar checker can detect dropped words, extra words, or, incredibly, words that have been misspelled in a way that creates another, correctly spelled word. These are the kinds of errors other grammar checkers and spell-checkers miss. PC-Proof will uncover errors involving subject/verb agreement, commonly confused words, the use of "a" and "an," double negatives, and the passive voice. It also detects other common mistakes like missing articles, misused possessives, missing infinitives, incorrect verb tense, missing punctuation, and more. It offers explanations of the errors it finds, as shown in Figure 3-2. This ain't no feeble style or readability checker. PC-Proof will make your memos shine.

Intellect Systems
P.O. Box 58213
Renton, WA 98058
Phone: 206/226-0429
Price: $40
Online filename: PC_PRO20.ZIP

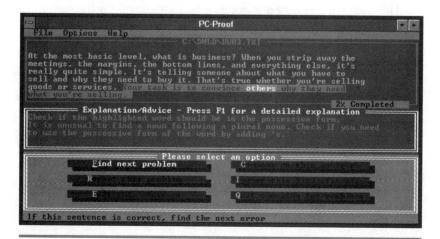

Figure 3-2   PC-Proof offers detailed explanations of the errors
                 it finds

Thelma Thistleblossom: Grammar & Style Checker

DOS

Thelma Thistleblossom will spruce up your writing as thoroughly as any erudite secretary. Designed for use on WordPerfect documents, it examines your literary output for such linguistic faux pas as rambling sentences, subject/verb disagreement, mistakes involving possessive pronouns, clichés, erroneous punctuation, and bumbling spelling. The checker's 85,000-word dictionary is included at no extra cost. Thelma highlights any problems it finds and provides an explanation of the problem (perfect for that guy in marketing who keeps asking you what his grammar checker means when it complains his memos contain 89 percent passive sentences). Then Thelma tells you how to fix it. Your project reports will never be the same.

> **Timp Software**
> **P.O. Box 37**
> **Orem, UT 84059**
> **Price: $25**
> **Online filename: TT5xx_1.ZIP and TT5xx_2.ZIP**

Critic

DOS

The critic is a compact readability checker that will sift through your prose and tell you how overly educated someone must be to read it. It will tell you if your sentences are too long, tell you if you use too many passive verbs, and check your grammar to boot. It can't read formatted files, unfortunately. You must convert the files to plain text before putting them to the test of the critic, but that's not hard.

> **James Wygant**
> **1130 S.W. Morrison, #220**
> **Portland, OR 97205**
> **Phone: 503/228-3632**
> **Price: $10**
> **Online filename: CRITIC.EXE**

Spell-Checkers

Today, a built-in spell-checker is standard in virtually all commercial word processors. Still, there are instances when you compose text outside your word processor when it would be helpful to have a spell-checker overseeing your typing: when you're jotting a note in your text editor that you plan to send to the recipient via e-mail, for example, or when you're typing entries into your phone log. Some of these shareware spell-checkers can help you out on those occasions.

WinSpell

WinSpell will oversee your spelling while you're in any Windows application, be it spreadsheet software or the Windows clipboard. As you type, it alerts you with beeps or messages to any potential misspellings. You can also look up individual words by using wildcard characters for the letters you're unsure of. You can activate WinSpell in just one window, as shown in Figure 3-3, or all windows, and turn it on or off as you wish.

WinSpell makes a special effort to ignore numerical data, a feature that is a godsend to anyone who includes numbers in memos or reports. WinSpell will even correct your spelling as you type online in an e-mail message or a computer "CB" conference, making you appear more

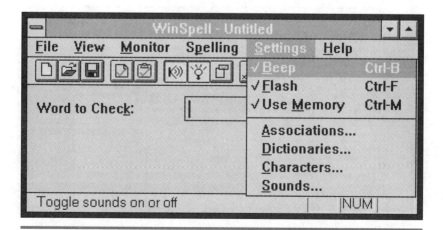

Figure 3-3 WinSpell's easy-to-use main menu screen

typographically coherent than you normally are. You can add words to WinSpell's dictionary of 120,000 words, create your own special dictionaries, and even save dictionaries as text files.

R and TH Inc.
1730 Sherbrook Dr., N.E.
Cedar Rapids, IA 52402
Phone: 214/783-8641
Price: $29.95
Online filename: WNSPL201.ZIP

ShareSpell

If you compose memos or e-mail in DOS, you'll want a copy of ShareSpell. This is the best spell-checker you'll find for scanning pure text documents, such as those created with basic text editors. After you're done writing your memo or letter, exit your text editor and then run the file through ShareSpell. When ShareSpell finds a misspelled word, it displays it in context with a list of potentially correct spellings, as shown in Figure 3-4. Highlight the right choice and ShareSpell replaces your error with its correction. Its disctionary of 112,000-plus words is comprehensive and conveniently compressed to occupy less disk space. The program is fast, and you can easily add your own words to the dictionary.

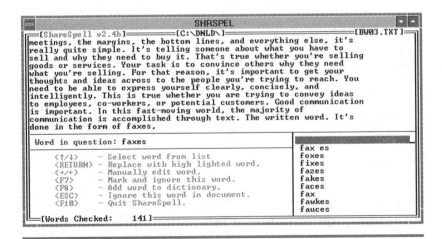

Figure 3-4   ShareSpell displays list of correct spellings

Acropolis Software
P.O. Box 5037
Fair Oaks, CA 95628
Phone: 916/967-4791
Price: $20 plus California sales tax
Online filename: SS24B.ZIP or SHRSPL24.ZIP

File Managers

If you use your PC for word processing, its hard disk can easily become as disordered as a jammed file drawer. Documents with inscrutable names like WILLY208.DOC clutter every subdirectory. Soon, your hard disk looks like bedlam itself. Your word processing software is never any help at straightening out the mess. Here are some shareware utilities that will make your document directories as orderly as Heloise's home office.

DocuPower Pro

Windows

DocuPower Pro is a must-have for Word for Windows users. It lets you create electronic folders in which to store documents, as shown in Figure 3-5. You can create a fax folder to hold your faxes, a letter folder to hold your letters, and so on. Yes, each document still goes by one of those egregiously unenlightening DOS file names, but DocuPower lets you add additional information to each name, like when the document was created and where it was sent. What a difference this information can make.

DocuPower Pro makes it easy to open, print, or insert documents into other documents just by pointing and clicking on the file descriptions. For those of us who never learn and keep assigning cryptic document names like "LETTER.DOC," DocuPower will search the file description to find the one you're looking for.

Total Systems Solutions, Inc.
1530 East 18th St., Suite 6H
Brooklyn, NY 11230
Phone: 718/375-2997 or 800/814-2300 (orders only)
Fax: 718/375-6261
BBS: 718/375-6261
Price: $39.95
Online filename: DP30W6.ZIP and DP30W2.ZIP

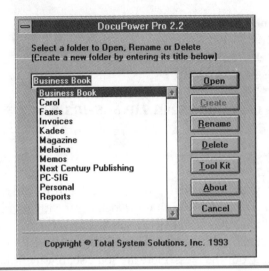

Figure 3-5   The folder selection screen of DocuPower

Word for Windows Accessories

Microsoft Word for Windows is one of the greatest word processors ever written, but it has some annoying quirks, like not permitting you to delete files within Word or taking so long to write to the screen that you might as well hang an "Out to Lunch" sign on your PC. Fortunately, the shareware forest is lush with add-on utilities and macros that make Word easy to bear. We'll start by giving you a taste of some popular Word add-on libraries, then move on to faxing goodies. As noted earlier, we can't even begin to chronicle all the useful stuff you'll be able to find online for Word. You'd be well advised to check out the Microsoft Word conferences on services like CompuServe and America Online. You'll find fonts, document templates, and special-purpose macros and utilities galore.

Word for Windows Office Power Pack (WOPR)

You'll find all the Word extras you crave in this highly acclaimed package of add-ons and macros. WOPR will let you accomplish feats as wide-ranging as printing pages front and back and squished two to a page, printing booklets with condensed type, and managing documents in a more sane manner than Word permits by giving them more self-explanatory names and popping them into the directories where they belong with the click of a mouse. You can also touch-type dingbats (typographical symbols like stars and arrows), create smart superscripts and subscripts, and print envelopes in a variety of shapes and formats. Use WOPR's toolbar editor to draw your own Word icons. The talents of this collection of software are truly abundant. It comes with the most humongous macro library you will ever download. Versions are available for both Word 2.0 and 6.0.

Pinecliffe International
Advanced Support Group
11900 Grant Place
Des Peres, MO 63131
Phone: 314/965-5630 or 800/659-4696 (orders only)
Price: $49.95 plus $4.50 shipping and handling
Online filename: WOPRx.EXE (at least 2 files), versions
are available for Word 2.0 and 6.0

Shareware in Action

Product: WOPR
Company: Jeffrey Weiss,
            Attorney at Law

New Hampshire attorney Jeffrey Weiss knows his way around the world of word processors. His first PC was a portable CP/M machine back in the first days of personal computing. Now he uses Word 6 to draft his legal documents, and he enhances Word with WOPR.

Of the many things people want a word processor to do, says Weiss, "Word provides the tools for about a third of them, but the user doesn't know the tools are there. For another third, the user needs to create macros." To meet most of the remaining third of their needs, users can turn to WOPR.

Mr. Weiss also finds Pinecliffe International, the developers of WOPR, an excellent resource for information on Word. The developers, he said, "are Word experts. As a result, WOPR provides workarounds for bugs in Word.

MegaWord

MegaWord is another must-have collection of Word add-ins, with over 30 extremely creative productivity enhancement tools, including a document recall feature that lets you preview, prior to loading, documents you've been working on. Its project manager feature lets you load a suite of documents at one swoop. It also offers a number of file management and printing utilities, plus a feature to make Word's File menu network friendly. Among other good stuff it can do: launch Windows applications from within Word, create switchable toolbars according to the document you're working on, and make your charts three-dimensional. A special CD-ROM feature lets you control your CD player from Word's toolbar.

> **Merlot International**
> **c/o Romke Soldaat**
> **1, Chemin des Moulines**
> **34230 St. Bauzille de la Sylve**
> **France**
> **Phone: 33-67-57-55-88**
> **CompuServe ID: 100273,32**
> **Price: $49 plus $5 shipping (You get $20 if you're a registered user of another designated Word add-in)**
> **Online filename: MW601.ZIP**

FileWare

Word for Windows has a way of making one feel isolated from the rest of his or her PC. If a document or graphic you need resides on another drive and you want to move it into your word processing directory, you have to go through all sorts of pointing and clicking acrobatics to get it to where you want it. If you have a copy of FileWare, you can create hard disk directories and move, delete, and rename files—all from within Word, as you can see in Figure 3-6. FileWare also includes a built-in address book, a bookmark function, and font analysis. Because of some idiosyncrasies with Word for Windows, there are separate FileWare versions for Word for Windows 2.x and 6.x. FileWare is so indispensable that it was chosen one of the top software add-in products in a *PC Magazine* review. It's also network compatible.

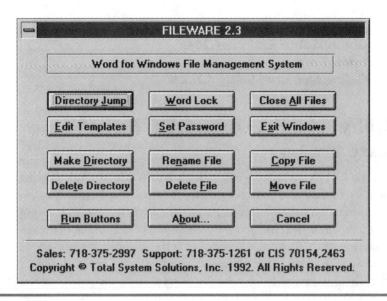

Figure 3-6   FileWare enables you to manage files from within
                 Word for Windows

Total Systems Solutions, Inc.
1530 East 18th St., Suite 6H
Brooklyn, NY 11230
Phone: 718/375-2997 or 800/814-2300 (orders only)
Fax: 718/375-6261
BBS: 718/375-6261
Price: $39.95
Online filename: FW31W2.ZIP and FW31W6.ZIP

John Navas's Send WinFax Button

Windows

Add a Send WinFax option to your Word File menu so that all you
need to do to send an active Word document out as a fax is click on Send
WinFax and out it goes. Installing Send WinFax is simple, too. Just click
on the Install option at the bottom of the documentation file and you've
got your new menu choice. This was downloaded an astonishing 2,500
times from CompuServe within a week after it was posted in a word
processing forum.

John Navas
CompuServe ID: 70244,2046
Price: Free
Online filename: SNDFAX.ZIP

The Andrew M. Freeman DDE Faxer & Template

Windows

Send Word documents to Delrina's WinFax Pro for quick faxing with the click of a button. This fax automater sends the fax recipient's name and number on to WinFax along with the active document. It comes with a fax template which will add the name and phone number of the receiver to the top of the document, along with the number of pages in the fax. When you're ready to send the document, click on the pull-down menu entry that this faxer adds to your Windows toolbar, and you'll be prompted with a dialog box for directions on sending the fax. It's super-easy to install. It works with Word for Windows 6.0 and WinFax 3.0.

Andrew M. Freeman
P.O. Box 189
Holbrook, NY 17741
CompuServe ID: 74250,1700
Registration $7
Online filename: FXDDEA.ZIP

AutoFax

Windows

Each time you want to send a fax with WinFax Pro, this spiffy Word macro will display a pop-up dialog box that will let you read, edit, and send faxes with just a mouse click. Enter the recipient's name, phone number, and other pertinent information in the dialog box. Part of the beauty of AutoFax is that it sends faxes without a cover letter, helping the environment as well as saving transmission time and paper.

MasterMind Software
CompuServe ID: 72630,555
Price: Free
Online filename: AUTOFX.ZIP

MergeFax

Use Word's mail-merge capabilities to send hundreds of personalized faxes to a mailing list. MergeFax works with WinFax Pro, and is perfect for public relations and sales people who need to send out lots of faxes on a regular basis. To install it, all you need to do is click on the install button in MergeFax's documentation file. MergeFax gives you button bars and other amenities to make fax broadcasting a snap.

> **BONZI SoftWare**
> **396 17th St.**
> **Paso Robles, CA 93446**
> **Fax: 805/238-5798**
> **CompuServe ID: 72053,2227**
> **Price: $55**
> **Online filename: MRGFAX.EXE**

Doc Browser

Ain't it a pain trying to shuffle your way through a 50-page document with that primitive Word Go To command? Doc Browser's special dialog box lets you click on the page number you want to go to, or head to the beginning, end, or middle of a document by specifying header or footer attributes.

> **Merlot International**
> **c/o Romke Soldaat**
> **1, Chemin des Moulines**
> **34320 St. Bauzille de la Sylve**
> **France**
> **Fax: 33-67-57-55-88**
> **CompuServe ID: 100273,32**
> **Price: Free**
> **Online filename: Included in MegaWord file**
> **MW601.ZIP**

FileDelete

Add a delete option to your Word File menu with this simple-to-install utility by shareware wiz author Gerald Henson. Now you can delete word processing documents as easily as you create them.

Price: Free
Online filename: WDDEL.ZIP

WordCab

WordCab is a simple front-end to Word that lets you search, sort, and store document files by English names rather than cryptic filenames, as shown in Figure 3-7. Filenames can be up to 64 characters in length, and don't need that annoying .DOC extension that Word gives files. If you've ever become exasperated with the way Word presents word processing files to you, and crave a more organized way to store them, this is for you.

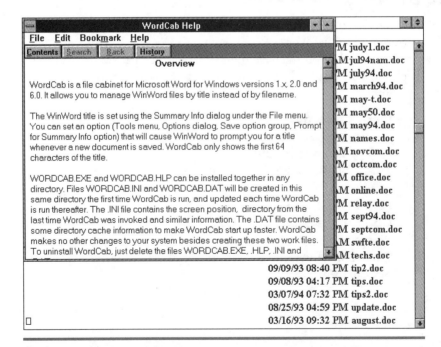

Figure 3-7 Sort and search word processing files with WordCab, a front-end to Word for Windows

Frank Ramos
CompuServe ID: 72202,2574
Price: Free
Online filename: WORDCA.ZIP

MACWIN

Windows

MACWIN is a little utility that makes Microsoft Word's agonizingly slow screen-write three to four times faster. It works by routing screen writes through your PC's BIOS in a more efficient way than Word uses. Be aware that some Windows' software installation programs experience problems with MACWIN, so you should remove MACWIN from memory when you're installing software, then replace it afterward.

MAC's Place BBS
P.O. Box 911
Dunn, NC 28335
BBS: 910/891-1111
Price: $5
Online filename: MACWIN.ZIP

MasterPrint

Windows

MasterPrint gives you better control over your printer while you're in Word. It provides a button panel from which you can print or fax selected text or selections of pages. Through MasterPrint's control panel you can also quickly change your printer's settings. Its fax feature lets you create a database of fax recipients so that you can easily send faxes from within Word.

Shawn Wallack
CompuServe ID: 72630,555
Price: Free
Online filename: MSTRPR4C.ZIP

Contract Template for Word for Windows

Windows

This Word for Windows template, designed by a lawyer, will let you update article and section numbering with the touch of a key, saving you typing time. It's easy to install and comes with great documentation. Press ALT-A when you want to type a new article, and ALT-N when you type a new section; Contract Template renumbers the entire document for you.

Hilary B. Miller, Esq.
112 Parsonage Rd.
Greenwich, CT 06803
203/861-6262
CompuServe I.D.: 76040,1743
Price: $15
Online filename: CONTRA.ZIP

WordPerfect Accessories

While add-ins for Word for Windows concentrate on filling in basic features that Microsoft forgot to include, add-ins for WordPerfect seem to focus on giving that word processor features that few people would ever consider giving to a word processor. Like a built-in blackjack player. Or the ability to act like a Rolodex at the pop of a button. There are also plenty of more prosaic WordPerfect macros floating around, like ones to automate faxing or to take addresses from a letter and print them onto an envelope. Again, you would be well advised to head to the WordPerfect forums found on CompuServe, GEnie, America Online, and many BBSs and check out the free macro collections there. Online you'll find a plenitude of templates, fonts, and information files that will help you get the most out of your word processor. Here are just a few of our favorite WordPerfect add-ins.

note

WordPerfect for Windows macros and add-ins will not work with WordPerfect for DOS, and vice versa. In fact, before you download a WordPerfect for DOS macro, always check to make sure that it's written for your version of WordPerfect. WordPerfect for DOS macros tend to work only with the version of WordPerfect that they're specifically written for.

Database Macro

If your entire life can be found in WordPerfect documents, then it pays to make WordPerfect act like a Rolodex, with card files containing pertinent information that you can view, edit, retrieve, and sort. You may want to store addresses and ideas, even recipes. The program works with WordPerfect for Windows.

> **Anthony Dobranski**
> **903 Second St.**
> **Alexandria, VA 22314**
> **CompuServe ID: 74007,46**
> **Price: Free**
> **Online filename: DB-WIN.ZIP**

WINFAX.ZIP

Here's a macro that allows you to fax a document without manually changing the printer setup. It works with WordPerfect for Windows 6.0 and Delrina's WinFax Pro.

> **Price: Free**
> **Online filename: WINFAX.ZIP**

FAX.WCM

Use this macro to automate the creation of fax cover sheets with WordPerfect for Windows. It will automatically insert in the cover sheet the name and firm of the recipient.

> **Kenneth D. Chesteka**
> **319 W. 10th St.**
> **Erie, PA 16502**
> **Phone: 814/454-5868**
> **CompuServe ID: 76525,1056**
> **Price: Free**
> **Online filename: FAXWIN.ZIP**

Word Six Tools

There are more than six tools here for WordPerfect for DOS 5.1 and 6.0. There are actually 15, and you can use them to generate a list of bookmarks contained in a document, extract comments from documents, print font lists and directory contents, list document reference targets, and much more.

> **David Seidman**
> **Software by Seidman**
> **2737 Devonshire Place., N.W.**
> **Washington, D.C. 20008**
> **Phone: 202/462-7381**
> **Fax: 202/462-8601**
> **CompuServe ID: 70441,2414**
> **Price: $25**
> **Online filename: 6TOOL11.ZIP**

WINENV.ZIP

This WordPerfect for Windows macro will copy a mailing address from the top of a letter and print it out on a long envelope. It's a great time saver when you want to print out an envelope for business correspondence without a lot of muss and fuss.

> **Price: Free**
> **Online filename: WINENV.ZIP**

Access

Here's a WordPerfect for Windows macro that will give you a pop-up menu through which you can have quick access to the Windows calculator, cardfile, and calendar, as well as to the DOS prompt. It's easier to use than ALT-TAB because you don't have to click your way to the utilities once you're in Program Manager.

> **Price: Free**
> **Online filename: ACCESS.WCM**

Blackjack

Install a blackjack game in your copy of WordPerfect for Windows, and make each foray into memo-writing a greater intellectual game of chance. This macro is written entirely in the WordPerfect macro language.

Price: Free
Online Filename: BLACK.ZIP

Medical Dictionaries for WordPerfect for DOS

Put words like actinomycosis, pericardium, and radiculopathies at your fingertips by installing these supplemental dictionaries of medical and pharmaceutical terms into WordPerfect for DOS. These are free, quick to download, and easy to install. You'll never again have to look up the spelling of "myeloproliferative."

Price: Free
Available on many online services and BBSs
Online filename: MEDDIC.ARC and MED517.ARC

CHAPTER 4

GRAPHICS AND PRESENTATION SOFTWARE TO MAKE THE WORLD SIT UP AND TAKE NOTICE

raphic images are assuming greater importance in our society the more electronically oriented we become. Computers give us the power to create and transmit pictures with an ease that would have boggled the great painters of yore. Today, graphics and video vie with the written word in enabling large numbers of people to communicate opinions and experiences, to learn, to empathize with others, and even to define their culture. Is it any surprise that the businesses that make the most money these days—Hollywood, Madison Avenue, Walt

Disney—are the ones that are best at manipulating the power of pictures?

You, my friend, can be every bit as good as Paramount in creating dazzling sales presentations or public relations slide-shows. You'll find shareware presentation programs that will endow your PC with the power of multimedia, helping you combine sound, graphics, and text with unparalleled ease. You can make a "talking brochure" that you can distribute to clients on floppy disks. You can create electronic publications with text, click-on buttons, graphics, sound, and more. Never again will "office communication" mean lugging a bunch of printouts to the photocopy machine.

Presentation Software

P.T. Barnum should have had it so easy. Now all you need to do to dazzle a crowd—or client—is to throw together a little music, a few PC screen pictures, add some text and maybe a dramatic voice-over, and you'll have a multimedia extravaganza good enough to feature in an IBM commercial. The shareware programs detailed in this chapter will let you do just that.

SuperShow IV

If you want multimedia presentation software, SuperShow IV is the real McCoy. It lets you script a slide show that combines pictures, text, and sound. You can fade from one screen to another, add kaleidoscope screen effects, draw boxes and circles, and clear the screen. There are other special effects too. The software supports digitized voice and MIDI music generated with SoundBlaster-compatible sound cards so you can add music and voice-overs to your slide show that will be heard over the PC's speaker.

SuperShow uses graphic files captured in the popular GIF format as well as files in the PCX format in its slide shows. If you don't have a screen capture program, you can use the one provided by SuperShow. Custom as well as standard computer fonts are provided to display text. To create a presentation, you'd use SuperShow's script-generator to create a script—a list of one- or two-word commands that instruct the program what you want displayed and how. That's not hard, even for the PC tenderfoot, because SuperShow offers pull-down menus containing the commands. It basically writes the script for you. Designing presentations couldn't be easier.

PC West
P.O. Box 31418
Phoenix, AZ 85046
Phone: 602/992-0310
Price: $89.95 plus $5 shipping
Online filename: SS4.ZIP

VIDVUE

Assemble slide shows using picture files from any of the major graphics formats with this impressive (although sometimes inscrutable) presentation program. Write your script in any text editor and, to display pictures, simply type in the filename of the picture file. VIDVUE won't write a script for you as SuperShow will, but, nonetheless, assembling a slide show with it isn't hard. A GIF screen capture and conversion utility is included. VIDVUE allows you to resize images, even full-motion AVI ones. It supports all the major graphics formats, and its script language lets you endow your slide shows with fairly sophisticated graphic effects like screen fades. You can even play multiple sounds while screens are displaying.

VIDVUE initially took us a long time to get to work. The demo slideshow included in the program wouldn't work initially because the slides weren't included. But once we figured out what was wrong and simply substituted our own graphic file names in the script that came with the program, VIDVUE worked like a charm. It lacks drawing tools like Multimedia Workshop below, but it still became our favorite of the programs in this chapter thanks to ease of use and adaptability (we could even incorporate in our slideshows pictures taken from Compton's CD-ROM Encyclopedia). It lacks a manual, but its help files are fine. Screen drawing aside, this program includes everything you want to do in multimedia.

Lawrence Gozum
100 Oriole Parkway #310
Toronto, Ontario M5P 2G8
Canada
CompuServe ID: 73437,2372
GEnie Mail: L.Gozum
Internet: l.gozum@geis.com
Price: $35
Online filename: VIDVUE.ZIP

Multimedia Workshop

Windows

Create a PC presentation with sound and animation using Multimedia Workshop. One of the things that makes it unique is that it comes with a full line of drawing tools with which to create your own graphics, something VIDVUE lacks. Link your pictures together, and then run them all at once in a continual display with sound. This is great for booths at trade shows where you want to run the same presentation over and over. A built-in indexing feature lets you search through your pictures easily. Figure 4-1 shows the array of tools you're offered when creating a presentation with Multimedia Workshop.

Multimedia Workshop uses a special graphics storage system that allows you to store up to 100 pictures on a single floppy disk, making your

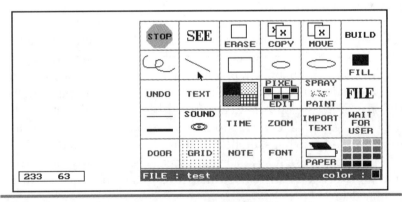

Figure 4-1   Working in Multimedia Workshop

presentations easily transportable. Needless to say, though, the faster your computer, the smoother the presentation will run. It will display GIF, PCX, TARGA, TIF, and PIC graphic files, and it plays sound through the PC's speaker and offers support for SoundBlaster sound cards.

Another Company
P.O. Box 3429
Ashland, OR 97520
Phone: 404/394-1000 or 800/444-2424 (orders only)
Attn: Gary Smith
Price: $99.95
Online filename: TMW10.EXE

Talking Slideshow

Talking Slideshow lets you put together a PC slide show with sound accompaniment (even your own voice) with astonishing ease. Simply create a series of Windows bitmap picture files, name them 1, 2, 3, and so on, and place them in Talking Slideshow's directory. Click on the play button. Talking Slideshow displays the picture and the associated sound file, then moves on to the next. Although Talking Slideshow supports internal sound boards, you don't even need one. It will play the sound through the PC's speaker. It lacks drawing tools like Multimedia Workshop, or special effects like screen fades but it's still slick and lots of fun.

Softline, Inc.
15377 N.E. 90th St.
Redmond, WA 98052
Phone: 206/861-5463
CompuServe ID: type GO IBMNET
Price: $9.95 plus $4 shipping; WA residents add sales tax
Online filename: !TLKSH.EXE

Quick Show Light for Windows

Quick Show lets you display a series of picture files in a sequence with sound. The documentation says it was "designed to be simple enough for children, politicians, and most species of single-celled organisms to operate." And indeed it is. Click your way to a slide show presentation in minutes. Quick Show supports just about every graphics format conceived, as well as sound formats.

This program is much simpler in concept than the others. It doesn't include drawing tools, and only offers two different picture transition types—a display in which squares of the picture are filled in quickly by random and a normal computer picture display. You can't cut and crop images either, although you can choose from different background colors and frame types. You can also select which area on the screen you want the image displayed. You choose how you want pictures displayed by clicking on buttons or choosing from lists in the pop-up menu displayed in Figure 4-2. With Quick Show you can display text with images as well as play sound. The program supports WAV, MIDI, and AVI files. This really works.

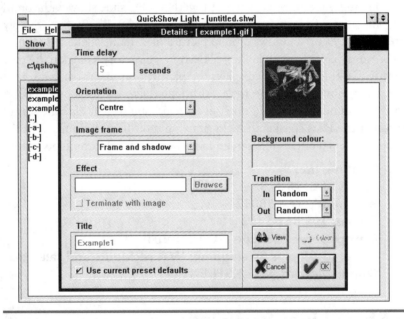

Figure 4-2　When you set up a Quick Show slide show, click on buttons to choose how you prefer each image—in this case, the frog in the upper-right corner—to be displayed

Alchemy Mindworks
P.O. Box 500
Beeton, Ontario LOG 1AO
Canada
Phone: 905/729-4969 or 800/729-4969 (orders only)
Fax: 905/729-4156
BBS: 905/729-4609
Price: $40 (Or submit proof that you have read Steven William Rimmer's novel "The Order"; mail bookstore receipt, copy of novel cover, along with comments about it to take advantage of this special offer.)
Online filename: QSHOW.ZIP

Lecture for Windows

There are times when you don't want to overwhelm your audience with graphics and sound, when you want to display facts, but don't need the flash. Lecture is an ideal tool for teachers and anyone else behind the podium. It works especially well when the PC's screen is projected for your audience. Lecture will read in plain text files and display them in a window on the screen. (Plain text or ASCII files are text files without the formatting of your word processor. All word processors will let you save files in this fashion. It's not hard to do.) As you talk, you can easily "turn pages" by clicking with the mouse or by pressing the space bar. You create slide shows by creating a simple script with Windows' Notepad, as shown in Figure 4-3. You use just five commands like "Mastertitle," "Subtitle," and "Point" to tell Lecture how to place text on the screen and the size of letters to display it in. It's very simple to use.

BarnOwl Software
P.O. Box 1115
O'Fallon, IL 62269
Phone: 618/632-7345 or 800/242-4775 (orders only)
Fax: 618/632-2339
Price: $29
Online filename: LECT-102.ZIP or LECTUR.ZIP

Figure 4-3   Create Lecture presentations with Windows'
Notepad using only five commands

Electronic Publications: Presentations for When You're Not There

Ever since Gutenberg, a printed book has been the most convenient way to circulate information. If your company doesn't have its own printing department, you may be getting sick of traipsing down the street or across town to a printer every time you need a brochure. Or, you may be getting tired of the cost of paper and four-color processing. You can skip the print-press shuffle and compose your own digital brochures on your PC; then, when that's done, you can distribute them by disk or modem. The software described next will give you the power to do all this, plus incorporate graphics and sound into your message. Before long, they'll have you convinced that anything on paper is strictly Pleistocene.

Softline Brochure for Windows

Use Brochure to create an electronic brochure in which you describe yourself or your product to potential customers, with up to 100 picture files capable of being displayed in slide show fashion on their PCs. You

Shareware in Action

**Product: Softline Brochure
for Windows
Company: Alta Copy
and Print**

When Ramey Bell of Alta Copy and Print in Bellevue, Washington, wanted to advertise his copy service, he wanted something his potential customers would notice. He didn't want to send them one more pretty brochure that might not even make it past the secretary or the mail room. Then he found Softline Brochure for Windows. For about the price of a four-color brochure, he sent self-running disks to targeted clients. When he followed up his mailing with phone calls, everyone who received a disk remembered him. Brochure, he said, helped him schedule appointments with new customers. "Brochure provides a different and unique way of advertising," he said, and called his first year of using Brochure "a great success" with an excellent rate of return.

can give your electronic brochures away at trade shows or send them out in mass-mailings with other promotional goodies.

This program is radically simply to use. You merely create a series of bitmapped images (the kind of screen graphics you can create with Windows and its built-in paint program, Windows Paint). You label them in the order you want them to appear as 1.BMP, 2.BMP, and so on. You create WAV sound files by either hooking a microphone to your PC or downloading some of the many public domain sound files found on services like CompuServe and America Online. Name them, similarly, as SOUND1.WAV, SOUND2.WAV, and so on, to correspond to the pictures you want to display. Place the files in the Talking Slideshow directory and click the play button in the program. The program displays the first image and plays the associated sound files. Then it moves on to the next and the next. Incredibly easy!

Brochure has features that will help you make your talking brochures as entertaining to watch as a video game. It lets you meld text, voice, and graphics in such an appealing fashion that you'll want to make your product catalogs into electronic ones. Brochure reads text files written in Write, the Windows mini-word processor; unfortunately, it won't read text files from any other word processor. The file can contain product info, new product announcements, a product catalog, or any other detailed information on your product. Your customer doesn't have to have any special sound hardware to run the brochures because the sound plays through the PC's speakers.

Softline, Inc.
15377 N.E. 90th St.
Redmond, WA 98052
Phone: 206/861-5463
CompuServe ID: 70253,1052
Price: $99.95 plus $4 shipping; WA residents add sales tax
Online filename: !BROCH.EXE

NeoShow and NeoShow Pro 2.0

Use NeoShow to author snazzy multimedia graphical presentations using sound and computer images. It's perfect for creating product presentations to run at tradeshows, in stores, and during client demos. First, create a computer image slide show by picking out the digitized pictures you want to display. (Unfortunately, you're limited to using PCX and GIF graphics files, but that's not too great of an inconvenience since those are the two most popular formats.) You add sound to your presentation by selecting VOC format sound files to play while each image is displayed. (Again, it's unfortunate that the program doesn't support more formats, particularly the common WAV sound file format, but those are the breaks.)

Built-in special effects let you control how images are displayed, by fade-in for example, or slide-in from one corner of the screen, at even a pixel at a time. You activate special effects by picking choices from a menu, which can be seen in Figure 4-4. You can also control the speed at which images display. A debug mode lets you run through the presentation quickly to see how (and if) it works, without having to wait for the special effects.

Each image in your slide show appears in a small window on the screen. NeoShow has a "build" option that you can use to automatically include all the images in a directory into your slide show. If you use the build option, the slides probably won't appear in the order that you want them to. That's not really a problem because you can easily rearrange the

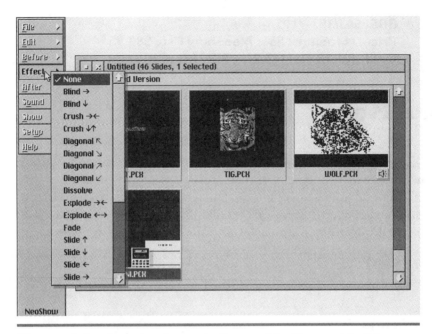

Figure 4-4 A menu of special effects in NeoShow, with slides for a presentation in the background

order of the slides by clicking on the window for a slide and dragging it to its proper place in the show.

NeoShow Pro differs from regular NeoShow in two ways. First, NeoShow Pro lets you record your sounds on SoundBlaster-compatible sound cards. The Pro version also gives you a compiler that allows you to create self-contained executable slide shows, which you can distribute on diskette for promotional purposes. The customer can fire them up just by typing the filename. The images and sound files are incorporated into the executable program, so you don't have to worry about forgetting to copy one of the files to your slide show diskettes.

OSCS Software Development, Inc.
354 NE Greenwood, Suite 108
Bend, OR 97701-4631
Phone: 503/389-5489
Fax: 503/388-8221

BBS: 503/383-7195
Price: NeoShow: $35; NeoShow Pro: $89.95
Online filename: NS.ZIP, NSPRO.ZIP

To Learn More

If you want to read more about multimedia, check out *The WAFFER!*
Multimedia Digest. It's a slick, information-packed publication that's run
in Windows, offering news, reviews, gossip, and gripes about the multimedia world. It's also free. You can find new editions posted regularly on
BBSs and online services. Look for files that are named WMD00*xx*.ZIP
or WMD00*xx*.EXE. The *x*'s and 0's will include the edition number.

CHAPTER 5

PRINTING SOFTWARE THAT BRINGS OUT THE BEST IN YOUR REPORTS

here is no peripheral with so much potential to wreak havoc as a printer. If lines in your report run off the page, or if Page 3 ends in the middle of Page 4, your career literally could very possibly be wrecked. Conversely, there is no peripheral with so much potential to make you look good. Unfortunately, sometimes it seems like getting your printer to print the way you want requires the effort of a NATO negotiation. There are literally thousands of shareware utilities out there that tackle such common printing problems as printing sideways, breaking pages properly, and handling fonts. Here are some of the most indispensable of those utilities.

Printing Sideways, Upside Down, and in Other Unorthodox Ways

Think of how much simpler the world would be if all the pages we had to print were 8 1/2" x 11" and all documents aligned themselves perfectly from the top of the page to the bottom. Until the laws of physics amend themselves to embrace sensible concepts, we're stuck with spreadsheets that must be printed sideways, employee handbooks that need to be printed two pages to a sheet, and printers that refuse to cooperate in all instances. The following utilities were designed to let you print in ways other than vertically and on materials other than typewriter pages.

On-Side

There is no conflict between man and machine more archetypal in nature than the one that occurs when what's on your screen is wider than the pages that come out of your printer. It happens all the time with spreadsheets. There are lots of hundred dollar programs that take care of this problem, but there are lots of shareware ones too that work just as well. The best is On-Side. It will print any file on its side, from spreadsheets to reports—something most word processing and shareware programs will not do. Unfortunately, you need a dot-matrix printer to use it. It won't work with a laser printer. But if someone sends you a plain text file, such as a humongous spreadsheet, using On-Side is considerably easier than getting out the tape and scissors.

Print your five-lane spreadsheet across multiple sheets of fan-folded paper and leave the perforations connected. On-Side works with any text file and can print out in a variety of fonts.

Expressware Corporation
P.O. Box 1800
Duvall, WA 98019
Phone: 206/788-0932 (tech support) or 800/753-3453
(orders only)
Fax: 206/788-4493
Price: $24.95 plus $5 shipping
Online filename: ONSIDE.ZIP

PPrint

DOS

PPrint is the Swiss Army knife of printer utilities. It slices, dices, prints page headers and footers, and can scale fish when dropped off the side of the Chrysler Building with a bungee cord. Seriously, PPrint lets you quickly print ordinary text files in ways that you normally could not without loading the file into a word processor and reformatting it. This capability is tremendously helpful if you are printing your electronic address book, word processing files that have been transmitted as text files through e-mail, or database files in text format.

You can print the files with page numbering, headers, footers, double-spacing, and line numbering. Tell PPrint what page to begin printing on and what page to end. You can't normally do that from the DOS command line. There's lots more you can do with it too. You can tailor PPrint to support any printer, but you probably won't have to configure it for yours, because it comes with great support for HP Laserjets and other leading printers.

> **PatriSoft**
> **5225 Canyon Crest Dr., Suite 71-358**
> **Riverside, CA 92507**
> **Phone: 909/352-2820 or 800/242-4775 (orders only)**
> **Price: $20 plus $4 shipping**
> **Online filename: PPRINT55.ZIP**

MultiLabel

Windows

Have you ever spent hours in a word processor, trying to line up columns and rows to print labels, but still couldn't make it work? Here's a lovely time and effort saver, MultiLabel.

MultiLabel lets Windows 3.1 users create customized labels on any Avery LaserLabel format or on custom-sized labels. The complete access MultiLabel affords to TrueType and Adobe Type Manager fonts and to PCX or BMP clip-art, along with the total control it allows over text and graphics alignment, make this program a must. You can print full sheets of identical labels. Plus, an address list database included in the program lets you store and select up to 750 names per file and print labels in a mail-merge style format. Other features include automatic serial numbers, line drawing tools, and support for all Windows-capable printers.

Labels are designed on a WYSIWYG display, complete with a layout grid, as shown in Figure 5-1. Text alignment can be automatic or you can use a precision text placement system, plus there's support for multicolumn label designs. MultiLabel is ideal for creating product labels, return address labels, or address labels using the built-in address book module. The interface uses onscreen visual aids, so you're never forced to hunt through menus for the tools you need.

MultiLabel
1472 Sixth St.
Los Osos, CA 93402
Phone: 805/528-1759
Fax: 805/528-3074
BBS: 805/528-3753
Price: $20
Online filename: MLTLBL.ZIP

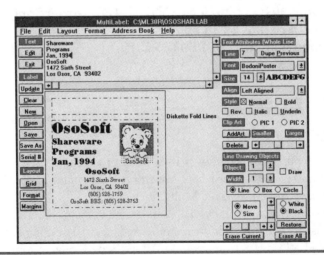

Figure 5-1   MultiLabel gives you a wide range of tools with which to design labels

Rockford!

Windows

Need business cards fast? Rockford!'s your program. Design and print professional business cards with this program for Windows 3.1. Use any TrueType or Postscript Type 1 font to lay out text, then add BMP or PCX clip-art images, lines, boxes, and circles, and even reverse (white on black) type. Use the WYSIWYG display to view your card just as it will print. Then, print your finished card as a camera-ready layout, or print sheets of finished cards on plain card stock or on pre-scored card stock from Paper Direct or other sources. Rockford! works with any Windows-capable printer.

From start to finish, you can have powerful cards in less than 10 minutes, using the logical onscreen tools. You control every aspect of the card, from text positioning and alignment to font sizes and graphics scaling, as shown in Figure 5-2. Why struggle with an ineffective, hard to use business card template in another program when you can design cards in minutes in a program specially set up for that chore?

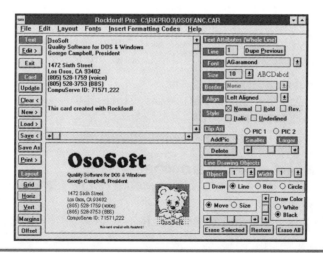

Figure 5-2   Use your PC and laser printer to create professional looking business cards with Rockford!

Rockford!
1472 Sixth St.
Los Osos, CA 93402
Phone: 805/528-1759
Fax: 805/528-3074
BBS: 805/528-3753
Price: $20
Online filename: RCKFRD.ZIP/ROCKFORD.ZIP

4Print & 4Book

Ever try to print a booklet on your laser printer with more than one page printed on a standard sized page? Unless you have expensive desktop publishing software it can be all but impossible. 4Print will print as many as four pages of text, at 66 lines and 80 columns per page, on just one 8 1/2" by 11" sheet of paper. Imagine the money this will save when you print up your employee handbook.

4Print offers lots of command line parameters that let you control how the output will look. It lets you add borders, the date and time, the filename, and the page count. 4Print automatically handles form feeds, tabs, and end-of-file markers. 4Book, a companion program included with 4Print, helps in creating good-looking booklets ready for a three-ring binder. Documents printed with 4Print are easy to read and nicely formatted. 4Print works with all HP Laserjet printers and compatibles.

Korenthal Associates, Inc.
511 Avenue of the Americas, Suite 400
New York, NY 10011
Phone: 212/242-1790
Fax: 212/242-2599
CompuServe: type GO KORENTHAL
Price: $49.95 (DOS only); $69.95 (DOS and Windows);
plus $5 shipping
Online filename: 4PRINT.ZIP

MicroText

MicroText lets you print up to four pages of text on one sheet of paper, much like 4Print. Its advantage over that program is that it offers menus, while 4Print requires you enter commands at the primitive DOS prompt. It doesn't offer as many features as 4Print, but it's just as functional and easier to use. MicroText will automatically wrap words to the width you specify. It will never break a word in two to wrap it. It will also strip out any extra blank lines. You can also configure it to print graphics characters, add margins, and print in one or two columns.

OsoSoft
1472 Sixth St.
Los Osos, CA 93402
Phone: 805/528-1759
Fax: 805/528-3074
BBS: 805/528-3753
Price: $15
Online filename: MICROTXT.ZIP

DMP

DMP is our favorite print spooler. It can spool to disk, spool to expanded or extended memory, and even to XMS extended memory. You can use DMP to send files to the printer, but wait to actually print them until it's more convenient for you to do so. The printing queue can hold multiple files—imagine a bunch of files standing in line waiting for access to the printer. You don't have to worry about over-running your DOS or Windows printer queue with too many files, or files that are too large, because DMP provides you with virtually unlimited room to store files. Highly configurable, it supports both parallel and serial printers. It also works exceptionally well when task-switching programs are loaded. It can even compensate for problems your printer is having, such as, for instance, its failure to send form feeds when it's supposed to.

DMP Software
204 E. Second Ave., Suite 610
San Mateo, CA 94401
Price: $29
Online filename: DMP*xxx*.ZIP

Windows Printing Helpers

If you've ever tried to print a plain text file from Windows—a file not created in a Windows word processor—you know the problems. Ordinary ASCII text files don't contain special fonts or formatting. What's more, Windows can be balky at printing anything from a DOS window. These utilities can help you out.

Drag and Drop Printing

Drag and Drop lets you print old-fashioned text files from within Windows with ease. Simply drag the name of the file from File Manager and drop it on the Drag and Drop icon. The file will be printed in the background. You can print files sideways; print with one of the TrueType fonts, screen fonts, or printer fonts; set the margins; add headers and footers, and more.

Drag and Drop will also print graphics and will let you specify dithering for graphic detail, darkness, and whether or not the graphic should be in color (assuming your printer is a color one). You can also select paper size. This is a very handy program, and exceptionally well done.

FLFSoft
P.O. Box 306
Oak Creek, WI 53154-0306
Price: $15
Online filename: DDP*xx*.ZIP

Print Screen Manager

When you press PRTSC while in Windows, Windows puts a copy of the PC's screen into its clipboard. Press the same key while Print Screen Manager is running and you have the choice of printing the screen, saving

Figure 5-3   Select Output Destination dialog box of Print
Screen Manager

it as a bitmap graphics file, or storing it in the clipboard. A dialog box, shown in Figure 5-3, prompts you for your choices. The uses for such a utility are as unlimited as the PRTSC button itself. Use it for capturing and printing portions of e-mail or pasting pictures of screens into reports or documention files.

> **Mallegrax Software**
> **21446 Firwood St.**
> **Lake Forest, CA 92630**
> **Price: $20**
> **Online filename: PSMAN.ZIP**

Fonts, Fonts, and More Fonts

The best thing about laser printers are all those fonts you can print with. Century Schoolbook, Helvetica Bold, Futura Light. You don't have to head to a printer to make your pages sparkle. The kingpin of shareware fonts is Gary Elfring of Elfring Soft Fonts. He sells fonts for Word, WordPerfect, Windows, and other programs. You can even order custom fronts from him, like a font that is a replica of your handwriting. Some of the packages below are shareware versions of ones he sells at retail.

You'll find lots more fonts available online on the major information services. Head to the support forums for your brand of word processing software. You'll find hundreds (and we mean hundreds) of free and nearly free fonts that are quick to download and easy to install. You'll find all the standard fonts, like Bauhaus Demi, plus lots of special purpose ones, like bamboo letters, and fonts that look like the letters were painted with a paint brush. See Chapter 2 for more information on hunting shareware online.

Top Fonts

Top Fonts is a truly impressive sampler package of text and display fonts for Windows and WordPerfect 6.0. Among the fonts included are Cooper Black, Cursive Elegant, Futura Black, Old English, and Nova. The package, which is a subset of the commercial package of the same name, also includes a tutorial on using the fonts.

Elfring Soft Fonts
P.O. Box 61
Wasco IL 60183
Phone: 708/377-3520
Fax: 708/377-6402
Price: $20
Online filename: TOPFONT.ZIP

ESF's TrueType Collection 1

Elfring's TrueType Collection 1 consists of ten scalable TrueType fonts for Windows 3.1 and WordPerfect 6.0 for DOS. Fonts include Century Bold, Cursive Elegant, Aapex, Century, Friz Quad, Friz Quad Bold, Old English, MicroStile, MicroStile Bold, and Zap Chance, shown here:

ESF's TrueType Collection 1 Preview

Aapex ABCEFGabcdefg
Cursive Elegant AB Cabc
Century ABCDabcd
Century Bold ABCDabcd
Friz Kat ABCDabcd
Friz Bold ABCDabcd
MicroStile ABCDabcd
MicroStile Bold ABCDabcd
Old English ABCDabcd
Zap Chance ABCDabcd

The collection includes a special setup program that will automatically install the fonts for you. A full tutorial on fonts that will prove helpful for many users is also included.

Elfring Soft Fonts
P.O. Box 61
Wasco, IL 60183
Phone: 708/377-3520
Fax: 708/377-6402
Price: $25
Online filename: ESFTT1.ZIP

Fonter

If you use Windows, you've probably accumulated a long list of fonts. But remembering which font looks like the one you want can be a chore. Fonter is designed to help you see your fonts clearly. Use it to view any installed TrueType or Adobe Type Manager Type 1 font in several ways. You can view a font sample, keyboard layout, or ANSI code chart on the screen. See a large default text sample or view your own text as it will appear in print.

Even better, Fonter lets you print font lists, with samples, of all the fonts you have or of selected fonts. You can control the text to be printed for quick comparisons. Or, you can print a full-page type specimen sheet, a keyboard layout diagram, or an ANSI code chart for access to foreign and symbol fonts. What's more, you can even save any character in a symbol or dingbat font as a 72-point BMP clip-art file. Fonter is easy to use, and the registered version even comes with two utilities to help you manage your fonts and detect defective fonts.

OsoSoft
1472 Sixth St.
Los Osos, CA 93402
Phone: 805/528-1759
Fax: 805/528-3074
BBS: 805/528-3753
Price: $20
Online filename: FONTER.ZIP

TSR Download

One of the problems with soft fonts is that they can be a pain to keep track of. The names are cryptic, you often forget which one you sent to the printer, and you never know when your printer will run out of memory. TSR Download is a memory-resident font manager that will pop up over any non-graphics application, locate all of your fonts, and translate their names into something in English.

You can tag an individual font or complete list of fonts for downloading to your printer. The program is so fast it can download 100K of fonts to the printer in seconds. TSR Download also remembers what fonts you've sent to the printer and how much memory they require. It will warn you when you're about to exceed the memory limit of your printer. You can control many basic printer functions with TSR Download, including selection of landscape or portrait modes, when to send form feeds, and how to set line spacing. You can also set the number of characters per inch and switch between manual and tray feed. TSR Download supports up to 100 fonts.

> **Elfring Soft Fonts**
> **P.O. Box 61**
> **Wasco, IL 60183**
> **Phone: 708/377-3520**
> **Fax: 708/377-6402**
> **Price: $34.95**
> **Online filename: TSRDLxx.ZIP**

JaDy FontEdit

Create your own soft fonts or edit ones you already have with this easy-to-use font editor, shown in Figure 5-4. Alter soft fonts to give them new effects, like italics, boldface, ghosting, and overlay. Tweek pixels and create typographical characters up to one inch in height. Use JaDy to create your own novelty fonts for special projects. (I remember once spending hours online and on the phone looking for a laser printer font similar to a whimsical typesetter's font I'd once seen. It was called Stars and Strips. I wanted to use it to make a corner of a tiny magazine ad especially eye-catching. I never did find a soft font version. Had I had a

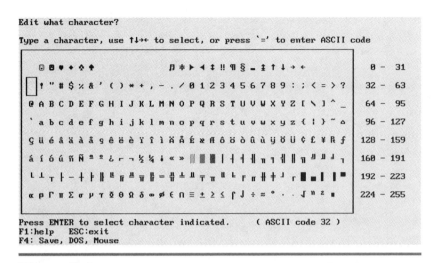

Figure 5-4   Create your own soft fonts with JaDy FontEdit

copy of JaDy, I'm sure I could have manually created something similar, and it would have been an appropriate way to solve the problem. After all, I only wanted to use the font for a couple of words.) Ghost effects are also great to use in newsletters. This program is not for everyone, but if there's a latent graphic designer lurking inside of you, you'll enjoy using JaDy.

John Derrickson
834 Chestnut St., #1204
Philadelphia, PA 19107
Phone: 215/922-1826
CompuServe ID: 70240,261
GEnie ID: J.DERRICKSON
Price: $30
Online filename: FONTJD.EXE

CHAPTER 6

DATABASE SOFTWARE THAT KEEPS YOUR WORLD IN ORDER

Your database software can be the difference between happy customers who keep coming back and irritated ones who keep flooding you with angry calls, complaining that you botched their orders. Database software is essential not just for keeping track of your customers, but for every aspect of business in which you have information to maintain and manipulate. Databases are the engines behind mass-mailing campaigns, card catalogs for market research, and electronic file cabinets used to store personnel files. Many businesses even use databases to store and search information on competitors and their products.

We won't lie to you and tell you that shareware database software will serve all your needs as efficiently as one of those pricey commercial database products like dBASE or Ingres. In fact, we should point out that price wars among commercial software producers, like Microsoft, Borland, and Lotus, have brought the price of commercial database software within range of many shareware products. In fact, many shareware packages run around $100, which is the price of many of the major commercial database software these days.

So why use shareware? If you run a small home business or are starting a business and are unsure of what your database needs will be six months down the road, or even if you're just short on cash and not quite ready to make a buying decision, shareware database software may serve your needs perfectly, providing an easy way to index, search, sort, and print information. Shareware is also great because it's compact. Who needs a huge database program to keep track of the hundred or so customers of a new business? Shareware also runs on many lower powered machines like 286s and those old 8086s you can find in the newspaper classifieds for $100. In short, shareware database software is a good deal for the new and small business. We've used shareware database packages for years for keeping track of book research, as well as customer and prospect lists for our own home businesses.

But even if your business already relies on a major commercial database package like Paradox, dBASE, or FoxPro, shareware offers something for you too. Information services like CompuServe have vast shareware file libraries of special purpose macros and software add-ins for these commercial programs. There are report writers, screen layout designers, letter and mail-merge utilities, and many other tools for writing custom applications in these databases' special languages. Skip to the end of the chapter for more information on these utilities and a list of our favorites.

What to Look for in a Database

What should you look for in shareware database software? A virtually limitless number of records and tables is good for starters. You also want to be able to specify fields for dates, currency, and solely numeric entries. And you want to be able to append to records a memo field that can contain a sizable amount of text for notes on customers or their orders.

An easy way to query the database, or to tell it what kind of information you want, is also essential. And fast record searching is also vital.

Eventually, as your business grows, you may find that there is something that you want to specify in your database's fields that your shareware won't permit. That's when it's time to migrate to a full-blown, programmable, commercial package with a fourth generation programming language that allows you to create a front-end for your database as well as a querying language with which your employees can query the database to search for information. But, who knows? Shareware may serve your needs for years to come.

Structured Databases

The traditional database is a structured one. You enter information into records with fields. Think of these as being like the card catalog at the public library. The record is like the 3" x 5" index card and the fields are like the categories for author, title, and so on. *Structured databases* are the workhorses of the database world. You use them for storing information that you want arranged in a structured way and output in a standard format, like mailing labels or invoices. A *free-form database*, conversely, is one in which less rigidly structured informational items—like ideas, notes for a book, or contacts for research—are stored with intuitive links that make them easy to find when you're in the midst of a midnight brainstorm. We'll talk more about free-form databases later. There are a number of powerful shareware databases that fall into the structured database category. Next, we'll discuss some particularly good ones and then describe a few of the better free-form ones.

PC-File

PC-File was one of the first shareware products ever, written by a former IBM executive back in 1982. It continues to be a favorite for businesses that want a powerful little database that's super-easy to use. Its ease of use cannot be overstated. PC-File is by far the easiest database to use on the market. A novice PC user with no experience with databases can have it up and running within less than an hour, if not minutes. PC-File is an all-purpose relational database with an easy to learn, "mouseable" interface that mimics Windows. When you start it, it gives you a list of the databases on your disk and asks which one you want to load and whether you want to search, modify, or delete records. It's ideal for keeping customer records and address and phone listings as well as for invoicing, sales tracking and analysis, inventory control, and much more. PC-File creates and uses files that are dBASE compatible so you can interchange files with other major database products. Its main limitation is that it doesn't have a developer's mode that lets you create database applications yourself.

You can use PC-File's unique *learn mode* to create a database through prompts which ask the user what to do next, and a database structure is built accordingly. Novice database users will appreciate the learn mode because it's so easy to use and doesn't require any prior knowledge of databases to set one up. With the learn mode and the extensive built-in help to print mailing labels, you can create customer support, dial phone numbers in your database, and graph information with pie, bar, and line charts. You can also build intelligent macros that you can use to automate repetitive chores.

When you create a database with PC-File, it gives you the option either of setting up the record screens using the standard format or of "painting" the screen. You're not really painting the screen as in a PC paint program. Rather, you type in each of the fields, then press the space bar to designate how many spaces each entry should get, as shown in Figure 6-1. If you select the second option you can customize up to five data entry screens, with up to 128 fields. Each field is placed exactly where you want it. You can tell the program to fill some fields automatically. Databases can be imported, exported, and cloned. PC-File can handle an almost limitless number of records and has many configurable options. You can even use it to create form letters and to print labels.

Buttonware, Inc.
P.O. Box 96058
Bellevue, WA 98009
Phone: 206/865-0773 or 800/528-8866 (orders only)
Fax: 206/865-0894
Price: $89.95
Online filename: PCF70A-D.ZIP

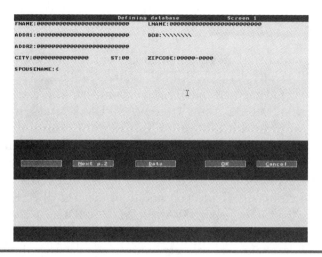

Figure 6-1 You set up a database in PC-File by designing the format for the records

Shareware in Action

**Product: PC-File
Company: State of
Louisiana Department of
Social Services, Office of
Community Services**

The Office of Community Services at the State of Louisiana Department of Social Services is responsible for investigating child abuse, finding prospective adoptive parents for children, and providing other social services throughout the state. The office's 60 field offices are connected by Novell LANs, and all workers have access to a computer. When this system was set up, the office wanted to provide a suite of applications to its employees, including a database. The top contenders were powerful, full-featured programs such as dBASE III, but most staff members would require training, and database management wasn't their main job. They needed a tool that would help them without burdening them. "So we chose PC-File," said Terry Skaggs, community services information management director. "We just ordered it, tried it out, and compared it to the other programs. It was simple, and a non-computer person could use it."

The Office of Community Services has now used PC-File for more than five years and has approximately 250 copies distributed throughout its offices. Employees "share ideas for using the program, but there are no required file types or formats," says Skaggs. Some use it for scheduling appointments and events, and some use it as a phone directory. Others use it to keep track of abuse cases and investigations or prospective adoptive parents. "Each person customizes the program—it's totally individualized."

WAMPUM

DOS

Here's another shareware mondo-classic: Ward Mundy's WAMPUM. A dBASE III clone, WAMPUM (Ward's Automated Menu Package Using Microcomputers) has thrilled data-indexing PC users since the days of the old 8086 PC. Ward wrote WAMPUM years ago in response to his annoyance with dBASE's $700 price (of course, commercial databases are nowhere near this price now), and used it to create databases for the court system of Atlanta, Georgia. What makes the program one of a kind is its *developer's mode*, which lets you write full-fledged custom database applications just like the dBASE language does. (You load it by typing **WAMPUM VOODOO**.) Ward hasn't rewritten WAMPUM much to keep up with the times, but it's still a powerful little beauty and will serve most user's database development needs. Granted, many commercial databases cost $100 these days while this costs $50, but WAMPUM gives you a complete dBASE-like programming language for designing powerful databases yourself, making it of interest to database programmers. Another unique feature not found in many database packages is WAMPUM's ability to create graphics databases made of PCX picture files. Use it to create databases of computer-scanned images like employee pictures, pictures of inventory and real estate, databases of office equipment for insurance purposes, even museum holdings.

If you want to run WAMPUM as a database and not a database development tool, load it by typing **WAMPUM**. You can load it as a pop-up memory resident program (it uses a paltry 20K of memory) and run it as a full-functioned relational database while your favorite application software chugs away in the foreground. It supports all the features of the dBASE language, including the ability to generate reports and labels. Other features include a phone dialer, a spreadsheet-like data manager, and built-in form letters.

Ward Mundy Software
4160 Club Dr.
Atlanta, GA 30319
Phone: 404/237-9420
Price: $50 ($150 for network version; $20 for user guide)
plus $5 shipping
Online filename: WAMPUM.ZIP

File Express

File Express began life as a simple database program in which records were stored in linear order, as shown in Figure 6-2. It's evolved dramatically, and the latest version includes basic relational capabilities that make it easy to exchange information between multiple databases. It also includes a built-in editor that you can use to create form letters.

File Express's most appealing feature, in our opinion, is that it can import and export eight different leading file formats including WordPerfect, Lotus, and dBASE. That means you'll be able to easily shuffle information between your databases and these applications. And File Express has tremendous data storage capability: 2 billion records per database, 200 fields per record, and 1,000 characters per field.

Recognizing that one of the primary uses of a database is for mailing lists, File Express includes some basic editing capabilities so users can write a letter from within File Express, incorporating data from a database. It also offers file-locking for network use, custom screen design, and macros.

One of the nicer touches in File Express allows you to change the format of your database at any time, adding new fields and removing existing ones or changing the length of fields and their organization.

```
Index:BYMONTH                       Quick Scan                     File:BIRTHDAY
√ Rec First Name    Last Name       Company                        Address
   20 Abe            Lincoln         Bright Lights                  3156 Flor
    1 Mary           Baker           Baker the Baker                16 North
    2 John           Wood            Woodworking by Wood            7345 S Pi
    3 Fred           Bennett         Baker the Baker                16 North
    4 Jim            Singer          Singer's Song Birds            100 Birds
    5 Margaret       Miller          M & M Candy Company            3618 Suga
    6 Ken            Williams        Baker the Baker                16 North
    7 Carol          Burnett         M & M Candy Company            3618 Suga
    8 Dave           Copperfield     Dave's Produce Stand           31933 Che
    9 Patricia       Young           M & M Candy Company            3618 Suga
   10 Beverly        Heart           Dave's Produce Stand           31933 Che
   11 Pat            Boone           M & M Candy Company            3618 Suga
   12 Mike           Hammer          Dave's Produce Stand           31933 Che
   13 Pegi           Fleming         Baker the Baker                16 North
   14 Diane          Cannon          Singer's Song Birds            100 Birds
   15 Steve          Martin          Singer's Song Birds            100 Birds
   16 Bob            Hope            Singer's Song Birds            100 Birds
   17 Terry          Wright          Bright Lights                  3156 Flor
   18 Wayne          Newton          Dave's Produce Stand           31933 Che
   19 Scott          Fitzgerald      Bright Lights                  3156 Flor
F1:First Name
Alt: <E>dit:OFF <D>elete <Z>oom <W>idth <T>ag <I>ndex <S>earch <A>dd      <Esc>
```

Figure 6-2   File Express displays your database records in "linear" fashion

Making such changes is usually a pain in other databases. Other virtues include word wrap, automatic addition of field names, calculable fields, and easily drawn lines and boxes.

The report writer can create reports in either columnar or multiline format. In addition, the program can sort up to ten fields at one time. It offers support for nearly 300 printers, and does math calculations with accuracy up to 14 digits.

> **Expressware Corp.**
> **P.O. Box 1800**
> **Duvall, WA 98019**
> **Phone: 206/788-0932 or 800/753-3453 (orders only)**
> **Fax: 206/788-4493**
> **Price: $99 plus $5 shipping**
> **Online filename: FE51.ZIP**

Wyndfields

Wyndfields is more limited in scope than PC File or File Express—it can handle only 70 fields per record, and its search routines are not as complex as those in other packages, but it's just enough database to accomplish many tasks, like printing mailing labels, creating form letters, and running mail merges with popular word processors. Its pull-down menus and mouse support make it a snap to use for those of us who don't like to devote a lot of time to learning our databases. The database maintains multiple indices for you, and numerous methods are available for extracting the information that you need.

For the advanced user, there are extensive string and math functions for use in searches and calculating fields. You can create records of up to 70 fields, and databases of virtually unlimited records as well as up to ten different indices, each with ten key fields in ascending or descending order.

> **WyndWare**
> **One Parker Place, Suite 308**
> **Janesville, WI 53545**
> **Phone: 800/475-1628**
> **Price: $70 (DOS version); $99 (Windows version)**
> **Online filename: WYNDFLDx.ZIP**

Free-Form Databases

There are times in the business world when a structured database won't do—like when you want to jot down those flickers of inspiration that hit you in the middle of the night. Or when you want to store those phone numbers that keep accumulating on your desk, but you're hesitant to put them in a standard phone card file because you're afraid you'll never remember the names. That's when a free-form database can come in handy. Free-form databases let you store bits and scraps of information the way they come in—in random, unconnected ways—and let you sift through them in a way that's more freely associative than structured.

InfoRecall for Windows

InfoRecall is specifically designed for storing personal business information: things like trade show contacts, meeting notes, and ideas. InfoRecall will, in other words, help you clean up your desk. You can store all those bits of paper on your desk or in your briefcase in *hypertext* fashion, with links formed to the items through keywords or data association. There are no forms to fill in, there is no structure. It's a "free-form database." You can search through the data for all records indexed by the keyword "contract" or "distributor," for example. You can even pull up records from multiple databases through hypertext links as well as create connections on the fly to link all records to a given subject. Searching for data is easy; you can search through one database, as shown in Figure 6-3, or all of them at the same time.

You can export the information to other Windows software, print it out, or fax it. You can switch between records by merely double-clicking on a word. Double-click on a record and it will pop open instantly. A Windows-style button bar gives you access to all the program's features. You can build multiple databases, interconnect them, and password-protect them so that only you can access them. A record can be up to 6,000 words in length.

Curtram, Inc.
200 Yorkland Blvd., Suite 801
Toronto, ON M2J 5C1
Canada

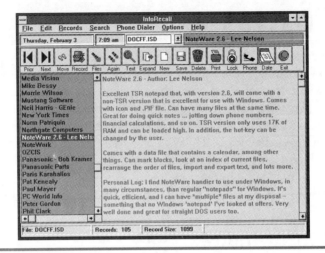

Figure 6-3 InfoRecall is a free-form database which allows for easy searching

Phone: 416/502-1311
Fax: 416/502-1345
Price: $69.95; $99.95 professional version
Online filename: INFOLT.ZIP

SureFire

SureFire is a hypertext-like database system with a built-in spreadsheet and word processor. Utterly unlike anything on the market, it lets you write a letter in which you can inject the address or other data at the pop of a key, calculate a customer's bill, and add data from a variety of databases. SureFire even includes a spell-checker that you can run on documents.

SureFire lets you create what are called *smart documents*. These are word processing document templates in which the software prompts you for information at designated points and automatically injects your choices. For instance, you could have a letter in which, when you reach the address line, a box pops up listing all the people you write regularly. Click on a name and his or her title and address are added to the letter. If you link your letter "smart document" to your daily expense log, details of your monthly reimbursable employee expenses will be injected into the

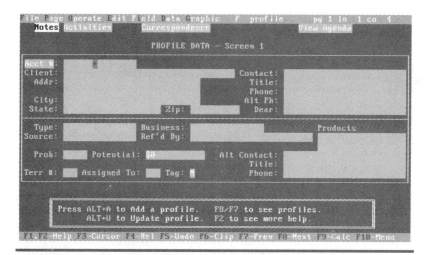

Figure 6-4   Creating the database portion of a "smart document" in SureFire

letter. Link the letter to a database and the customer's name and address and details of the order will be added to the letter at your bidding. Figure 6-4 shows the creation of a "smart document."

Piaf, Inc.
3918 Orchard Ct.
Boulder, CO 80304
Phone: 303/786-8222
Price: $79
Online filename: SUREFI-x.ZIP

Pop-Up Database Utilities

No discussion of database software would be complete without recommendations on pop-up database utilities. In general, pop-up utilities allow you to do things inside a software application that you are not normally allowed to do. Nowhere is the ability to do what is normally forbidden more essential than in the structured database world, where sometimes it seems like your entire world is a prison of blinking cursors and fields that beep at you when you try to type in something that you're not supposed to.

PopDBF

Pop up PopDBF over a spreadsheet or word processing document and get instant access to dBASE files at the touch of a key. You don't need to have a copy of dBASE per say. But many databases and other software programs use dBASE compatible files. You can read any of these files, whether or not they were generated in dBASE, with PopDBF. Browse, edit, append, delete, and search database records without ever leaving your application—and without having to load some bulky database program. Use it to search your client database while you're writing a letter or creating an invoice. Figure 6-5 shows the database screen of PopDBF which you will see when you pop it up over an application. From here you can choose the database records that you want displayed. Get quick access to your market research database while assembling research reports. PopDBF will let you do other things to the data too, like print it, compress it, or delete it.

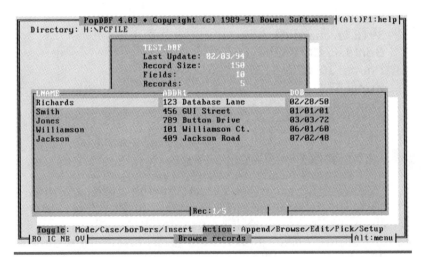

Figure 6-5   From PopDBF's database screen, you can easily browse through database entries

Lighthouse Software
P.O. Box 9601
Peoria, IL 61614
Phone: 309/673-9886
Fax: 309/673-9895
Price: $35 plus $5 shipping
Online filename: POPDBF*xx*.ZIP

buttonFile

buttonFile is a teeny database program that's ideal for storing all those snippets of ideas, contacts, and research notes—the sorts of things that might clutter your desk or briefcase or that, if you're really organized, you might store on cards in note card boxes. buttonFile stacks its records on your screen like recipe cards, as shown in Figure 6-6. You can click through the cards with your mouse, or else search them with plain English phrases like "begins with...," "sounds like...," and "contains...." You can also view them in a spreadsheet table or print them.

Design and print mailing labels, envelopes, and 3" x 5" phone file cards. buttonFile contains over a hundred predefined forms for printing different kinds of labels and forms including diskette labels, envelopes,

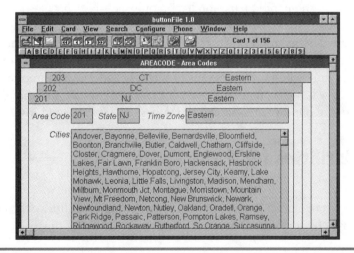

Figure 6-6   Using buttonFile is just like flipping through a stack of index cards displayed on your PC screen

and Avery and Dennison tractor-feed forms. It allows you to speed-dial any number in your databases or speed-dial through a list of frequently dialed numbers. You won't find any programming languages, macros, or query languages in buttonFile, but you will find all the database basics to help you store, search, and print those little information files that clutter up our lives. Because it imports dBASE, Windows, and WordPerfect files, buttonFile makes a great companion to those workhorse applications.

Buttonware
P.O. Box 96058
Bellevue, WA 98009
Phone: 206/865-0773 or 800/528-8866 (orders only)
Fax: 206/865-0894
Price: $69.90
Online filename: BFILE1A-E.ZIP or BFxxx.ZIP

Database Add-Ins

If your company uses one of the major database packages on the market, like Paradox or FoxPro, hustle yourself onto one of the information services like CompuServe or America Online that offer user support forums for these products. You'll not only be able to get some free technical support (we've found that the support that software companies offer online is generally far superior to the advice you get on the phone) and share tips with other users of your database software, you'll also find libraries full of literally thousands of macros, add-ins, and information files that will help you get the most out of your database software. Here are a few of our favorite shareware database macros and add-ins.

Paladin Utilities for Paradox for DOS

This popular collection of over 140 Paradox utilities will make database creation easy. There are routines for data and time functions, input/output, look-up functions, creating dialog boxes, and messaging. There are also workspace and utility routines.

> **dp Solutions**
> **P.O. Box 629**
> **Mount Holly, NJ 08060**
> **CompuServe ID: 75300,1734**
> **Price: $35**
> **Online filename: PALA40.EXE**

Report Utility for Paradox for DOS

Report Utility will make report generation with Paradox a breeze. Simple to install, it lets you easily move, copy, or summarize any field on a Paradox report.

> **The C Group, Inc.**
> **1454 Rockaway Pkwy., Suite 252**
> **Brooklyn, NY 11236**
> **BBS: 718/241-0225**
> **CompuServe ID: 76670,2602**
> **America Online ID: MarkSCohen**
> **Price: $15**
> **Online filename: RPTUTIL.ZIP**

Code39 for Paradox for Windows

Here's a Paradox script that allows you to print the scanner-standard Code 39 bar codes used in retail pricing, shipping, and inventory on your HP Laserjet printer. The script lets you set the size of the bar code box; then it will convert your string parameter to Code 39. Also included are several printer control functions for things like drawing a box around the bar code and setting the printer to start printing at a particular point on the page.

> **Price: Free**
> **Online filename: CODE39.SC**

Documentation Generator for Paradox for DOS

DOS

Paradox users have to jump through hoops to print the structure of a database table. You need to head to Paradox's restructure feature and press PRTSCRN, but that's frustratingly slow. Plus, if your table definition is longer than one screen, you have to repeat the process for each screen. What a bummer. Documentation Generator is a script that lets you print lists of tables and fields conveniently. Simply play the script through the Paradox menu and select the tables you wish to print. Documentation Generator sends the tables to a text file so you can pull them up in your word processor while you're writing documentation for your Paradox application.

> **Ton Reesink**
> **Aronskelkweg 105**
> **2555 GP The Hague**
> **The Netherlands**
> **CompuServe ID: 100121,641**
> **Price: Free**
> **Online filename: DOCGEN.ZIP**

Screen Layout Designer for dBASE

DOS

Screen Layout Designer is a data entry screen design tool. It reads the header of a dBASE file and places the fields, complete with title, on the screen. It has a slick drag-and-drop feature that allows you to reposition fields by clicking on the field and dragging it to where you want it. You can also change the color scheme, create menus, and add boxes, text, or other trim. You can design up to 20 screens with up to 512 fields in one session. Save the screen as a text file containing dBASE-type "@ SAY" and "@GET" commands and you can pull the screens right into your dBASE or Clipper applications.

> **PDM Associates**
> **17 Heathlands**
> **Shedfield, Southampton**
> **Hants S0 2JD**

England
CompuServe ID: 100116,370
Price: $40
Online filename: SLD.ZIP

3-D Macros for FoxPro for Windows

Windows

Here's a macro library that will give your FoxPro screens dazzling 3-D effects. Create raised and recessed panels, shadowed text, and other dimensional effects. It's easy to use 3-D Macros. Once you load the macros with FoxPro, you can use hotkeys to set up the 3-D effects. The registered version includes a Qedit macro library, a thermometer bar macro, and a utility for adding passwords to FoxPro databases.

JSA/Micro
P.O. Box 890214
Oklahoma City, OK 73189
CompuServe ID: 73767,1325
America Online ID: JSA-Micro
Price: $14.95
Online filename: 3D.ZIP

WMsgBox for FoxPro for Windows

Windows

If you're frustrated with the limitations of the FoxPro MsgBox() function, WMsgBox will let you position message boxes anywhere on the screen, plus display text in the font and style you specify. It will also display icons for you, and give you a choice of buttons to display on the screen.

Tri M. Ly
CompuServe ID: 73062,512
Price: Free, but author requests you donate $5 to your favorite charity
Online filename: WMSGBO.EXE

ADSTools for Access

ADSTools adds an icon menu bar to your Access development screen to speed up development. It doesn't allow you to do anything you couldn't do otherwise, but it makes some Access features available with the click of a mouse.

Synergystic Productions Unlimited
1503 Nance St.
Houston, TX 77002-1127
Phone: 713/228-4959
Fax: 713/228-5848
CompuServe ID: 72322,765
Internet: taylorbr@blkbox.com
Price: $20
Online filename: ADSTxx.ZIP

CHAPTER 7

SPREADSHEETS AND ACCESSORIES

n years past, when a copy of Lotus 1-2-3 commanded a princely $400 price tag, one of the hottest shareware products was a 1-2-3 clone called As-Easy-As. But since the prices of spreadsheet packages have plummeted into the affordable range, shareware spreadsheets are less attractive. As with shareware word processors, shareware spreadsheets are functional, but their single authors simply cannot keep pace with the teams of programming wizards at the Lotuses, Borlands, and Microsofts of the world.

It's likely that you already own a copy of Microsoft's Excel, Borland's Quattro Pro, or Lotus's 1-2-3. You'll find thousands of pre-written macros for these packages in the online tech support forums of these vendors on the major information services. While some are shareware, most are free. You'll find printing drivers, bookkeeping worksheet templates, document managers, calendar planners, worksheets that will download stock quotes for you from CompuServe and feed them into a spreadsheet, and worksheets for developing five-year business plans. You'll also find many, many files that contain discussions and explanations of how to solve common problems like running Lotus 1-2-3 for DOS under Windows.

We couldn't possibly tell you about all the downloadable spreadsheet utilities you'll find useful—that alone could fill up this book! Thus, we've selected a sampling of the kinds of add-ons and programs available to give you a feel for what's out there. We encourage you to head to your favorite online service or bulletin board to check out the libraries of spreadsheet utilities yourself. You should be able to quickly locate the relevant add-ons. For instance, if you look on CompuServe, you can find a plethora of files by simply typing **GO BORLAND** (for Quattro Pro), **GO EXCEL** (for Excel), and **GO LOTUS** (for 1-2-3) at any prompt.

Finally, if you're one of those rare birds who still doesn't own a spreadsheet program, you may want to get your feet wet by trying a few shareware ones. There's even a shareware spreadsheet program that's completely memory-resident. You can pop it over any other application and calculate rows and numbers to your heart's content. If you're an accountant, you'll love it.

Accessories for Microsoft Excel for Windows

Excel for Windows is fun to use, and these shareware templates and macros make it even more of a pleasure. Rearrange your office, track stock performance, and speed up the laborious weekly process of tabulating hours on employee time cards. These add-ons help you do all those things. You'll find more handy templates and add-ons in the Microsoft support forums on all the major online services.

Save Excel Document as Icon

If you're like most people, at one time or another you've probably had problems finding a spreadsheet you've previously stored. Did you name it Budget1 or Numbers2? What directory is it in? Sometimes you can spend more time *finding* a spreadsheet than you spend working on it. If you're not a brilliant file manager, the Save Excel Document as Icon macro is for you.

This macro will make it easy to find Excel spreadsheets because they'll appear as icons in any Windows program group you specify. Simply place the macro in Excel's XLSTART subdirectory. The first time you save your spreadsheet, a dialog box will appear and prompt you for the icon name and program group that you want to put it in. Next time you want to load that spreadsheet, just click on that icon.

> **Save As Icon**
> **Frank Reidelberger**
> **CompuServe ID: 73230,650**
> **Price: Free**
> **Online filename: SAVICO.ZIP**

Office Floor Planner

If you are considering remodeling your business and want to play around with designs and layouts *before* hiring an architect—and don't want to spend hundreds of dollars on a computer aided design (CAD) program—Office Floor Planner might be just what you need. Of course, it won't generate floor plans that you can actually build from, but it will certainly help you with some of the major layout decisions before you bring in a consultant and the builders.

Office Floor Planner is an Excel spreadsheet that includes drawing tools for laying out your office space. You start with a sample office with doors, windows, and office dividers already in place. You'll have to move these and resize them to represent your floor plan. (Each cell on the spreadsheet represents two feet.) Then you can place desks, chairs, computers, and other objects wherever you want, as shown in Figure 7-1. We had fun resizing a computer to take up half a room and labeling it

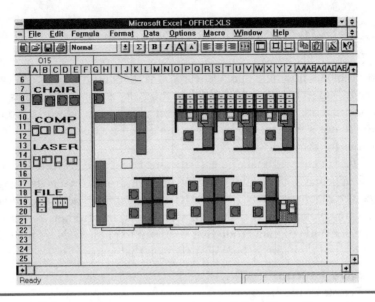

Figure 7-1   A floor plan designed with Office Floor Planner, an
Excel spreadsheet

"Univac 2000." We put a window in our normal office and made it twice
the size it really is.

You *could* use Office for laying out any type of room and even for
landscape design, but Decisions Inq has other tools for these tasks.
They're available when you register Office Floor Planner.

Decisions Inq
3329 W. 3rd Ave.
Vancouver, B.C.
Canada
CompuServe ID: 73314,1473
Price: $10
Online filename: OFFICE.ZIP

Business Bookkeeping Worksheet

If you run a small, cash-based business you'll love this bookkeeping
template for Excel that automates the calculation of receipts and expenditures according to the Dome Simplified Monthly Bookkeeping Record
procedure. In the Merchandise & Materials column, track the office

supplies you pay for by check or cash. Calculate all other expenses in the Other Expenditures column. This is perfect for home business entrepreneurs who still keep their receipts in a shoe box and are hesitant to take the plunge into spreadsheets.

Price: Free
Online filename: BUSINE.ZIP

Time Card

Help your payroll office out by giving them this Excel template in which you can easily enter and tabulate data taken from employee time cards. It's a very simple utility. Just load it in Excel, then enter into the grids time card data for each employee, as shown in Figure 7-2. The template automatically calculates how many hours they've worked in a week, plus has room for notes on employee attendance, sick days, and vacation. It's great for small business owners who hate futzing with time cards each Friday.

Price: Free
Online filename: TIMECA.ZIP

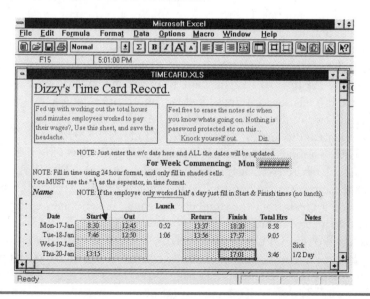

Figure 7-2   Time Card is a nifty little Excel template which calculates how many hours employees have worked in a week

Stock Price Check

Give your copy of Excel the remarkable capability of dialing CompuServe, downloading selected closing stock prices from the service's free Basic Quotes, then logging off and feeding them into a spreadsheet with which you can track your portfolio's performance. Obviously you need a modem, but you don't need communications software, because Stock Price Check will call CompuServe for you—automatically. It will take the ticker symbols from your spreadsheet. This is the program all you stock pickers have been waiting for.

Price: Free
Online filename: DOSTCK.EXE

Accessories for Borland Quattro Pro for DOS and Quattro Pro for Windows

There are very few shareware macros and templates available for Quattro Pro, probably because there are so many free ones available from Borland International. The shareware utilities that do exist are generally excellent and are available on many of the online services. These utilities are excellent. Most of them are for the DOS-based Quattro Pro (all the macros listed are for the DOS version of the product unless otherwise noted). Some that you might want to check out include packages of Quattro Pro macros for things like loan amortization tables and spreadsheet utilities (online filenames: QPROMA.ZIP and UTLDSK.ZIP for DOS Quattro Pro and AMORT.ZIP for Windows Quattro Pro).

There's a spreadsheet template that will help you develop a five-year business plan based on sales projections (online filename: BUSPLA.ZIP), an expense report template (online filename: EXPENS.ZIP), and, when you need a break from the number crunching, poker games written in Quattro's macro language (online filenames: WPOKER.ZIP for Windows Quattro Pro and QPOKER.WB1 for DOS Quattro Pro). If you insert clip-art into spreadsheets, you'll want a copy of a macro that will let you view clip-art without leaving Quattro (online filename: ARTVUE.WQ1). If you store names and phone numbers of clients inside spreadsheets, you'll appreciate a pop-up phone dialer that will dial the phone numbers that you highlight on the screen (online filename: DIAL.WQ).

P&F Macro

If you use Quattro Pro for DOS spreadsheets to track stock prices, you'll appreciate P&F Macro, which lets you print high/low bar graphs for the quotes. Quattro Pro already has a high/low graph feature, but it prints in graphics that are not easily yanked into a text editor or word processor. The ASCII text output of P&F Macro, shown in Figure 7-3, uses X's and O's to depict the bars of the graph so it can be printed on any printer—even a daisy wheel printer. If you have a laser printer and are not looking for a pretty page, you'll like the speed at which P&F Macro prints text.

```
17-Jul Point & Figure for ZIGO size 0.25 number 3
 8.75
 8.50
 8.25 X
 8.00 X O X X
 7.75 X O X O X O
 7.50 X O X O X O
 7.25 X O O O X
 7.00 O X X O
 6.75 O X X O X X O X X X
 6.50 O X O X O X O X O X O X O X O X
 6.25 O X O X O X O X O X O X O X O X O
 6.00 O X O O O X O O O X O X O
 5.75 O O O O X O
 5.50 O
 5.25
 5.00
 4.75
```

Figure 7-3 P&F Macro prints fast high/low bar graphs from stock quotes stored in Excel

Guy Symonds
6328 Vermont
St. Louis, MO 63111
CompuServe ID: 76347,3301
Price: $10
Online filename: P&FQPR.ZIP

Accessories for Lotus 1-2-3 for DOS and 1-2-3 for Windows

Macros, templates, and add-ons for Lotus 1-2-3 and all its different (and often incompatible) versions jam the file libraries of many online services. If you log on to any business-related computer bulletin board or online service, you'll find everything from spreadsheet printing utilities to expense account spreadsheet templates, budgeting worksheets, and travel expense spreadsheets. Once again, we think the best place to look for Lotus accessories is the Lotus conference on CompuServe (type **GO LOTUS** at any prompt). The first thing you should do is download a file called 123UTIL.LST, sometimes called 123UTL.ZIP, along with a file called 123UTV.ZIP. These files list all the shareware utilities available for Lotus, where you can find them, and how to contact the vendors. They also list which version of 1-2-3 each utility works with. Many of the listed utilities are shareware, but some of them are free.

Super Macro Library for Lotus 1-2-3

One of the most popular macro libraries for Lotus, Super Macro gives you the equivalent of three disks full of macros. There are over 250 macros, including some for printing mailing labels, creating a spreadsheet calendar (shown in Figure 7-4), printing letters that incorporate spreadsheet data, inserting and deleting ranges, searching and replacing, and expanding Lotus's menu bar. The program's macro manager can give you a list of macros while you're inside Lotus. You can search through the list to find the macro you need and load it by pointing and shooting. These macros work with 1-2-3 versions 2.2 or later and 1-2-3 for Windows version 1.1.

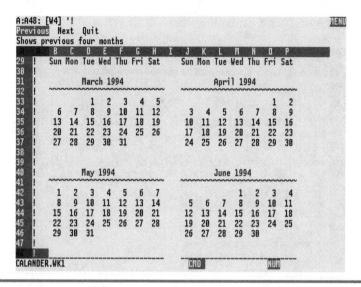

Figure 7-4   This macro from Super Macro Library for Lotus lets
you create a spreadsheet calendar

K.I.T.A.L. Software
P.O. Box 748
Karmiel 20100
Israel
Phone: 972-4-9987255 (evenings & weekends Israel time)
Price: $50 (or $59 for disks)
Online filename: SUPRMAC.ZIP

FileControl

DOS

FileControl, shown in Figure 7-5, is essentially a spreadsheet for
keeping track of your spreadsheets. You start by adding the spreadsheets
in a particular directory to FileControl's spreadsheet. Once your spreadsheets are listed in FileControl, you can open them by selecting the Open
item on the FileControl menu. You can also delete, copy, and move files
and directories. For those of us who create a lot of spreadsheets but never
get around to deleting old ones, one of FileControl's conveniences is that
it provides an easy way to delete spreadsheets. FileControl lists spreadsheets with a 200+ character description, so you'll always know what's

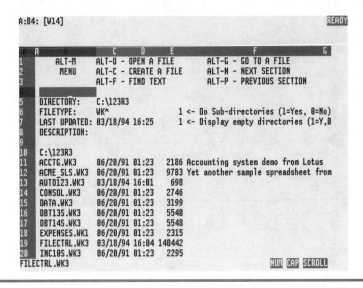

Figure 7-5   FileControl catalogs your Lotus spreadsheets

in a spreadsheet. There is also a version of FileControl for Microsoft Excel, shown in Figure 7-6.

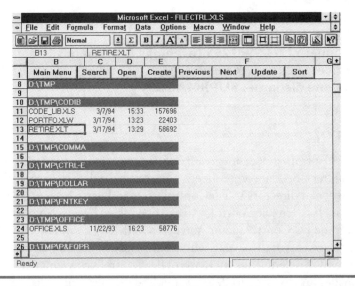

Figure 7-6   The Excel version of FileControl lets you keep tabs on your voluminous spreadsheet collection

Macro Systems
1008 Lawndale Rd.
Wilmington, DE 19810
Phone: 302/475-0142
CompuServe ID: 72774,416
Price: $29 ($10 extra for manuals and disks)
Online filename: CTRL-L*xx*.ZIP (Lotus version);
CTRL-E*xx*.ZIP (Excel version)

Shareware Spreadsheet Programs

PCs have been dubbed "spreadsheet boxes" because for many years the only reason businesses bought them was to run Lotus 1-2-3. However, you may be one of those rare individuals who is unsure if you need a spreadsheet program. Some PC users claim that spreadsheets are more convenient for tracking home office expenses and investments than programs like Quicken or Managing Your Money, but will *you* find them to be more convenient? Some users rely on them to create graphs to incorporate in reports, but maybe you'll be one of the many who prefer to use the graphing feature built into your word processor instead. How do you know if spreadsheet software is for you? Try out one of these shareware programs. They have all the graphing and equation solving abilities that most spreadsheet users require, and can best the original Lotus 1-2-3 in their features. Should you find yourself becoming a spreadsheet jock, you can always migrate to one of the heavy-hitters like Excel or Quattro Pro, but on the other hand, you may well find all the features you need in these shareware models.

As-Easy-As

As-Easy-As is an old-time favorite Lotus 1-2-3 clone. While it can read Lotus worksheet files, calculations between Lotus and As-Easy-As are not always compatible so it may be unable to process a Lotus-engendered spreadsheet. You enter "slash" commands into As-Easy-As, similar to what you do in Lotus, except that As-Easy-As gives you pull-down menus that make operations a bit clearer for the spreadsheet wary, as shown in Figure 7-7. It has some other advantages over the DOS version of 1-2-3, such as a few more ways of graphing, but overall it's not nearly as functional as Excel. Why would a business want to use it? Because it offers all the features that casual spreadsheet users need, including graphing, macros, and all the basic spreadsheet formulas. It's also slim on disk space and memory requirements, making it convenient to use on laptops. Plus, it's available in several foreign language versions, including Chinese.

As-Easy-As can plot 11 different kinds of graphs, and run a full range of calculations, from financial to statistical and including user-defined ones. It also includes a macro language similar to Lotus's for automating operations. In addition, you can link spreadsheets so that calculations and entries in one will adjust the entries in another. As-Easy-As is a great little spreadsheet program to get you started if you've never used a spreadsheet before, but the chances are good that if you have aspirations to become a spreadsheet jockey, you'll outgrow it before long.

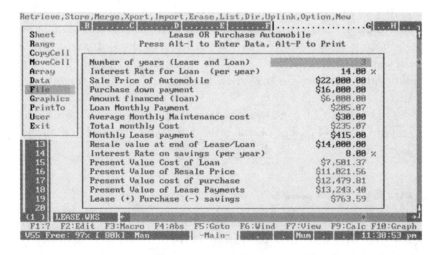

Figure 7-7 As-Easy-As is a full-featured spreadsheet program that's a lot like Lotus 1-2-3

Shareware in Action

Product: As-Easy-As
Company: Foodmaker, Inc.

Foodmaker, Inc., wanted to offer a straightforward spreadsheet program to the managers of its Jack-in-the-Box restaurant chain. The company surveyed the marketplace with a list of needs in hand. The right program, said MIS department senior analyst Aiala Reizer, had to be:

▷ Compatible with all versions of Lotus 1-2-3

▷ Not too big, so it didn't consume too many system resources

▷ Not too expensive, because it needed to be installed at many sites

▷ Easy and inexpensive to customize

The company considered writing its own program, but abandoned this plan after seeing As-Easy-As. "As-Easy-As," said Ms. Reizer, "met all our requirements. We have now been using it for nearly three years."

More than a thousand Jack-in-the-Box franchisees now use As-Easy-As to help calculate inventories, perform quality assurance, and meet all their other spreadsheet needs.

Trius, Inc.
231 Sutton St., Suite 2D-3
P.O. Box 249
North Andover, MA 01845
Phone: 508/794-9377
Fax: 508/688-6312
BBS: 508/794-0762
CompuServe ID: 71333,103
Price: $69
Online filename: AEA*xx*.ZIP

Alite/R

Alite/R is a toned-down version of As-Easy-As that can run memory resident. Pop it up over other DOS applications like your database program when you need quick access to a spreadsheet or some figures.

It's useful for accountants and also comes in handy if you're a laptop user, because it requires a spare 150K of memory, as you can see in Figure 7-8. Like As-Easy-As, it's mostly Lotus compatible, reading WK1 and WKS spreadsheets, but not completely compatible in the way of spreadsheet calculations. It includes a macro language, uses Lotus-like "slash" commands, but also includes pull-down menus and a list of mathematical functions that you can scroll through to pick the one you want to use. It plots S-Y, line, bar, and stacked bar graphs, as well as pie charts, but it prints out only on a dot-matrix or 9-pin printer.

Trius, Inc.
231 Sutton St., Suite 2D-3
P.O. Box 249
North Andover, MA 01845
Phone: 508/794-9377
Fax: 508/688-6312
Price: $20
Online filename: ALITE.EXE

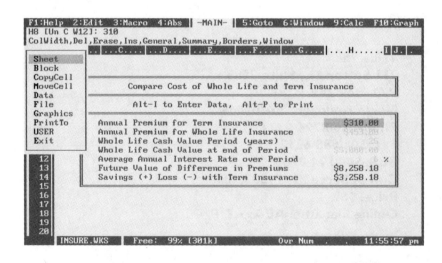

Figure 7-8   Alite/R's slim memory requirements make it ideal for laptops

CHAPTER 8

SOFTWARE TO MAKE DESKTOP PUBLISHING PROJECTS SHINE

en years ago, a curious little machine briefly found its way into the business world's heart. It had a big plastic dial. Letters were embossed around the edge of the dial. You would turn the dial and punch out headlines for things like mock-ups of ads and newsletters. It would print near typeset-quality headlines on clear plastic tape similar to the tape in a handyman's labeling gun. To change the font, you would adjust the plastic dial. It was a clumsy set-up, and it was easy to go through a roll of tape before you got a headline printed the way you wanted. But every marketing department had one of these contraptions.

Who would have guessed that just a few years later desktop publishing would be born, bringing the potential to infuse every desk with the power of a printing press and a room full of layout artists with pica rulers dangling from their belts? No business deserves to be without desktop publishing software and a laser printer. Even if you're in business for yourself, the ability to design and print snappy brochures, proposals, newsletters, and even ads will do more to enhance your professional image than a new suit or business cards.

Top-of-the-line desktop publishing software, like PageMaker or QuarkXPress, is every bit as complex a tool as a room-sized printing press. Yes, it's expensive—you're talking $400 to $700—but, if you need to import a wide variety of graphics and word-processing files into your page layouts, if you expect lots of high-quality fonts, and if you require automatic indexing of documents, color printing, and the ability to run it on a network, then this is one tool you can't cheap-out on.

If your desktop publishing needs are tame—say you want to design a newsletter in black and white—you may be able to get by with the design features in more sophisticated word processors like Microsoft Word. You can also buy a low-end desktop publishing program for around $100. But first, we have a $69 shareware desktop publishing program that you should take for a spin. It may well suit your needs (it's won just about every award the shareware industry gives out). At the very least it will give you an idea of the sort of things you'll need in your desktop publishing software.

Beyond full-fledged desktop publishing software, the shareware world offers realms of utilities for working with graphics: programs that let you edit, cut, dither, and even convert your graphics into clip-art, as well as ones that help you organize your fonts. You'll find utilities that will let you read Mac desktop publishing files with your PC, and that turn your PC ones into something a Mac can digest.

In the desktop publishing forums of major online services you'll also find thousands of shareware fonts for use with your desktop publishing software. (See Chapter 5 for recommendations on shareware fonts.) Some of the most popular ones are exotic fonts with letters that, for example, look like they were painted with a thick paintbrush or built out of bamboo. You'll also find an appealing range of clip-art that you can incorporate into your brochures and newsletters, everything from a "Banker in Frankfurt" to a picture of a "Man in Paris with a Bird." There are also free templates to help you design newsletters, ads, and brochures. We can't cover here all the things available online that you'll find useful.

Instead, we urge you to check out the desktop publishing forums on CompuServe (type **GO DTP** at any prompt), General Electric's GEnie, or on America Online. You'll find so many good things in these forums to use with your desktop publishing software that you'll never give another thought to trading in your PC for a Macintosh.

Font Managers

Fonts are like socks. If you're not careful, they end up all over the house. For some of us, a sock organizer is the only reason we never show up at work in the morning barefoot. Similarly, font managers are the only way we can find 14 point Bauhaus when we need it and keep 8 point Futura from ending up in the spreadsheet directory. If left unmanaged, fonts can multiply as quickly as unpaired athletic socks, and the chance of finding them when needed becomes as remote as locating two matched socks when you're in a hurry.

The best thing about font managers, though, is that they let you preview and compare fonts so that you can easily select the lettering you want to use in a project. You can print out samples of particular characters, like dingbats, to see exactly how they'll look in your report or newsletter. You can even organize your fonts by categories—group all the fonts you like to use in business letters in one category, for example, and store the ones you use for creating mass mailings in another. Some font managers will even let you edit individual characters in a font's character set just as if you were a professional typeset designer.

The following font managers are comparable in capabilities, letting you easily view and print out font samples, as well as organize them. All will work with virtually any laser printer. Which one you like the best will be a matter of personal preference.

Printer's Apprentice

Windows

Printer's Apprentice is the Cadillac of shareware font managers, and at only $20 it's a bargain that shouldn't be passed up. It does what all font managers do: it serves as a handy pop-up utility to view and inventory burgeoning collections of TrueType & Adobe Type 1 fonts. It lets you print complete sample character charts for any selected font, plus keyboard layouts, and specimen sheets. A button pad lets you pick the type of

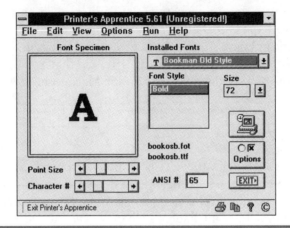

Figure 8-1   Use the button pad of Printer's Apprentice to print specimens of any selected font

sample sheet you want to print of a selected font, as you can see in Figure 8-1. Printer's Apprentice also includes a few extra features that none of the other font managers in this chapter have. You can organize your fonts by name, style, use, or purpose. You can print keyboard layouts for the different fonts—useful for using wingdings or other non-letter forts. You can also edit individual characters—ideal for the super-fussy among us. *PC Magazine* called this the best Windows font utility on the market.

> **Lose Your Mind Development**
> **c/o Bryan T. Kinkel**
> **506 Wilder Square**
> **Norristown, PA 19401**
> **Phone: 215/275-7034**
> **Price: $20 ($5 for manual)**
> **Online filename: PA561.ZIP**

Font Monster

Use Font Monster to view your TrueType and Type 1 fonts. Print sample charts of the fonts' characters and lists of the names of your fonts. You can also rename, edit, and resize fonts. Font Monster will also let you create font groups that you can install by clicking on a Program Manager icon. Font Monster is almost, but not quite as feature-packed as Printer's Apprentice. Whether you like it more than the above will be a matter of personal taste. A sample screen of Font Monster is shown in Figure 8-2.

note

The author is living in Taiwan and requests that Font Monster be registered by contacting the Public (Software) Library at the address below. The Public (Software) Library can only accept registrations; it cannot provide tech support.

Leaping Lizards
Public (Software) Library
P.O. Box 35705
Houston, TX 77235-5705
Phone: 713/524-6394 or 800/242-4775 (orders only)
Fax: 713/524-6398
CompuServe ID: 71355,470
Price: $25
Online filename: FMONS3.ZIP

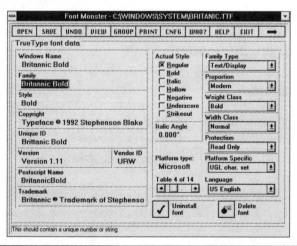

Figure 8-2   Font Monster lets you preview and organize your burgeoning collection of TrueType fonts

Font Book

Organize your fonts with Font Book by creating "books" of fonts for different purposes. You might store all the fonts you use with your desktop publishing software in one book, for example, and fonts you use with your word processor in another. Font Book will display their names in list style. You can view or print symbol sets, character sets, or a text sample of a chosen font. As shown in Figure 8-3, you can view characters in italic, underlined, or bold format and in any point size. Font Book is more austere in features than Font Monster or Printer's Apprentice; it doesn't allow you to edit fonts or catalog them in as many ways. But it's a very useful program nonetheless.

Mark Cohen
c/o The C Group, Inc.
1454 Rockaway Parkway, Suite 252
Brooklyn, NY 11236
BBS: 718/241-0225
CompuServe ID: 76670,2602
America Online ID: MarkSCohen
Price: $15
Online filename: FONTBK.ZIP

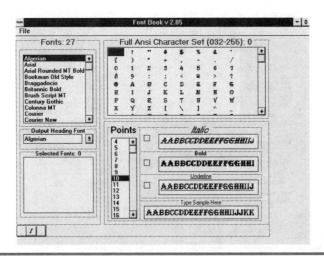

Figure 8-3   Font Book makes it easy to view and catalog fonts as well as print samples

FontShow

Here is a simple, but elegantly useful (and cheap!) font previewer. With just a few mouse clicks you can preview a font used in sample text. View a line, a paragraph, or a full page. View a font's complete character set in normal, bold, or italic, as shown in Figure 8-4. It's easy to zoom in on a character to display an enlarged version of it. FontShow lacks many of the features of the other font managers, such as the ability to create font catalogs for individual uses or print keyboard layouts, but many people don't need all those features anyway.

Glenn Alcott
86-22 60th Rd.
Elmhurst, NY 11373
CompuServe ID: 76044,747
Price: $10
Online filename: FONTSH.ZIP

Figure 8-4 Pop up FontShow over your work area and preview fonts through sample text

CleanTTF

Cure font bloat with this simple, but indispensable utility that will clean out your hard disk subdirectories of all the TrueType fonts that you're not using. CleanTTF checks your Windows configuration file to see which fonts are installed, then it creates a file listing all the fonts on your disk that aren't presently installed. It gives you the option of backing up the fonts, then wiping them from your disk, or just deleting them outright. If you're a font addict, CleanTTF will free up megabytes on your disk.

> **Solid Oak Software**
> **P.O. Box 6826**
> **Santa Barbara, CA 93160**
> **Phone: 805/967-9853**
> **Fax: 805/967-1614**
> **Price: $15**
> **Online filename: CLNTTF.ZIP**

Desktop Publishing Software

Desktop publishing software is nothing less than a miracle. It gives your lowly PC capabilities that Guttenberg could only have dreamt of. Create newsletters, brochures, mass-mailings, and even books with the panache of a professional graphic designer. Spin text around on the page, illustrate it with computer graphics, set it in different type fonts with just a few mouse clicks—desktop publishing software will let you do all these things. If you're as yet without a DP software package of your own, try this shareware one. You'll find it has many of the capabilities of $400 DP software packages.

EnVision Publisher

DOS

Just when the world said that full-featured desktop publishing software was beyond the capabilities of shareware authors, EnVision Publisher came along and caught everyone's breath. EnVision offers all the tools you'd expect in a basic desktop publisher. It's not a Windows-based program, but who says you need Windows to do desktop publishing. Lots of small businesses use EnVision to create black and white signs, brochures, and newsletters, and find that it suits their DP needs just fine.

The user interface is very Windows-like with a button bar on one side of the screen that gives you access to commonly used functions. Dialog boxes prompt you for settings on margins, columns, and other layout decisions. EnVision will import clip-art, so long as it's in PCX format, and text in the formats of leading word processors.

You can align the text in columns, rotate it, justify it, set it in bold or italics, and fill the background with a fill pattern. EnVision comes with 68 scaleable fonts (you get the fonts when you register the program). You can zoom in on pages and even create style sheets to hold the basic elements of your design. Lots of templates are included for newsletters, menus, letterheads, invoices, and envelopes.

The most recent version includes a spell-checker. You can save the entire document or individual pages of it. It saves documents in TIF, bit-map, and PCX formats, which makes it convenient for faxing. It supports just about every printer known to man. Admittedly, EnVision does not occupy the same lofty graphics design strata as PageMaker, but what can you expect for $69? It's the recipient of *Shareware Magazine's* Editor's Choice Award and winner of numerous shareware industry awards including Best Application Software of the Last 11 Years.

Software Vision Corp.
9400 4th Street N., Suite 202
St. Petersburg, FL 33702
Phone: 813/577-6048 or 800/388-8474
Fax: 813/576-5924
CompuServe ID: 70304,64
Price: $69
Online filename: EVPxxA.ZIP and EVPxxB.ZIP

Shareware in Action

Product: EnVision Publisher
Company: Wendy's of Missouri

When Jennifer Buchert became director of marketing a year ago at Wendy's of Missouri, owner of Wendy's restaurants, she found an operation in need of computerization. The company had never used a desktop publishing program, and even its word processing software provided only minimal formatting capabilities. Ms. Buchert had used PageMaker with a Macintosh, so she knew what the company was missing. But Wendy's was using PCs, and like many companies contemplating desktop publishing, resisted the high price tag of the software she suggested. Then the controller heard about EnVision Publisher. He gave Buchert a copy to try, and within a few days, she knew it would fit the bill just fine. "I had no problem switching from PageMaker," she said. It doesn't have PageMaker's Select All feature, but otherwise, "I haven't missed any other features."

Buchert now uses EnVision Publisher to communicate with 20 Wendy's restaurants and produce a monthly newsletter and calendar. She also uses it to produce small print ads. Before, the department had to rely on outsiders to create any artwork, but now it can produce its own. She has even promoted the program to others within Wendy's. "We use it for internal signs, too, such as signs in kitchens. The person who makes these signs isn't especially computer literate, but now she uses my computer whenever she needs signs," said Buchert. "EnVision Publisher is a nice step toward making even your internal communications attractive."

Software to Store and Manipulate Clip-Art and Graphics

Windows

When you create a document for the very first time in a desktop publishing program, the first learning curve hurdle you need to jump is finding out how to import text from your word processor into the document. The second hurdle is learning how to import graphics. The problem with graphics is that you don't just drop the picture on the page like you can text. You must rotate it, resize it, scale it, convert, cut it, and perform a dozen other manipulations. These handy programs will help you get your computer pictures ready for use in a desktop publishing publication by letting you edit, paste, and convert the images before you load your DP software. They'll also help you catalog your computer pictures so that they'll be easy to find in the future.

ThumbsUp!

If you have a lot of graphics files or clip-art floating around various directories on your hard disk, ThumbsUp! will help you get the clutter under control. It will search your disk's subdirectories for the graphics files you specify—be they Windows bitmaps, metafiles, or icon files; TIFs or GIFs; CorelDRAW!, Targa, Macintosh, Micrographx, Lotus, Auto-CAD, or PC Paintbrush pictures. It will then display them in a thumbnail view so that you can catalog them, move them to different subdirectories, or organize them into a slideshow (see Figure 8-5 for a screenfull of thumbnails).

You can also copy, paste, crop, convert, and edit pictures. Thumbs-Up! will also let you organize them into graphic art databases. This is an ideal program for anyone who frequently incorporates computer-gener-

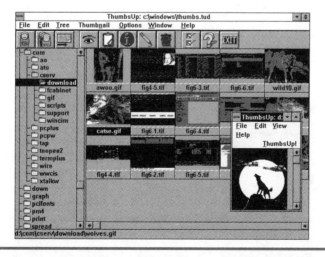

Figure 8-5   ThumbsUp! displays "thumbnail" versions of picture files and will print, copy, paste, crop, and convert images

ated art into desktop publishing projects like newsletters, press releases, and mass-mailings.

Cerious Software
5424 Chedworth Dr.
Charlotte, NC 28210
Phone: 704/529-0200
CompuServe ID: 71501,2470
America Online ID: CeriousSW
Internet: cerious@vnet.net
Price: $50
Online filename: THUMBS.ZIP

Image Gallery

Use Image Gallery to assemble a scrapbook of picture files with miniature screen shots that you can browse through, as shown in Figure 8-6. The name of the file is displayed by each image so you can find it easily. You can append comments or captions to each picture and search through your gallery by keywords or by looking at the images themselves. You can store galleries in either landscape or portrait mode. Each gallery can store up to 65,280 pictures, provided you have enough disk space to

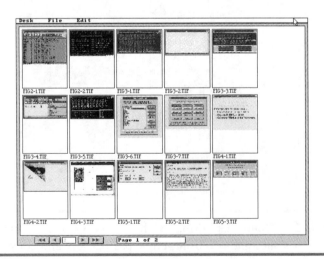

Figure 8-6   Image Gallery displays a collection of TIF files

handle them. It supports all the major picture formats including PCX, GIF, TIF, BMP, Targa, WPG, EPS, MSP, GEM/IMG, and MacPaint.

Alchemy MindWorks
P.O. Box 500
Beeton, Ontario L0G 1A0
Canada
Phone: 905/729-4969 (orders); 905/729-3831 (tech support)
Fax: 905/729-4156
Price: $40 plus $5 shipping
Online filename: GALLRY.ZIP

Paint Shop Pro

Windows

You can't use Paint Shop Pro to draw pictures. Rather, you use it to manipulate computer graphic images for inclusion in newsletters, brochures, and the like. Flip, rotate, shrink, stretch, or resize images. Increase the color depth, boost the brightness, adjust the contrast, or deepen the gray scale—all from simple menus like the one shown in Figure 8-7. Turn a picture into a negative of itself (how many times have you searched to high heaven for a program that will do this when you're importing PC screen

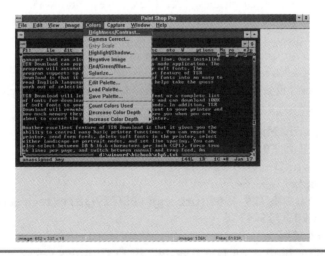

Figure 8-7 With Paint Shop Pro you can manipulate graphic images in a myriad of ways

captures into desktop publishing documents?). Paint Shop Pro comes with a standard set of filters, but it also lets you create your own. You can change colors in an image with a standard palette or a customized one.

Paint Shop Pro will also convert pictures from one graphics format to another, including TIF, GIF, PCX, WPG, BMP, IMG, PIC, RLE, DIB, JAS, MSP, RAS, and TGA. It can handle all the most common bitmap formats. You can even convert PC graphics to Mac ones, and vice versa, and you can work with multiple images at the same time. Paint Shop Pro will also capture images, and it works with all TWAIN compliant scanners.

> **JASC, Inc.**
> **10901 Red Circle Dr., Suite 340**
> **Minnetonka, MN 55343**
> **Phone: 612/930-9171**
> **Price: $69 plus $5 shipping**
> **Online filename: PSPx.ZIP**

Graphic Workshop

Use Graphic Workshop to convert picture files between just about any image format. Formats supported include BMP, DLL, GEM/IMG, GIF, Halo CUT files, IFF/LBM, MacPaint, MSP, PCX, PIC, RLE, TGA, TIF (from full color to gray scale), 24 bit files, TXT (ASCII files), and WPG. The main screen shows the available functions, as seen in Figure 8-8. You can also use Graphics Workshop to rotate and flip images, scale images, sharpen and soften them for special effects, even capture Windows screens or portions thereof. There's a full range of half-toning and dithering features. You can even convert full-color digitized photographs to black and white clip art in any of the supported formats.

> **Alchemy MindWorks**
> **P.O. Box 500**
> **Beeton, Ontario L0G 1A0**
> **Canada**
> **Phone: 905/729-4969 (orders); 905/729-3831 (tech support)**
> **Fax: 905/729-4156**
> **Price: $40**
> **Online filename: GWSWIN.ZIP (Windows version);**
> **GRFWRK.ZIP (DOS version)**

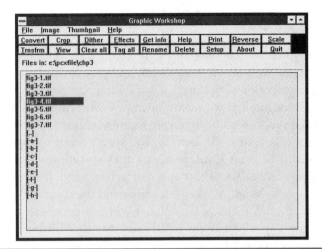

Figure 8-8   Working from Graphics Workshop for Windows'
main screen, you can perform a wide array of functions

VPIC

VPIC is a handy picture viewer that lets you convert graphics files to and from numerous uncommon graphic formats. Some of the formats supported by VPIC that you won't find in most other picture viewing programs include Dr. Halo CUT, Deluxe Paint LBM files, binary image files (BIFs) from black and white image capture boards, Targa TGA files, and ColorRIX/EGA Paint files. It also supports bit-mapped graphics, PCX, and PIC files. You can display pictures from the Macintosh but you can't print them out or convert them to another format. With VPIC, you can save any image to a GIF file in regular, inverted, mirrored, or rotated fashion. Unfortunately, you can't save images to any other file format.

Bob Montgomery
543 Via Fontana, #203
Altamonte Springs, FL 32714
CompuServe ID: 73357,3140
Price: $25
Online filename: VPICxx.ZIP

Painting Programs

You say you're no painter, that you're a clutz with a charcoal drawing pencil, a hazard with an illustrator's ink and pen. Still, there are times when you're preparing something for work—a report perhaps, or a chart illustrating some marketing or sales principle—when the kind of illustration you need simply can't be found anywhere as clip-art, which is so easy to incorporate in your document. So you spend about twenty minutes dabbling with Microsoft Paint, trying to draw something on your own. Your drawing isn't bad, but Paint annoys you to no end. It's a crude tool: its subtlety means Magic Marker-thick lines and the colors look like they came from a 9-crayon box of Crayolas. Try one of these paint programs instead. They may not make you into Renoir, but they'll make it easier to achieve artistry in pixels.

NeoPaint

NeoPaint is one of the best paint programs you'll find in the shareware world or the commercial one. It offers oodles of paint tools usually found only in pricey programs, like airbrushing, flipping, rotating, stretching, tile fill, scaling, smudging, blurring, and fading. If you're a PC artist, everything you could want is here (see Figure 8-9 for a sample of what can be done with a potato). You can view and edit multiple images in adjustable windows with video modes up to 1024 x 768. NeoPaint reads and writes 2, 16, and 256 color PCX, GIF, and TIF files. It will even convert between different formats, colors, and resolutions.

It comes with 12 fonts in multiple sizes and with bold, italic, outline, underline, and shadow effects. A unique feature is its "stamp pad," which you use to add clip-art to your drawing. A zoom feature lets you magnify drawing areas. You can even create 3-D objects and rotate them through space. You can print your pictures to Epson/IBM dot matrix printers, HP LaserJets, Postscript printers, and compatibles.

OSCS Software Development, Inc.
354 N.E. Greenwood Ave., Suite 108
Bend, OR 97701
Phone: 503/389-5489
Fax: 503/388-8221
Price: $45 plus $5 shipping
Online filename: NEOPNT.ZIP

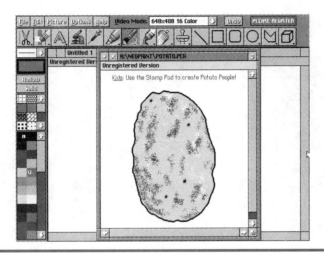

Figure 8-9   Working with a picture in NeoPaint

MVP Paint Professional

MVP Paint was designed by hit shareware game producers Epic MegaGames to produce the stunning graphics in its games. It includes lots of sophisticated graphics design features that you won't find in other paint programs (even commercial ones), like an unparalleled array of drawing tools, colors that can be blended and mixed, and tools for changing proportions easily and resizing elements. The program's icon-based interface makes it easy for even novice computer graphics designers to use. A unique palette manipulation feature lets you choose from 262,144 breathtaking colors. As you can see from Figure 8-10, it will even hide its menu when extremely large images are onscreen. You'll have a ball using this to design sizzling graphics for newsletters, brochures, and reports.

MVP Software
1035 Dallas S.E.
Grand Rapids, MI 49507-1407
Phone: 616/245-8376 or 800/968-9684 (orders)
Price: $49.95 (professional)
Online filename: MVPP2.ZIP

Figure 8-10   Experimenting with MVP Paint

Computer-Aided Design Software

Windows

Computer-aided design or CAD software differs from a paint program in that it lets you draw to scale and in multiple dimensions. Generally the stuff of architects and aircraft designers, CAD software also comes in handy when you're designing the layout of offices or special-purpose precision tools for use in manufacturing or the research sciences.

GammaCAD

GammaCAD is a computer-aided design program that allows you to draw objects to scale in two dimensions. While CAD software is used most widely in technical fields like architecture, engineering, and electronics, it also comes in handy anytime you want to design something to scale—be it office or landscaping plans or promotional posters—then plot it with different dimensions. CAD software goes beyond a paint program in that it enables you to paint with precision, to rotate and animate objects, and to create three-dimensional effects.

Sophisticated CAD packages cost $500 and upwards, but if you're not designing high-precision aircraft and have only an occasional need to organize objects three-dimensionally, a shareware package like GammaCAD might foot the bill. It doesn't go so far as to let you animate objects or work with layers of objects like some CAD packages do, but it's impressive nonetheless. (One of the authors of this book is using it to design a new addition to his house—which he needs to house his mounting library of shareware; you can see a floor plan in Figure 8-11.)

You can draw with lines, arcs, circles, and points. Enter coordinates for an element, pick a position on the screen, then start drawing. You can also add text, as well as symbols. You can copy, scale, or rotate elements until the drawing is to your liking. Zoom or pan the drawing to look at different parts in detail. (Figure 8-12 shows the same subject from different perspectives.) You can also specify line type (solid, dashed, dotted), color, and width. For text, you can choose font, size, color, angle, and justification. You can paste GammaCAD drawings into your word processor or desktop publishing software by cutting and pasting via the Windows clipboard. GammaCAD is as easy to use as it is powerful. It includes built-in help screens to get you up and running and dialog boxes to guide you along. Status messages display pertinent program information at a glance. GammaCAD supports a wide variety of printers and plotters.

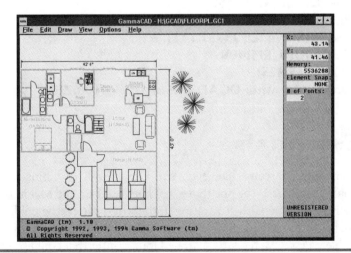

Figure 8-11   Creating a floor plan with GammaCAD

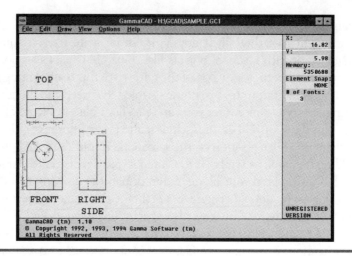

Figure 8-12   GammaCAD drawing from different angles

Gamma Software
P.O. Box 8191
Fort Collins, CO 80526
Phone: 303/490-2928 or 800/747-9960
CompuServe ID: 73737,1721
GEnie ID: T.EMMER
Price: $15-$25
Online filename: GCAD.ZIP or GCAD100.ZIP

Random Essentials

Sometimes it seems like even the Great Wall of China isn't as formidable a barrier as the one that exists between PCs and Macintoshes. This barrier is particularly frustrating in the world of desktop publishing. All the best printers and graphic arts studios seem to rely on Macs. Most offices have PCs. (We recently searched for a printer that could print out some drafting designs that had been created with a PC. No luck. Every printer in the city used Macs.) Here's a utility that will help you leap the Great Wall.

MacSEE

If you've ever wanted to run a Mac-generated desktop publishing file on a PC, or vice versa, you'll appreciate MacSEE. MacSEE, shown in Figure 8-13, can convert between the two languages as proficiently as a United Nations translator can between Swedish and Arabic. Use it to read or write Mac 3.5" high-density disks in your PC. (It won't read low-density disks. You need special hardware to do that.) You can also use it to access Mac-formatted hard drives and CD-ROMs.

The shareware version will only transfer files of 16K bytes or less in length between PCs and Macs. If you pay the registration, you get a version that can handle larger files. The registered version also gives you complete access to the Mac file system, letting you rename, delete, and make folders. The shareware version won't let you do those things.

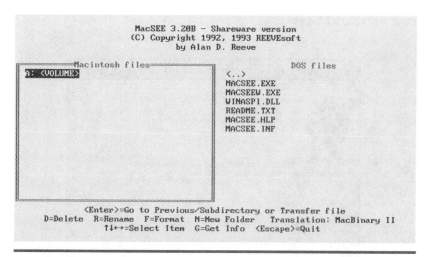

Figure 8-13 MacSEE lists PC (DOS) files on one side of the screen, and Mac files on the other

REEVEsoft
P.O. Box 1884
Clemson, SC 29633
Phone: 803/654-7378
CompuServe ID: 71521,2200
Internet: reevesoft@delphi.com
Price: $79.95
Online filename: MACSEE.ZIP

The Sign Maker

The Sign Maker may not make your store more profitable, but it will make it much easier to create professional looking signs that communicate such essentials as "This Way to the Washroom" or "Sorry, We Do Not Have a Pay Phone." Sign Maker is an extremely simple drawing program that accommodates the two most vital tasks of retail sign-making: writing in big letters and incorporating cute graphics. It lets you design signs for different sizes of paper and print them out in different formats, like landscape. It also includes a small selection of fonts. Figure 8-14 shows an example of a sign that was created in a short amount of time with Sign Maker.

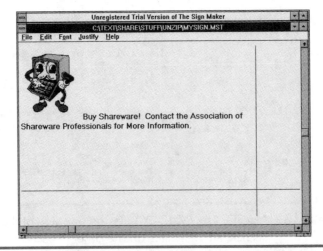

Figure 8-14   This professional-looking sign was designed in
under two minutes with Sign Maker

Michael Dum
4342 S.W. Lagrange St.
Port St. Lucie, FL 34953
Phone: 407/336-2791
CompuServe ID: 75540,1735
Price: $50
Online filename: SIGNMK.EXE

CHAPTER 9

COMMUNICATIONS SOFTWARE FOR NAVIGATING THE INFORMATION HIGHWAY

ew things are as critical to a business as good communications, whether it's by phone, fax, computer modem, or ordinary U.S. Mail. The shareware in this chapter is for use in communicating with a computer modem or fax/modem. A modem is a device plugged into your computer or found inside your computer that enables your PC to communicate over phone lines with other computers, or online information services like CompuServe. If the modem can also send faxes to other computers and fax machines, then it's a fax/modem.

There are many types of communications or telecom software. You use general-purpose communications software, like the commercial best-seller Procomm Plus by Datastorm, for calling BBSs, online information services, and other PCs. Special-purpose communications software is online service-specific. This software is designed for automating access to and speeding up the use of just one online service, like MCI Mail or America Online. Often called front-end programs, they'll automate your use of the service to the extent of retrieving your mail for you, capturing messages in the public forums you specify so that you can read them later offline, while the toll charge clock isn't ticking, and often even download-ing files for you. Needless to say, such software can save you oodles of money. A third type of communications software is fax software, which you use for sending and receiving faxes.

Through the years, shareware authors have embraced the genre of communications software as exuberantly as Renaissance painters created frescoes. Since the livelihood of shareware authors revolves around their frequenting online services and bulletin boards, who else could be so attuned to what modem users need in software? You'll find that shareware used for performing basic modem chores like dialing online services is generally more sophisticated than what you'll find in stores. Shareware authors rush to incorporate leading-edge features and file-download protocols into their wares—a job that often takes commercial software vendors years to implement.

There are exceptions. Shareware communications authors some-times forget to include features that corporate PC users need. Like high-quality terminal emulations. Or the software "hook" that's needed to integrate a communications program into a TCP/IP network, the kind found in many offices. But fear not, corporate modem users, because we'll tell you about a shareware communications program from a leading American university that will work better in most corporate mainframe, hyper-networked environments than anything from IBM.

Windows communications is another bugaboo for shareware. Com-munications software for Windows is a nasty trick to write. There are few shareware communications products available for Windows. There is, however, one general communications program for Windows that wins raves, and several utilities that you don't want to be without if you do anything under Windows.

There's also no good fax software available as shareware.

But be warned: as we pointed out in Chapter 2 your online sessions will be faster if you choose communications software that's DOS-based. If you run Windows we advise that you choose a DOS-based communications program and run it in a DOS window. You'll be guaranteed better performance online with faster software downloads that way. (Be sure to read our tips in Chapter 2 for speeding up communications under Windows.)

Basic Communications Software

Choosing the communications software that's best for you is as personal a decision as choosing the right car. For dialing online services and BBSs, you'll find that all the products listed below are as good as any commercial package. They include all the super-fast file transfer protocols, built-in host modes that let your PC answer calls like a mini-BBS, a scrollback buffer that lets you read e-mail messages that have scrolled off your screen, and in some cases, built-in editors for writing e-mail offline and limited multi-tasking ability. For the corporate computer user who's linked to mainframes and mini-computers, there's a shareware program that can perform feats in a networked business environment that no other commercial communications program can begin to accomplish.

Telemate

DOS

In a recent casual survey of computer bulletin board frequenters, Telemate was voted the most popular shareware communications program. Its ability to multi-task, letting you view scrolled screens and files in one window, while a file transfer proceeds in another, and you write e-mail in a third, is what makes it so special. Figure 9-1 shows how to edit in Telemate while downloading a file at the same time.

The scrollback buffer is probably the most utilitarian scrollback buffer of any communications program ever written. Use it like a word processor, cutting and pasting portions of the screen to the e-mail messages that you're writing. No other communications programs outside of Windows let you do all these things.

Telemate includes a very Windows-like editor and clipboard for composing e-mail and cutting and pasting text between its windows. Write your message in the editor, then simply paste it onto the terminal

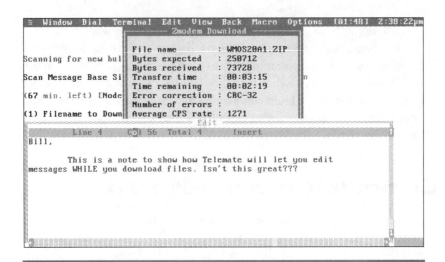

Figure 9-1   Editing while downloading in Telemate

screen and it will be sent to its destination. Figure 9-2 shows Telemate with several windows up.

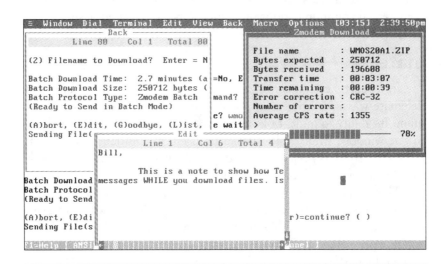

Figure 9-2   You can use Telemate to multi-task as you would in Windows

Telemate includes all the most popular protocols, including Zmodem, Ymodem-G, and CompuServe B+, plus you can add your own. There's also a good script language with a learn mode that will generate scripts that can automatically log you onto your favorite bulletin boards and online services. Terminal emulations include DEC VT-100, VT-52, and others. Its host mode is tops. Callers can upload, download, leave messages, and chat. Telemate is easily configurable to your preferences, plus it makes use of expanded and extended memory, and even video RAM as virtual memory to store data.

White River Software
P.O. Box 78081
Limeridge Mall Postal Outlet
Hamilton, Ontario
Canada L9A 5H7
Price: $49
Online filename: TMxxx-x.ZIP (4 files)

Unicom

Unicom puts the Windows environment to good use to make communications as simple as ever. It gives you a real dialing directory to pop up and place calls from, whereas most Windows communications software puts you through the rigmarole of having to snarf through the File menu for phone numbers. This makes it a populist favorite among BBS users.

Use Unicom to download files in one window while you work on applications like spreadsheets in another. Unicom gives you all the major file protocols, like Xmodem and CompuServe B+, plus a script language with a learn feature that generates scripts that allow you to set up the program to log on to online services automatically. Figure 9-3 shows Unicom's main screen.

Initial versions of Unicom were featherweight compared to commercial Windows communications software, but the current version is a powerhouse with a full range of terminal emulations, DDE support, and a script language. One unique feature of Unicom allows the use of its clipboard to cut and paste data from your system directly into the Windows' clipboard of a remote PC.

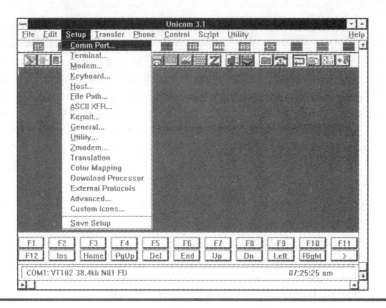

Figure 9-3   Unicom's main screen

Unicom is also equipped with keyboard macros that you can assign to on-screen buttons so that you can point and click your way around your favorite information services. A record mode lets you automate repetitive tasks, like cutting and pasting screen contents.

Unicom's host mode is pretty high-powered compared to that of most Windows communications software. You can specify a caller's amount of access to your hard disk, plus assign caller passwords and time limits on the system. This feature comes in handy if you want to give callers remote access to certain files on your disk, but not the entire disk. Callers can access your computer while you work on files in the foreground.

When you download Unicom, you'll find that before you register it, you'll be bugged by all the pop-up screens reminding you to send in your money. Users find this annoying, but it is of course the point. When you pay for Unicom, you'll be given a password to make the reminders disappear.

Unicom
Data Graphics
P.O. Box 58717
Renton, WA 98058
Phone: 206/432-1201
Fax: 206/432-8673
Price: $69.95
Online filename: UCxxx-X.ZIP (2 files)

Telix

Telix is a communications program that, with its pop-up phone directory, is much like Procomm and Qmodem, as you can see in the command summary screen in Figure 9-4. Telix is also included on the disk that accompanies this book so you can take a look at it yourself. But what makes this product so special is its powerful script language. This script language, which is more like the difficult programming language of C than the English-based languages found in other communications programs, is not for everyone. If you're a real computer jock, you'll be able to program Telix to do things you can't do with other shareware programs. You can use it, for instance, as remote control software to let you dial in

```
                   Telix v3.22 Command Summary

         Main Functions                          Other functions

Dialing directory..Alt-D  Queue Redial #s....Alt-Q  | Run editor........Alt-A
Send files.........Alt-S  Receive files......Alt-R  | Local echo........Alt-E
Exit Telix.........Alt-X  Run script (Go)....Alt-G  | Screen Image......Alt-I
Comm Parameters....Alt-P  cOnfigure Telix....Alt-O  | DOS command.......Alt-V
Key defs./macros...Alt-K  Terminal emulation.Alt-T  | Translate Table...Alt-W
Capture toggle.....Alt-L  Scroll Back........Alt-B  | Chat Mode.........Alt-Y
DOS Functions......Alt-F  Jump to DOS shell..Alt-J  | Status Toggle.....Alt-8
Hang-up modem......Alt-H  Clear screen.......Alt-C  | DOORWAY mode......Alt-=
Usage Log toggle...Alt-U  Misc. functions....Alt-M  | Printer on/off...Ctrl-@
                                                    | Send BREAK.....Ctrl-End
        Select function or press Enter for none.    | Add LF Toggle.....S-Tab

Copyright (C) 1986-94 deltaComm Development, PO Box 1185, Cary, NC 27512 USA

  Time .. 14:30:58   Online .... No      | Capture ... Off
  Date .. 03-06-94                       | Printer ... Off
  Baud .. 38400      Terminal .. ANSI    | Script ....
  Comm .. N,8,1      Port ...... COM1    | Reg. Key .. TELIX.KEY
  Echo .. Off        Add LF .... Off     | Dial Dir .. TELIX.FON
```

Figure 9-4   The command summary screen of Telix

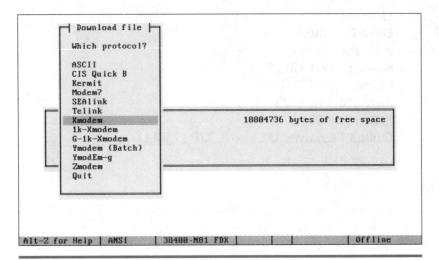

```
┤ Download file ├

Which protocol?

ASCII
CIS Quick B
Kermit
Modem7
SEAlink
Telink
Xmodem                          18004736 bytes of free space
1k-Xmodem
G-1k-Xmodem
Ymodem (Batch)
YmodEm-g
Zmodem
Quit
```

```
Alt-Z for Help | ANSI    | 38400-N81 FDX |       |    |       | Offline
```

Figure 9-5   Telix's file transfer options

and run application software from another PC. Some businesses program Telix to transfer data between PCs at night when no one is around. Telix can start dialing other PCs at the time specified, log on, check the disk space available, transfer the files, leave e-mail to the PC's user, then log off and shut itself down. But as we said, you have to be a real programming jock (or at least have a talented programmer in your office) to make use of stuff like this.

Other Telix attributes include all the leading file protocols, as shown in Figure 9-5, multiple dialing directories, and DEC VT-100 and VT-52 terminal emulations.

> **Exix, Inc.**
> **P.O. Box 130**
> **West Hill, Ontario**
> **Canada M1E 4R4**
> **Price: $39**
> **Online filename: TLXxxx-x ZIP (4 files)**

MS-Kermit

DOS

If you're a corporate modem user, you *can't* be without Kermit. This *wunderkind* from the kids at Columbia University can do things in a 7-bit networked mainframe environment that no other communications software—either shareware or commercial—can touch. It's become the mostly widely used communications software in the world, with versions available for DOS, UNIX, VMS, OS/2, and many other computer operating environments.

Don't confuse this full-fledged communications package with the file transfer protocol of the same name. Kermit, the file transfer protocol, is also the work of Columbia University and, under the right circumstances (like on a corporate network), it's one of the things that gives Kermit, the communications software, its edge.

MS-Kermit lacks fancy menus and other feel-good features. To use it, you load it and enter commands from the primitive DOS command prompt as in Figure 9-6. This is not something that will endear it to the PC tenderfoot, but the last time we spoke with Frank da Cruz and his development team at Columbia, they were hard at work on a menu-driven Kermit. So, instead of downloading Kermit, we suggest that you call Columbia at the number we give below and obtain the software directly from them.

Why do you want to use Kermit? Because it transfers files like greased lightning on 7-bit corporate networks. You won't get Xmodem or other

```
Ask, Askq (read keybd to variable)   Open Read/Write/Append file  scripts
Bye        (logout remote server)     Output text      (for scripts)
C or Connect  (become a terminal)     Pause [seconds], MPause [millisec]
Clear    (Input, comms recv buffer)   Pop, End (exit current macro/Take file)
Close      (logging and script file)  Push      (go to DOS, keep Kermit)
CLS (clear screen at command level)   Quit       (leave Kermit)
CWD or CD  (change dir &/or disk)      R or Receive  (opt local filename)
Decrement/Increment variable number   Read (line from a file to variable)
Define/Assign   (a command macro)     Reinput  (script input, reread buffer)
Delete   (a file)                     Remote   (prefix for commands)
Directory (filepsec)                  Replay    (file through term emulator)
Disable  (selected server commands)   Run       (a program)
Echo text (show line on screen)       S or Send   local file   new name
Enable   (selected server commands)   Server [timeout] (become a server)
EXIT     (leave Kermit)               Set       (most things)
Finish   (to remote server)           Show      (most things)
Get      (remote file opt new name)   Space    (free on current disk)
GetOK    (get Yes, OK, No response)   Stop     (exit all Take files & macros)
Goto     (label, Take file or Macro)  Take     (do a command file)
Hangup   (drop DTR, hang up phone)    Transmit filespec [prompt] (raw upload)
If [not] <condition> <command>        Type     (a file)
I or Input [timeout] text (scripts)   Wait [timeout] on modem \cd \cts \dsr
Log (Packet, Session, Transaction)    Write  FILE or log file    text
Mail      (file to host Mailer)
MS-Kermit>
```

Figure 9-6   MS-Kermit is run from the DOS command prompt, something novice users may not appreciate, but Kermit fans (and there are millions of them) don't mind protocols to work there. It offers superior performance in connections to IBM mainframes, over X.25-based networks, and many TELNET and most RLOGIN connections. It will also work over networks that don't like certain control characters, like Xon/Xoff flow control characters.

Other features corporate users like include a built-in TCP/IP connection, top-notch terminal emulations, lots of customizability, foreign character sets including Hebrew, plus features to accommodate physical handicaps. (You will not find a Hebrew character set or features to accomodate physical handicaps in any other telecom program.) And the built-in file protocol of Kermit is one of the best in the world.

"Wait a minute," you say. You've heard that the Kermit file protocol you have in your present communications software is kind of crummy. You've been told not to use it under any circumstances. That's because the way the Kermit protocol is implemented in most general communications software packages is awful. Cheap knock-offs of designer goods, you might say. The Kermit file protocol in the MS-Kermit software really sings.

So why is Kermit called Kermit? Kermit began as a volunteer project at Columbia over a decade ago. Countless programmers from all over the world have worked on it. Columbia wanted to make the software available free to the public, but didn't want anyone to benefit financially from it. (They blanch at the idea of the program being called "shareware" because it's technically not. But we just had to include it anyway.) The late Jim Henson, creator of *Sesame Street*, granted Columbia use of the copyrighted name "Kermit," thereby prohibiting anyone from selling the software under the name Kermit. However, ever since Walt Disney bought the rights to all the *Sesame Street* characters, Disney lawyers have been gnashing their teeth over this peculiar use of their frog's name. ("Whatever you do, don't make jokes about frogs when you write about us!" Frank da Cruz begged in total seriousness when we contacted him.)

Let's all be glad the software isn't called MS-Piggy.

Kermit Distribution
Columbia University Academic Information Systems
612 W. 115th St.
New York, NY 10025
Phone: 212/854-3703
Fax: 212/663-8202
Internet: kermit.columbia.edu

Price: Free. (But we suggest ordering the software together with Christine M. Gianone's excellent book "Using MS-DOS Kermit"—$34.95 from Digital Press at 800/344-4825. The book-software set can also be ordered from Columbia University.)
Online filename: MSVIBM.ZIP

Specialized Front-End Software for Online Services and Bulletin Boards

When you call an information service like CompuServe and use a general communications program like Procomm Plus, you must type in all the CompuServe commands yourself. There are drawbacks to this. First, you need to know the commands. Second, your use of the service will be slower than if your PC enters the commands for you. Both of these things can translate into longer time spent online and, hence, bigger online bills.

Programs like OzCIS and AutoSIG don't like to advertise that they will help you keep your online bills down by automating your use of CompuServe, uploading and downloading messages for you, searching for files, even scanning public conferences for topics of your interest. They like to stress in their manuals that they will make the services easier for you to use and to help you get more out of them. That they do. But they also help you keep your bills low.

Either way, these programs *are* indispensable for anyone who calls online services. If you use CompuServe, GEnie, or Prodigy, you should download all the applicable front-end programs for the services and try each of them out. You'll find that the time and effort spent online pulling hairs, trying to remember commands, and searching for information can be saved by simply loading one of these and watching the software do all the hard work for you.

CompuServe

CompuServe offers the most good things online for business users of any online service. There are databases galore filled with business news, financial and background information on companies and investments, plus hundreds of public forums on topics ranging from investing to entrepreneurship that are full of fascinating discussions. CompuServe's prices have been falling the past few years, but you're still charged by the hour to read many of the forums and databases. These programs will speed up your access of the services and (hopefully) keep your online bills down.

OzCIS

DOS

CompuServe navigators go in and out of fashion. Some subscribers prefer TapCIS, some AutoSIG. More users these days are switching to the Cadillac of CompuServe navigators: OzCIS. OzCIS will download your private e-mail, capture to disk public messages in the forums that you specify, and even search for and download files for you. You can set up OzCIS to automatically log on to CompuServe, perform all the tasks that you specify as in Figure 9-7, which shows how forums are configured, then quickly log off. Or else you can use it to log on to CompuServe and navigate it yourself. OzCIS will put the entire labyrinthine service into pull-down menus, making files and forums super-easy to find.

OzCIS is one flashy program. It offers windowing so you can view messages as you write replies, multiple split-screen editors, a clipboard for cutting and pasting text from messages, and a built-in GIF picture viewer. You can store impossible-to-remember CompuServe user IDs in its

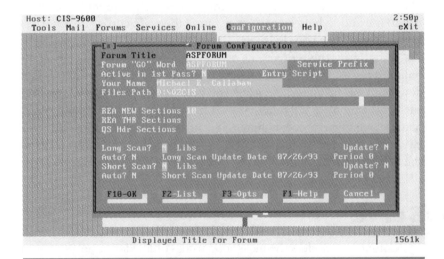

Figure 9-7   Configuring a forum in OzCIS

phonebook. It also offers a script language with GOTO, JUMP, and GOSUB commands.

You can use it to automate just about anything you want to do on CompuServe, from retrieving and answering private mail, to capturing to disk messages from public forums, to searching for files. Get quick access to CompuServe weather, news, stock trends, graphs, and quotes through OzCIS's pull-down Service menu.

OzCIS has a few flaws, including editors that are clunky to use (they use old WordStar-like commands that you practically need a keyboard template to remember) and some people find it difficult to set up. It also requires a lot of computer hardware. The current version demands a PC with a 80386 processor and at least 4 megs of memory. It can only be found in the IBMCOM Forum on CompuServe in Library 12. Toned-down versions requiring a 80286 PC can be found on many other online services and bulletin boards, but you won't find OzCIS supporting PCs any less powerful than that.

note

The current version of OzCIS is only found on CompuServe in IBMCOM Forum, Library 12. Type **GO IBMCOM** at any CompuServe prompt. The software is stored in three files.)

> **Ozarks West Software**
> **14150 Gleneagle Dr.**
> **Colorado Springs, CO 80921**
> **Fax: 719/260-7151**
> **Price: Free to home users, $50 for business users**
> **Online filename: OZCISx.EXE**

AutoSIG

DOS

AutoSIG is one of the easiest CompuServe navigators to use. It's also free. The work of Don Watkins, sysop of the IBM forums on CompuServe, and programming whiz Vern Buerg, AutoSIG will significantly cut your access time to the service by automating private message retrieval as well as capturing disk messages from the public forums that you specify. You can also use it to automate searches of file collections on CompuServe, but it wasn't originally designed for that and, consequently, is a bit clumsy to use that way.

AutoSIG has one main screen at which you configure the program show in Figure 9-8, tell it which public forums you want to read, and instruct AutoSIG to dial CompuServe. Once connected, it will head to the forums you specify, quickly capture a list of messages headers, then log off. Offline, you can scroll through the headers, mark those messages that you want to read, then log back on to CompuServe. AutoSIG will download those messages and log off. You read and write replies to the messages offline. Once you're done, tell AutoSIG to dial CompuServe again and it uploads the replies into the appropriate forums.

You can set up AutoSIG to search and download files, but it's not very good at it. You need to install in the program another shareware utility called ATOBRO to enable AutoSIG to download file catalogs and let you search them offline.

AutoSIG comes with a script language that is the most extensive of any script language found in any of the CompuServe navigators. It includes commands for IF, THEN, GOTO, ELSE, plus the usual ones like WAIT, PAUSE, and SEND. Lots of AutoSIG scripts for doing things like downloading stock quotes can be found on CompuServe.

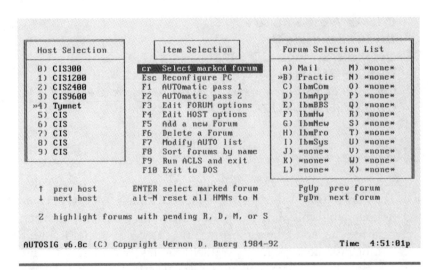

Figure 9-8   The main screen of AutoSIG

note

Also look for ATOBRO.ZIP to automate file searching.

Price: Free
Online filename: AUTOSIG.ZIP or ATOxx.ZIP

TapCIS, The Access Program for CompuServe

DOS

TapCIS is the crown prince of CompuServe navigators. It's feature-rich, well supported, and comes at a kingly price. Registration is $79. Is it worth it? Lots of CompuServe users think so. (We personally prefer the freebies AutoSIG and OzCIS, but we like TapCIS too.)

One of the virtues of TapCIS is that a cottage industry has sprung up selling TapCIS add-on utilities. These script utilities set up TapCIS to automate just about anything a business user would want to do on CompuServe, from downloading company reports to feeding captured stock quotes into spreadsheets. The TapCIS support forum on CompuServe is loaded with these. (Type **GO TAPCIS** at any CompuServe prompt.)

You'll find all of TapCIS's chores listed on one main screen in the program shown in Figure 9-9. They're divided into online and offline operations. Offline, you can write messages with the built-in editor, read downloaded messages, and mark downloaded message headers from a forum. You can set up TapCIS to dial CompuServe, head to a designated forum, download the messages or headers, and then quickly log off. You answer the messages offline. TapCIS will also retrieve private mail. TapCIS is also better at searching online libraries and retrieving files than any other CompuServe navigator.

Its drawbacks include the failure to list completely all of its commands on the menu. You must continually flip through the manual for commands. It also doesn't let you import text into messages the way that AutoSIG does. That's a *real* pain. Loading TapCIS scripts is also a pretty clunky procedure. Nonetheless, this is a must-have program for CompuServe users.

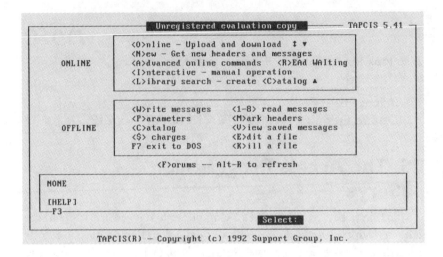

```
┌─────────────── Unregistered evaluation copy ───────── TAPCIS 5.41 ─┐
│                  <O>nline – Upload and download  ↕ ▼                │
│                  <N>ew – Get new headers and messages              │
│         ONLINE   <A>dvanced online commands    <R>EAd WAIting      │
│                  <I>nteractive – manual operation                  │
│                  <L>ibrary search – create <C>atalog ▲             │
│                                                                    │
│                  <W>rite messages       <1-8> read messages        │
│                  <P>arameters           <M>ark headers             │
│        OFFLINE   <C>atalog              <V>iew saved messages      │
│                  <$> charges            <E>dit a file              │
│                  F7 exit to DOS         <K>ill a file              │
│                                                                    │
│                     <F>orums –– Alt-R to refresh                   │
│  ┌─────────────────────────────────────────────────────────────┐  │
│  │ NONE                                                         │  │
│  │                                                              │  │
│  │ [HELP]                                                       │  │
│  └─F3──────────────────────────────────────────┌──────────┐────┘  │
│                                                 │ Select:  │       │
└─────────────────────────────────────────────────────────────────┘
      TAPCIS(R) – Copyright (c) 1992 Support Group, Inc.
```

Figure 9-9   The TapCIS main screen for logging on to CIS and
downloading messages

The Support Group, Inc.
Lake Technology Park
McHenry, MD 21541
Phone: 301/387-4500, 800/ USA-GROUP(orders only)
Fax: 301/387-7322
Price: $79, including $15 of CompuServe time
Online filename: TAP.EXE (Type GO TAPCIS at any
CompuServe prompt.)

CompuServe Information Manager

CompuServe offers two nearly free navigators that every new CompuServe user should get. They'll make your use of the service so much easier you'll find yourself unable to live without them. They will not *automate* your use of the service like other front-ends will. Remember, CompuServe has a financial interest in seeing you spend as much time as possible online. But they will put the whole Byzantine service into snappy pull-down menus and, in the case of the Windows navigator, buttons and

Figure 9-10   Use icons and buttons to click your way to favorite places with WINCIM

icons too like in Figure 9-10. Overall, they'll transform CompuServe from a bewildering maze into an enjoyable experience.

CompuServe Information Manager for Windows, or WINCIM, is a jewel. Easy to identify icons let you point and click your way to news, travel, investment information, public forums, the reference library, and games. Click on buttons on the top of the screen to get to your favorite places online, to read your mail, and to see your local weather forecast.

While you're online, easy to comprehend button bars (you don't have to squint at them for 30 seconds to figure out what they mean) let you retrieve files and messages from forums, join computer-CB conferences, and much more. To get your mail, simply click on the mailbox at the top of the screen. To disconnect, click on the connected cables. A built-in GO-command glossary will prove indispensable.

CompuServe Information Manager for DOS arranges the service in pull-down menus instead of buttons and icons, but it will similarly speed you around the service. To find your way to forums and search for files, you merely pull down self-explanatory menus and click on choices. You'll never have to enter another CompuServe command again. The program similarly automates retrieval of mail.

Both programs, although they offer little in the way of automation, are worth their weight in gold. To download either Information Manager version, type GO CIM at any CompuServe prompt. You can also order both from CompuServe by typing GO ORDER. They cost $25 when purchased that way, but you'll receive a $15 credit toward CompuServe online charges.

CompuServe Information Service
5000 Arlington Centre Blvd.
Post Office Box 20212
Columbus, OH 43220
Phone: 800/848-8990
Price: $10 download charge offset by a $10 credit toward CompuServe online charges
Online filename: WINCIM.ZIP and DOSCIM.ZIP

America Online

In less than a year, America Online has blossomed into America's favorite family-oriented online service. It's cheap to use, the special software that you run on your PC and use to call the service is free, and it's simple enough that just about anyone can use it. For business callers, the Home Office Forum and the Microsoft Small Business Center are tops for cheap advise and conversation with other small business owners. This is a service you can't afford not to join.

America Online

DOS

Windows

America Online is the country's fastest growing online service, with all the features home or business PC users would want in an information service, including e-mail, Internet access, computer forums, stock quotes, news, and more. You need special software for signing up for America Online and for accessing it. But it's free, and you can download it from just about any BBS or online service—or obtain it directly from America Online.

There are both Windows and DOS versions of America Online's software. Both use a fun, warm-and-fuzzy graphical interface shown in Figure 9-11 that makes it easy to click your way around online. Just click on the icons to get to weather, stock quotes as in Figure 9-12, or—one of our favorite places—the Microsoft Small Business Center, where you can hobnob with members of the Retired Executive Corps or download information files on subjects like how to know when it's time to form an S corporation. If you've never used a modem before, America Online is a great way to get your feet wet.

Unlike other online automation programs discussed in this chapter, America Online's software won't make your online access faster (America Online is very slow), but at a $3.50 per hour access fee, America Online is one of the best bargains going online.

note

A Windows version of this product may be found in a ZIP file on some BBSs.

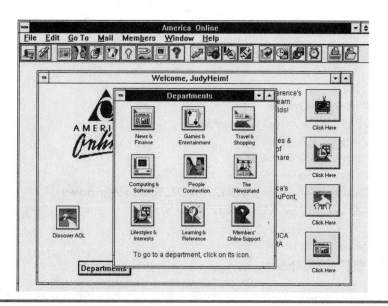

Figure 9-11 Using the Windows version of America Online's software you can point and click your way to just about anything online, even Internet and the information super-highway

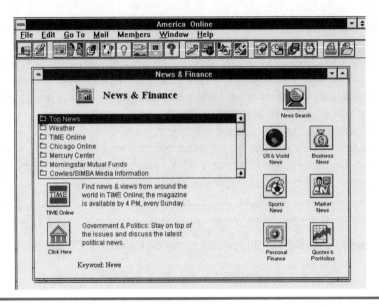

Figure 9-12   America Online takes you straight to the business
news with market reports and financial research

America Online
8619 Westwood Center Dr.
Vienna, VA 22182
Phone: 800/827-6364
Price: Free
Online filename: MAKEWAOL.EXE (Windows);
AOL-1.ZIP & AOL-2.ZIP (DOS)

Prodigy Services

Everyone likes Prodigy. Its graphical user-interface is fun and cute,
and its appealing mix of news, financial and consumer information, and
home and hobby conferences makes it an online service on which it's easy
to kill a couple hours. A joint venture of IBM and Sears, Prodigy has
weathered hard times as rough as any faced by its two corporate parents
in the past decade, but not only does Prodigy survive, it seems to keep

getting better. It offers some of the most innovative financial information services for small investors found in the online world, like a daily glimpse into the stock picks of top high-priced financial newsletters—and it costs only $1 to read.

Pro-Util

If you're a Prodigy regular, you'll want a copy of Pro-Util. Prodigy is agonizingly slow to use. (One of us embroiders while waiting for Prodigy menus to update.) Pro-Util will speed up your access a bit, although not a lot because Prodigy is...well, Prodigy. There's just not a lot that can be done about it.

Pro-Util runs on top of Prodigy's special-purpose software, endowing Prodigy with features it really should have, but doesn't—like macros and the ability to print screens and save data to disk. It also lets you write e-mail offline, and import files into your messages from major word processors like Word for Windows and WordPerfect. You can check your messages with a spell-checker, and address them with Pro-Util's built-in address book. Enter ticker symbols for public companies you're interested in and Pro-Util will head out online and gather all the company news on them. You can even set up the software to log on to Prodigy and download data in the middle of the night when you're not around.

There are lots of Prodigy add-on utilities, but Pro-Util is our favorite, and the one that's easiest to set up.

Royston Development
4195 Chino Hills Pkwy, Suite 365
Chino Hills, CA 91709
Price: $24.95 plus $3.50 shipping or $2.75 to download
from Prodigy
Online filename: Download it from Prodigy by clicking
on "jump" on the bottom of the screen, then type
ROYSTON in the dialog box.

General Electric's GEnie

General Electric's GEnie has taken a beating the past few years from America Online and Prodigy. Those services offer a colorful, easy to use interface that you can point and click your way around with a mouse. GEnie, on the other hand, gives consumers a Pleistocene user-interface that's like dialing into an old mainframe. You type in cryptic commands and the system responds by scrolling menus over the screen, but ever so slowly. Sometimes the system "hangs" and you must sit there waiting for it to revive itself. It's very frustrating. GEnie, however, does offer some good online conversations, especially in its message area for small businesses. We've found business owners exchanging advice and "war stories" of a depth and caliber not seen on any of the other online services.

Aladdin

DOS

Aladdin is a free front-end program for General Electric's GEnie information service, shown in Figure 9-13. It automatically retrieves mail so that you can read it and respond to it offline. It will also capture to disk messages in the public forums, or "roundtables," that you specify, so that you can peruse them offline and even answer them. This software

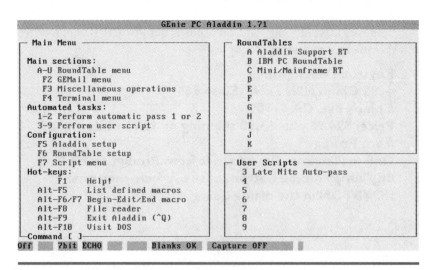

Figure 9-13 Aladdin's main screen

makes it tolerable to use GEnie, which otherwise has an unpleasant user-interface that sometimes freezes up, occasionally kicks back garbage to you, and in general is heinously slow to use. In fact, you may find GEnie intolerable without Aladdin.

Aladdin's script language and a wide variety of free scripts found on GEnie let you automate such tasks as stock quote retrieval. These scripts are easy to set up and use. A terminal mode lets you "break in" to an automated session and issue commands to GEnie directly.

Aladdin's only drawback is that, because General Electric often makes changes to its clunky software, when Aladdin users log on they sometimes discover unpleasant surprises, like Aladdin downloading thousands of already read messages (thanks to the message pointers being moved), or some such nonsense. Still, if you use GEnie, you'll want Aladdin.

General Electric Information Service (GEnie)
401 N. Washington St.
Rockville, MD 20850
Phone: 800/638-9636
Price: Free
Online filename: ALAD172.EXE (type ALADDIN at any
GEnie prompt to download it)

Computer Bulletin Boards

Computer bulletin boards are like the cozy roadhouses tucked along the information highway. They're the haunts of regulars who often have great conversation and good software to share. You need only basic all-purpose communications software to dial computer bulletin boards. Programs like Telemate, Telix, or Unicom will work fine. But if there's a particular BBS you frequent you might find that it's quicker to call and retrieve your e-mail if you use a communications program designed specifically to automate your call to the board. You will need to find out the kind of BBS software that the board uses in order to find an applicable program (most BBSs list the brand of software they use on their intro-duction screen). You might also want to solicit recommendations from other callers to the board.

RoboComm

RoboComm will automate your access to computer bulletin boards that run PC Board and Wildcat! software. Its ability to capture to disk messages for offline reply, and scan for new files in BBS libraries make it indispensable for anyone who dials BBSs long-distance. (Come on, admit it: your first month of modem ownership you dialed zillions of BBSs and ended up with a $300 phone bill that you consequently scurried to hide from the rest of the family.)

You can set up RoboComm to call a list of BBSs. For each board you call you

create an Agenda of Things to Do as in Figure 9-14. Among the tasks you can schedule are downloading of public and private messages, scanning for new files in selected file areas, and uploading and downloading files to designated systems. You can even tell it to call a BBS at a designated time when you're not there. When RoboComm finds new files on a system you call, it adds the filename to its database. After it gets done with its calls, you can scroll through the database, highlight the filenames and descriptions you want, and tell RoboComm to dial those BBSs again and retrieve the files.

If you're a shareware author (or an aspiring one) you can use RoboComm to "broadcast" new versions of your software to multiple

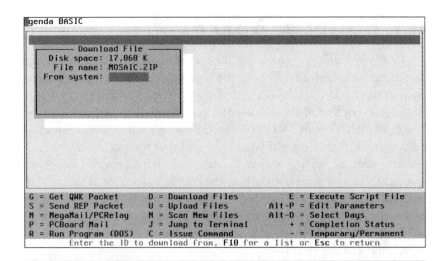

Figure 9-14   Creating an "Agenda" in RoboComm

systems. RoboComm will keep a log of all activities attempted and completed.

RoboComm has other talents. It automatically scans file downloads for viruses. It lets you run any other DOS software while it's busy offline. It also includes a script language.

Parsons Consulting
5020 S. Lake Shore Dr., Suite 3301
Chicago, IL 60615
BBS: 312/752-1258
Online filename: ROBO*xx*-A.ZIP, ROBO*xx*-B.ZIP

Speed Read

Speed Read automates mail retrieval from computer bulletin boards that use the popular QWK mail format. There are hoards of BBS mail readers out there, but Speed is our favorite. One of the main reasons is that it's so easy to set up and use. (Sometimes it seems like the BBS world revels in BBS-related software that has more parts to assemble than an artificial Christmas tree.)

You set up Speed Read to dial up and download messages from the public conferences you specify on a bulletin board. It will also capture private mail. After it logs off, you can read, print, sort, and delete messages, and answer messages by attaching files to your replies and carbon copy other users. You can even compress messages to save disk space. After you're done, Speed Read will log back onto the bulletin board and transmit the messages, posting them in their appropriate places on the system.

When you download Speed Read, you'll need to enter an access code each time you use it until you pay the shareware registration. This isn't a gratuitous annoyance, and you can't blame the author for including this because BBS users are notorious for not paying their shareware registrations.

J.E. Smith
344 Observatory Dr.
Birmingham, AL 35206
Price: $25
Online filename: SPEED140.ZIP

MCI Mail

An e-mail box on MCI Mail is a must-have for the techno-chic. Use it to send mail to users on any online service in the world (literally) including CompuServe, Prodigy, AT&T Mail, and Internet. There are no hourly online charges, just a small per-message or monthly fee, so most subscribers dial it with all-purpose communications software and take their time reading and writing messages online. If you want to automate the retrieval of mail there are lots of options, both in the shareware and the commercial world. On the commercial side, there's MCI Mail's MCI Express and the MCI mailer found in Norton/Symantec's Norton Desktop. In the shareware world, our favorite is MailRoom.

MailRoom

Windows

MailRoom automates sending and retrieval of e-mail via MCI Mail. MailRoom's easy menus, as shown in Figure 9-15, let you compose e-mail messages offline with MailRoom's built-in editor, then dial the service and let MailRoom address and send the messages for you. After it's done, it

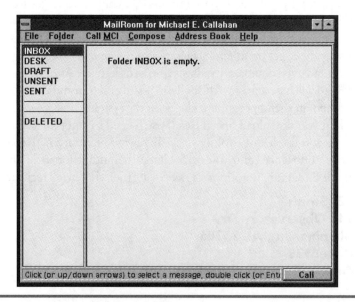

Figure 9-15   MailRoom's main screen

will download your waiting e-mail, then log off. You can read the messages offline, and store and sort the messages. One big advantage is that MailRoom saves all your messages to disk; if you want to save e-mail to disk when you dial MCI Mail with an all-purpose communications program you must invoke the file capture command to save messages. That can be a hassle. MailRoom also includes a handy address book for storing e-mail addresses that you can refer to while you're composing messages. MailRoom also has a script language you can use to automate frequently performed tasks on MCI Mail like uploading and downloading binary files and broadcasting messages to more than one address in your message book.

Sierra Solutions
2016 Kelton Ave.
Los Angeles, CA 90025
Phone: 310/478-2531
Price: $85
Internet: ftp.cica.indiana.edu
Online filename: MRMCI*xxx*.ZIP

Internet

Internet isn't really an online service in the sense that Prodigy or America Online are. It is not a business and it lacks any governing body. Rather, it is a web of electronic links between universities, businesses, government agencies, and commercial online services. To tap into Internet, you can't just call up an Internet Corp. (assuming one existed) and ask to subscribe. Getting onto Internet is a more circuitous process. If your employer isn't already on Internet, you need to tap into Internet through a commercial service that links into Internet. Most online services provide some sort of limited Internet access. (At this writing Delphi, in Boston, is the only major service that provides full mail, newsgroup, and TELNET access. See Appendix A for information on online services.) You can also tap into Internet via the following shareware program.

WinNet Mail

Windows

The Internet is lauded as the "information highway," but sometimes it seems more like an Alabama clay road still under construction. WinNet Mail smoothes out the information highway by giving you easy access to Internet mail as well as those raucous Usenet news groups. It won't give you access to Internet services like Gopher or TELNET but the average person really doesn't need those anyway. If you want low-cost access to "the Net" and you want it through Windows, WinNet Mail is something to consider.

WinNet Mail lets you set up an Internet account through a special connection through Computer Witchcraft. Unfortunately, it requires a call to the 508 area code, which may be long-distance for you. But phone charges aside, it will cost you only about $10 per month. Write e-mail with its built-in editor and automatically launch mail onto the Internet with the scheduling feature. Retrieve mail as easily and reply to it offline. WinNet will show you the message you're replying to as you reply. Figure 9-16 shows the WinNet editor.

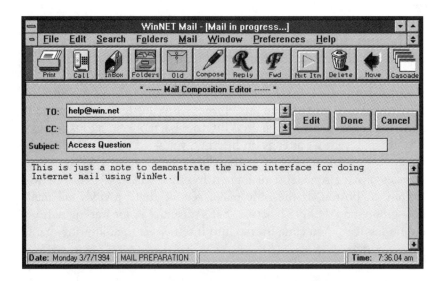

Figure 9-16   Creating a message with WinNet

Through WinNet you can access those famous Usenet public discussion groups, which range in topic from politics to car repair. You can exchange e-mail with computer nerds all over the world. WinNet puts all your Usenet mail into folders, organized by topic so that all you need to do to read it is to click on the appropriate button. That's the easiest way we know to read Usenet mail. WinNet also lets you read all your mail offline, so it doesn't cost you an arm and a leg to get all that mail.

Computer Witchcraft, Inc.
P. O. Box 4189
Louisville, KY 40204
Price: Software is free; average cost per month for the service is approximately $20. A long-distance call is involved to connect to the service.
Phone: 502/589-6800
Online filename: WINMAIL.ZIP or WNMAILxx.ZIP

Omnibus Navigators

Popping up on the market more and more frequently these days are e-mail readers that will retrieve e-mail from a number of different online services, including CompuServe, MCI Mail, and even some BBSs. Their advantage is that they simplify your life. You don't have to fire up five different communications programs each morning just to check on your e-mail on lots of different systems.

RFD Mail

Windows

Retrieve e-mail automatically from CompuServe, GEnie, MCI Mail, and BBSs with this colorful all-purpose online navigator. RFD Mail puts all your e-mail in one place and gives you a simple-to-use graphical interface for reading and answering mail from multiple services. No more thrashing between myriad communications programs and information service front-ends. Click on the Inbox icon to read your mail. Click on the address book icon to address e-mail to friends on different systems. Use different "e-mail signatures" for the different systems you call. Built-in binary file transfer features let you upload and download attached files to the messages. RFD Mail will only call systems that communicate

ASCII characters; that means you can't use it to call Prodigy or America Online, but you can use it to call most other online services and BBSs.

Performance Designs
CompuServe: 73017,1375
GEnie: PERFOM.DES
Internet: rfdmail@world.std.com
Price: $29.95
Online filename: RFDMAI.ZIP

Remote Software and Other Handy Stuff

Ever start working on something on your home computer, only to discover that you left some essential spreadsheet or word-processing file on the PC at your office? Remote software lets you dial up your office PC and pick up those files, or even work on application software as if you were sitting right in front of that faraway PC. Of course, there are commercial programs like Norton-Lambert's Close-Up that do this, but our shareware one is a bunch cheaper at $35, and just as functional.

Other shareware communications utilities can make your life easier. Use a pop-up dialer to easily dial phone numbers in a customer database (even voice calls!). Then turbo-charge your online sessions by giving Windows a new communications driver that will take advantage of high-speed serial ports in ways that Windows ordinarily will not.

Elsewhere

Elsewhere is a remote control program in the genre of Carbon Copy, but it was written to be lean and mean. Requiring only 8K of memory on the host PC (the PC you call into to run software), it's ideal for computer consultants who need to dial into a far-off customer's computer to update applications, troubleshoot, or run programs. Ordinary PC users will find it useful for accessing the office PC from their home PC at night, or while they're out on the road with a laptop.

Password protection shields the far-off PC from intruders. If you buy the $35 version, you'll get a file transfer module that will let you shuttle files between connected PCs with Xmodem and Ymodem. (O.K., it doesn't offer super-fast Zmodem, but Ymodem isn't bad.) You'll definitely need this. When you're connected to a remote PC with Elsewhere you won't get a menu like you do with other remote control programs, so this is not a program for amateurs. But it is easy to toggle between the remote PC and your own PC while online.

Remote control programs are often testy. Some will work with certain video boards and application software, and some will not. It's definitely the sort of software that you need to test-drive before you buy, and you can do that with Elsewhere. Don't expect to run Windows applications remotely, though—that's a toughie for any remote control software.

> **Kevin Kiley**
> **1222 5th St.**
> **Sarasota, FL 34236**
> **Price: Free, unless you want tech support, then it's $20, or $35 if you want the file transfer feature too.**
> **Online filename: EW_V*xx*.ZIP**

dbDIAL

DOS

dbDIAL is an electronic Rolodex that can dial the phone numbers for you. It can store up to a billion phone numbers (almost enough space for your little black book, right?), with a note space beside each for jotting reminders. Pop it up over other applications like client databases and dial numbers right off the screen. Use it to place voice and fax as well as data calls. dbDIAL will keep logs of your phone numbers, making it great for tax purposes, or for logging calls to, say, troublesome insurance companies.

You can search through dbDial's phone number files using various criteria. dbDIAL can also place names, addresses, and phone numbers into the Windows clipboard or the DOS keyboard buffer for easy transfers to other applications.

> **ZPAY Payroll Systems, Inc.**
> **2526 69th Ave., South**
> **St. Petersburg, FL 33712-5631**
> **Phone: 800/468-4188 (orders only)**
> **Fax: 813/866-8034**
> **Price: $49**
> **Online filename: DBD-1.ZIP & DBD-2.ZIP**

CHCOMB

If you run a communications program in a DOS window under Windows, you'll want to give Windows a new communications driver. The driver in Windows 3.1 does not support the high-speed 16550A UART when you run communications software under DOS. Support for that chip is *essential* for high-speed modem communications. If you don't have it, you'll get lots of errors during high-speed downloads, if your downloads work at all. CHCOMB will provide that support. It comes with simple to understand directions on installing it.

Cherry Hill Software
7 Valley View, Suite 18
Watervliet, NY 12189
Phone: 518/786-3153
Fax: 518/786-3158
Price: $10
Online filename: CHCOMB.EXE

CHAPTER 10

SOFTWARE THAT MAKES WINDOWS AND DOS EASIER TO LIVE WITH

GUI and CHUI. They're pronounced "gooey" and "chewy," the first like a wad of caramel, the second like the name of the big wookie in *Star Wars*. A GUI is a *graphical user interface*; that's what Windows is. A CHUI is a *character-based user interface*; that's what DOS is.

To some of us, however, they will always remain Gooey and Chewy. Like the caramel and the wookie. Sticky and not too bright. Trying to get into lockstep with these two characters is like getting sucked into a Bing Crosby and Bob Hope road movie. The misadventures come easily, but you never get anywhere.

That's where DOS and Windows enhancements fit in. Whether you're stuck at the main screen of the Windows Program Manager or stalled at the enigmatic DOS prompt, nine times out of ten you will either be unable to do what you want or you won't have the foggiest idea of how to do it. The utilities programs in this chapter can help protect you and your employees from spending hours staring at the screen, wondering what to do. The Windows add-ons will give you extra button bars for neglected features like the ability to quickly view files or directories. The DOS add-ons will not only give you new and useful commands to use, they also protect you from the inscrutabilities of the DOS command line by presenting a cozy, simple menu from which you can fire up your favorite applications, such as your word processor or spreadsheet program. You'll never have to touch DOS again (well, hopefully not).

Obviously, the DOS enhancement utilities aren't as popular as they once were, thanks to the spread of Windows. But if you have a less than up-to-date PC with an older (read *slower*) processor, like an 8082 or 286, you may find running Windows intolerable and hate to leave your DOS prompt. Or else you may have passed on that old PC to an employee, in which case they may appreciate a DOS menuing program through which they can access the programs they need.

Either way, you'll never want to brave the perils of Gooey and Chewy without these tools by your side.

Windows Enhancements

When Windows first came to market, long-time PC users howled about the many things that Windows would not let users do. It wouldn't let you delete files. It gave you no easy way to manage directories. The Program Manager tended to become cluttered by application icons and there was no easy way to reorganize them by embedding them in nested folders like Mac users can do. Years later, Windows still suffers these grievous omissions, but software entrepreneurs have leapt to the rescue with Windows add-on utilities that will give Windows capabilities you've always dreamed of—like the ability to easily read simple text files and use the popular compression program PKZIP without exiting to DOS.

Drag And Zip

Most files that you download from BBSs and computer information services are compressed with PKZIP to save time in downloading, and also to save space on the computer on which they're stored (see Chapter 11, "Tools and Toys," for more on PKZIP). Once you download a file you must "unZIP" it, but if you're a Windows user that means exiting to DOS to do so. Drag And Zip spares you the hassle by letting you Zip and unZIP files by merely dragging the filename from the Windows File Manager and dropping it on the Drag And Zip icon.

Dropping them on the Drag And Zip icon brings up the Drag And Zip dialog box, which is shown in Figure 10-1. Just type in the Zip filename and click on OK. To add a file to a ZIP file, drag the filename to the icon, then type in the name of the already Zipped file. To Zip or unZIP a file,

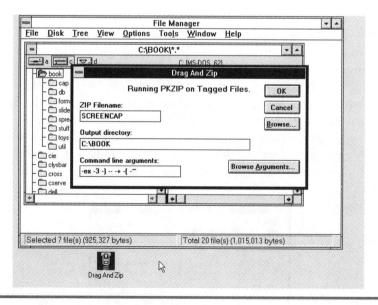

Figure 10-1   This dialog box appears when you drop a file on the Drag And Zip icon

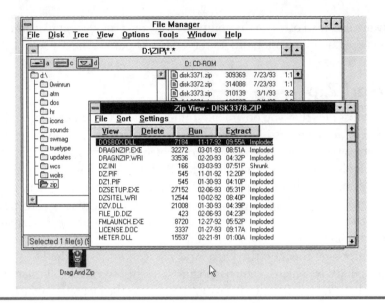

Figure 10-2 Drag And Zip lets you look inside Zipped text files before you uncompress them

merely drag the filename from the Windows File Manager and drop it on the Drag And Zip icon.

Another terrific feature of Drag And Zip is its file viewer, shown in Figure 10-2. It lets you look inside Zipped archive files before you uncompress them. You can even read the contents of a Zipped text file and run executable program files without hassling to unZIP them first.

If you insist on making your life difficult, you can click the Browse Arguments button to bring up a dialog box, shown here, that will allow you to set any of the many PKZIP command line options.

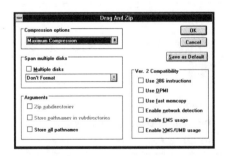

But Drag And Zip never lets things get more complicated than a plain-spoken dialog box. In fact, we like this easy-to-use program so much, we included it on the disk that comes with this book.

Canyon Software
1537 Fourth St., Suite 131
San Rafael, CA 94901
Phone: 415/382-7999
Fax: 415/382-7998
Price: $30
Online filename: DRAGZP.ZIP

WizManager

WizManager is a handy utility that adds a button bar to your Windows File Manager screen, giving you point-and-click access to file and directory management functions that Windows otherwise hides in out-of-the-way places, as you can see in Figure 10-3.

Shareware in Action

Product: Drag And Zip
Company:
Hewlett-Packard—
Corvallis Ink Jet Site

The Hewlett-Packard Ink Jet Site in Corvallis, Oregon, makes ink pins for Hewlett-Packard's ink jet printers—at a rate of one pin every three-quarters of a second. Procurement engineer Mike Griebel is responsible for sending tooling files for these pins to shops throughout the world. The files he sends are large—40MB and bigger—too large to send conveniently over a modem.

Until recently, Griebel had to use a DOS program to compress the thousands of pin tooling files created at Hewlett-Packard so they could be sent efficiently to the PC systems at the shop sites. "Typing the DOS commands took forever," he said, "and I had to remember all the commands." Then he discovered Drag And Zip. "Drag And Zip cuts the file size to about a third, and it takes about one-tenth the time to send the file. All I have to do is press a key and type in the filename."

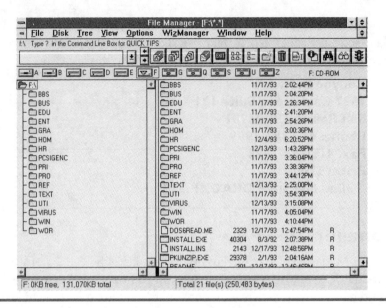

Figure 10-3 WizManager gives you point and click access to file directory management functions

With this utility, you can list directories and sort by the file's name, type, size, and date. You can view a file's contents and create, delete, rename, and search directories and files. You can also print directories and disk information. You can do all this by clicking buttons and highlighting directory and file names. WizManager lets you add your own buttons to its colorful button bar so that you can do things like launch applications, display picture files, or play special sound effects (like the *Star Trek* ones with which one of the authors of this book is driving the rest of us crazy).

You'll find Drag And Zip included on the disk that comes with this book. If you try out no other Windows enhancers, be sure to check out Drag And Zip.

Mijenix
6666 Odana Rd., Suite 326
Madison, WI 53719
Phone: 608/277-1971
CompuServe ID: 75430,1545
Price: $39.95 plus $4 shipping and handling
Online filename: WIZMGR.ZIP

Plug-In for Program Manager

Think of Plug-In for Program Manager as one of those useful little appliances, like a cassette recorder, that you can plug into the dashboard of your car. Its purpose is to provide meaningful and useful additions to the Windows Program Manager, like the ability to organize your applications into nested folders so that Program Manager does not get so cluttered with icons. Plug-In lets you customize your startup group of applications. Its quick-install feature lets you instantly install any new Windows application, displaying its documentation as it begins.

When you install Plug-In, it will change your Windows icons to something a bit more friendly. The Windows cursor will become a hand reminiscent of that on a Macintosh, as shown in Figure 10-4, and the hourglass will turn into a clock. You can also turn the clock into the head of a guy with a big nose who will open his mouth and smile, telling you to wait, whenever the sands of time would otherwise appear on the screen.

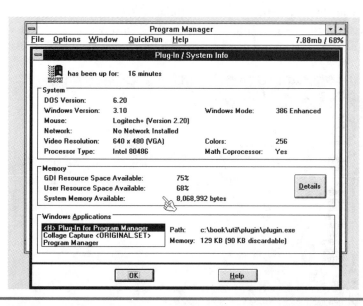

Figure 10-4 Plug-In's System Info feature turns the Windows cursor into a helping hand

Planet Crafters, Inc.
2580 Runic Way
Alpharetta, GA 30202
Phone: 404/740-9821
Fax: 404/740-1914
BBS: 404/740-8583
CompuServe ID: 73040,334
Internet: 73040.334@compuserve.com
America Online: DMandell
GEnie: D.MANDELL1
Prodigy: VSFB48A
MCI Mail: 572-7179
Price: $20 plus shipping and handling
Online filename: PLUGIN02.ZIP

Command Post

Windows

Command Post is another long-time Windows add-on favorite. It gives you file management abilities similar to WizManager plus the ability to create your own menuing interface for Windows, as you can see in Figure 10-5. The difference between Command Post and all the rest is

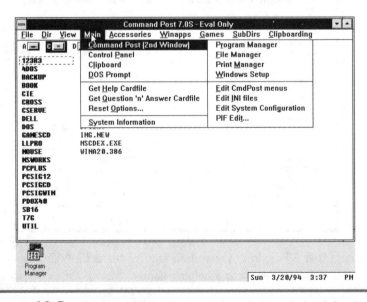

Figure 10-5   Command Post gives you the substance behind the icon

that Command Post displays file directories and filenames in much the same way as DOS does—with long lists.

To run programs or display files you click on them. You can delete, move, and copy directories and files by dragging and dropping the filenames. It also puts all your Windows applications into pull-down menus. You click on their names in order to run them. This spares you the tyranny of icons. Command Post also includes a special batch language so that you can automate the running of applications and opening of files. Command Post is for those of us who have never quite trusted Windows, with its happy-face icons and feel-good dialog boxes.

> **Wilson WindowWare**
> **2701 California Ave., S.W. #212**
> **Seattle, WA 98116**
> **Phone: 206/937-9335 or 800/762-8383 (orders only)**
> **Fax: 206/935-7129**
> **Price: $49.95**
> **Online filename: CP-xxx.ZIP or CMDPSTxx.ZIP**

File Commander

File Commander is a subset of Command Post. As shown in Figure 10-6, it lets you add four pull-down menus to Windows, with up to three layers of customizable sub-menus through which you can run applications. It also includes extensive scripting ability with 200 functions that let you automate such Windows operations as loading applications, resizing and moving windows, and accessing files. You might consider it a sort of shell to run over Windows.

> **Wilson WindowWare**
> **2701 California Ave., S.W. #212**
> **Seattle, WA 98116**
> **Phone: 206/937-9335 or 800/762-8383 (orders only)**
> **Fax: 206/935-7129**
> **Price: $49.95**
> **Online filename: FC-20K.ZIP**

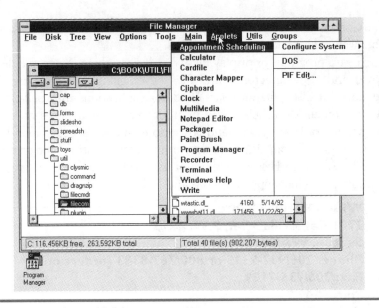

Figure 10-6 File Commander puts Windows utilities and
applications in easy-to-use pull-down menus

QRead

One of the most popular shareware utilities ever is a DOS text reader
called, unassumedly enough, List. It was written years ago by one of the
greatest PC programmers ever, Vern Buerg. Buerg wanted to distribute
List for free—and did so for a long time—until his friends badgered,
pestered, and goaded him (as well-meaning friends often do), and he
finally tacked to List's documentation file the request for a non-manda-
tory $10 donation. Being an unmaterialistic sort, Buerg was embarrassed
and even disconcerted by the checks that flooded in, although eventually
they provided a nice living for him. Now called List Plus, the program is
still popular, despite the onslaught of Windows (see Chapter 11, "Tools
and Toys," for more about List Plus).

QRead is for Windows what List Plus is for DOS: the indispensable,
consummately useful text reader. Simply drag a filename from the File
Manager window and drop it on the QRead icon. The file will pop up in
front of you, as shown in Figure 10-7. With QRead you can also search

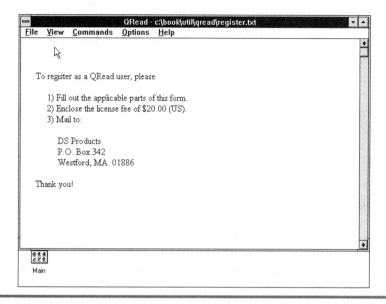

Figure 10-7   QRead gives you a quick and easy way to read text
files in Windows

through the text file for a particular word or phrase, copy part of the text
into Windows' clipboard, print and delete files, and filter out junk
characters. This is another program you *have* to have.

DS Products
P.O. Box 342
Westford, MA 01886
Price: $20
Online filename: QREA*xx*.ZIP or QREAD.ZIP

SmartCat

Isn't it funny how the people who live with bills and papers and
magazines strewn about their office are always the first ones to latch onto
a disk cataloger as some kind of software savior? SmartCat will catalog
all your disks and diskettes for you. It will scan your disk and add all the
filenames to a catalog along with the file's size, the last time it was
updated, and the name of the subdirectory it's stored in. It will even peek

into archive files and add the filenames it finds to your catalog. Once it finishes cataloging, it will record information about the disk, such as its size, available space, and volume label.

SmartCat can also scan the disk for viruses while cataloging. Even better, it lets you run an application from its catalog list. Now that's cool. You can also use it to search for files, specifying things like name, date range, and file size. The results of a typical search are shown in Figure 10-8. It will search not just your hard disk, but your floppy catalog too. Its only limitation is that file catalogs cannot exceed 3,000 items. It's easy to exceed that on a moderate-sized hard disk.

Shareable Software International, Inc.
P.O. Box 59102
Schaumburg, IL 60159
Fax: 708/397-0381
Compuserve ID: 76226,2652
EXEC-PC: Bill Dickson
Price: $39.95
Online filename: SMTCSX.ZIP

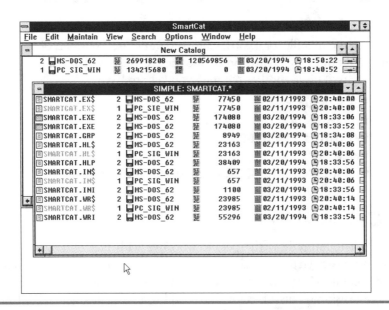

Figure 10-8   These are the fruits of a SmartCat search for
SMARTCAT

DOS Enhancements

DOS is like a no-frills checking account. It's serviceable, but essentials are missing. It would be nice if you had something else to look at on the screen besides that enigmatic DOS prompt, for instance, or if you could execute commands by pointing and shooting. The ultimate DOS enhancements are commercial multi-tasking programs like Quarterdeck's Desqview which enable you to run multiple DOS applications in windows that you can move between, like those in Windows. They also offer other needed features to DOS, like macros to automate chores. They're cheap too (usually under $100). There are shareware DOS multi-taskers, but none can approach Desqview in quality and low price. These multi-taskers are nowhere near as popular as they once were, thanks to the proliferation of fast 386 and 486 PCs that have made Windows a usable commodity. If you have an older PC, though, like a 286 or 8086, you'll want to use Desqview, or a menuing program which will list all your applications on the screen and make it easier to run them. There are lots of good shareware menuing programs. Our favorite is described below.

AutoMenu

DOS

AutoMenu is another shareware oldie-but-goodie. It's a menuing system that you install on employees' PCs to shelter them from the treacheries of DOS. For instance, you can list on the menu WordPerfect, Lotus 1-2-3, Calculator, or any other applications they frequently use, as shown in Figure 10-9. All they have to do is toggle to that application and AutoMenu loads it for them. They can also perform rudimentary DOS commands from the main menu, like copying files, all without touching DOS. (You can also keep them from accessing DOS completely, thereby preventing them from wreaking accidental havoc.)

We're constantly amazed by the number of PCs that we find AutoMenu running on. We even spot it on the PCs of fairly sophisticated users. It makes the world a simpler place, and we need more software that does that. AutoMenu is ideal for older PCs, like 8086s and 286s, that aren't up to power to running Windows at full blast.

AutoMenu's many features include network and mouse support, password protection, a few built-in games, and excellent documentation. For a long time it was the top DOS menuing software on the market—until Windows came along that is. Here's a bit of shareware trivia: Its author, Marshall Magee, was an ardent crusader, in the early days of shareware, for making this quixotic software genre appear respectable to big companies. For a long time he was the only shareware author who insisted on wearing a suit and tie. He was founding president of the Association of Shareware Professionals.

Magee Enterprises
P.O. Box 1587
Norcross, GA 30091
Phone: 404/446-6611 or 800/662-4330
Fax: 404/368-0719
BBS: 404/446-6650
Price: $69.95
Online filename: AUTO50.EXE

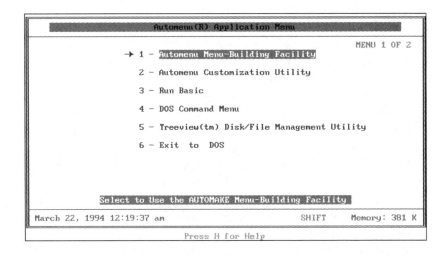

Figure 10-9   AutoMenu spares employees the vagaries of DOS

4DOS

4DOS is like a DOS replacement. You use it to replace the nutmeat of DOS, a program called COMMAND.COM. With 4DOS you get new DOS commands, plus some old DOS commands with new capabilities. It works with most PC hardware and software, including memory-resident software, as well as with networks. The only hitch we could find in using it is that, although the manual claims it will work with Windows and even includes a PIF file for doing so, it kept locking up our PC when we tried.

When you install 4DOS, your old DOS prompt will look the same. The difference is that you'll have over 40 more DOS commands. You can do things like copy a list of files all at once, get the name of a subdirectory where a program is run, and execute several commands in a row. 4DOS will also give you a list of all the commands you've recently entered and let you point and shoot to execute some of them again, as shown in Figure 10-10. 4DOS also provides built-in help screens (something DOS certainly doesn't do). Just type **HELP COPY** for a screen full of advice on using the copy command.

Admittedly some of these things are a bit techy, and not everyone is going to consider 4DOS the ideal DOS add-on for them. But some of the DOS command enhancements, like the ability to point and shoot commands, do come in handy.

JP Software Inc.
P.O. Box 1470
East Arlington, MA 02174
Phone: 617/646-3975 or 800/368-8777 (orders only)
Fax: 617/646-0904
CompuServe ID: 75020,244
MCI Mail: 470-7811
Price: $69 plus $6 shipping and handling
($12 outside the U.S.)
Online filename: 4DOS*xx*.ZIP

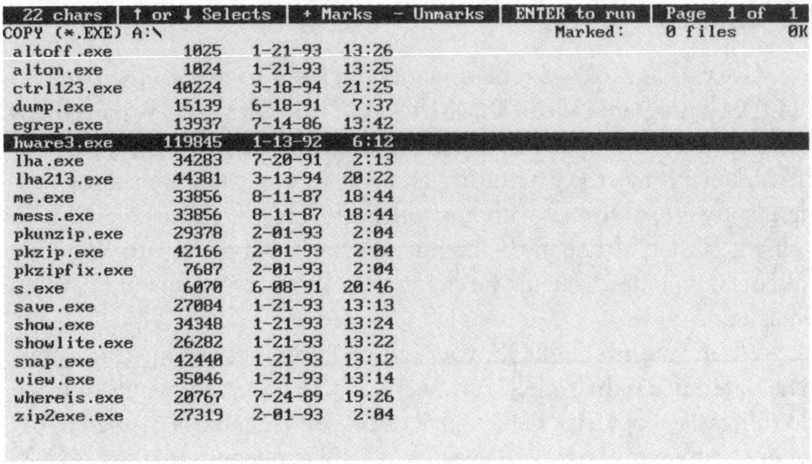

```
 22 chars │ ↑ or ↓ Selects │ + Marks   - Unmarks │ ENTER to run │ Page  1 of  1
COPY (*.EXE) A:\                                        Marked:     0 files      0K
  altoff.exe       1025   1-21-93   13:26
  alton.exe        1024   1-21-93   13:25
  ctrl123.exe     40224   3-18-94   21:25
  dump.exe        15139   6-18-91    7:37
  egrep.exe       13937   7-14-86   13:42
  hware3.exe     119845   1-13-92    6:12
  lha.exe         34283   7-20-91    2:13
  lha213.exe      44381   3-13-94   20:22
  me.exe          33856   8-11-87   18:44
  mess.exe        33856   8-11-87   18:44
  pkunzip.exe     29378   2-01-93    2:04
  pkzip.exe       42166   2-01-93    2:04
  pkzipfix.exe     7687   2-01-93    2:04
  s.exe            6070   6-08-91   20:46
  save.exe        27084   1-21-93   13:13
  show.exe        34348   1-21-93   13:24
  showlite.exe    26282   1-21-93   13:22
  snap.exe        42440   1-21-93   13:12
  view.exe        35046   1-21-93   13:14
  whereis.exe     20767   7-24-89   19:26
  zip2exe.exe     27319   2-01-93    2:04
```

Figure 10-10   With 4DOS loaded, you can execute many DOS commands point-and-shoot style

CHAPTER 11

TOOLS AND TOYS

magine yourself trying to navigate through a busy day without your appointment book in your pocket. Unthinkable. Or try figuring the lunch tab without that slim little calculator in your wallet. And don't forget how much more stress-ful a stress-filled day would be without those wind-up toy sharks in your desk drawer that are always good for a chuckle.

Our desk drawers and pockets are filled to the brim with small tools, as well as with some toys. Without them our days would be littered with inconveniences. Our PCs should similarly be filled with tiny tools: pop-up appointment books and diaries, file viewers, automatic software runners, and a game or two to break up a rough day. The nice thing about choosing your tools and toys from among shareware is that there is such a wide variety of utilities to select from, and you only have to pay for the ones you really want to keep.

note

 If what you're really looking for is something more sophisticated, check out the personal information managers, which combine phone books with notepads, calculators, and other desktop utensils, described in Chapter 22.

Back Soon!

 If you leave your computer on for a long time with the same screen displayed (such as when you leave your desk), you risk having your monitor suffer "phosphor burn-in." That's when the lines of word-processing documents or spreadsheets are literally burned into your screen from being displayed for too long without moving. Windows comes with a built-in screen saver that will blacken your screen when you're away from your desk so that the monitor doesn't become afflicted by phosphor burn-in. But when you work in DOS, there is no automatic screen saver to protect your monitor. Now, however, you can turn to Back Soon!.

Back Soon! is the perfect PC screen blanker for anyone with a desk job. When you head out to lunch or the copy machine, load Back Soon! and it will blacken the screen as well as display a message for anyone who may come looking for you, explaining where you went and when you'll be back. The message orbits the screen so it will not be burned in. Your visitor can also leave a message for you on the screen. As shown in Figure 11-1, you will be alerted to any waiting meassage. Since Back Soon! is password protected, only you can access the messages, and no one will be able to access anything on your PC while you're gone.

When you load Back Soon!, a menu opens from which you can choose any of a variety of messages—such as messages that say you've gone to lunch, gone for coffee or out on errands, or to the copy machine.

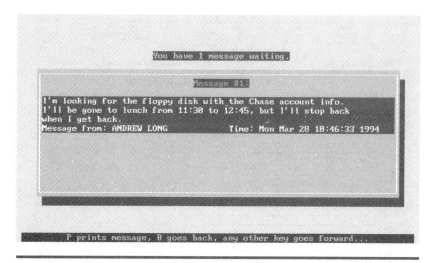

Figure 11-1   Enter your password and Back Soon! says if anyone left you a message

But it's also easy to create your own message. The program is not a TSR, so you'll have to load it each time you plan to leave your PC unattended; it does, however, come with WordPerfect and Quattro macros so that you can load it without exiting those programs. It's a DOS program, but you can use it in Windows.

> **Tay-Jee Software**
> **P.O. Box 835**
> **Lexington, VA 24450**
> **Price: $20 ($5 discount if you pay with cash, check, or money order)**
> **Online filename: BKSN10.ZIP or BACKSN.ZIP**

Reminder

Are you the type who sticks 3M Post-It Notes on your PC's monitor to remind you of things you need to do during the day? Get rid of the paper and make your reminders electronic with this little "sticky notes" utility. Use it to post bright yellow notes on your Windows' screen, like the one shown in Figure 11-2, to remind yourself of birthdays, meetings,

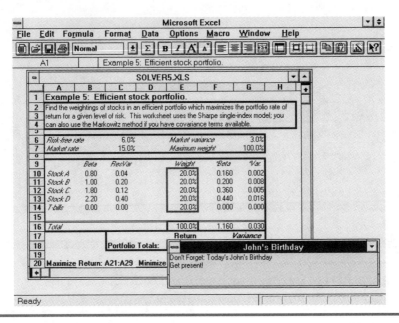

Figure 11-2   Reminder brings you electronic versions of 3M
Post-It Notes

phone calls that need to be made, and other important chores. It's a
program that's easy to load, type a reminder into, and unload when you're
done. You can place it anywhere on the screen, and you can set it to
appear on all active Windows screens, or just the one you specify. There
are several programs like this available as shareware. This is one of the
simplest.

Vance Kessler
2835 Binghampton Lane
Lawrenceville, GA 30244
Price: "Whatever amount you feel it is worth"
Online filename: REMIND.ZIP (note: you'll find lots of
files online with the name REMIND.ZIP, so you'll have
to look carefully)

WinUpD8R

Windows

If you have more than two PCs in your life, you know what a hassle it can be to keep files current on both. Say you have a laptop PC that you take on business trips. You use it to run spreadsheets, write letters, work on reports, even record phone numbers and information on customer contacts. When you get back to the office you need to update all those directories and files on your office PC. What a pain! WinUpD8R will bring sanity and automation to the chore.

First, run WinUpD8R on your laptop PC. It will show you the directories you specify and copy their contents, including their directory structure, to a floppy disk. Now insert the floppy in your office PC. Load WinUpD8R on that PC and it will copy the files into the applicable directories on that PC when you click on the UpD8R button. A batch mode lets you automate the procedure both ways so that you can update files on both PCs simultaneously. Its options, as shown in Figure 11-3,

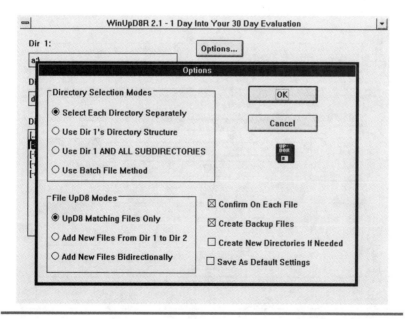

Figure 11-3   Copy files and directories from one PC to the other by specifying what needs to be updated in WinUpD8R's simple pop-up box

include the ability to create file backups and new directories when needed. We think this program is so handy we've included it on one of the disks that's packed with this book.

Open Windows
P.O. Box 49746
Colorado Springs, CO 80949
CompuServe ID: 75236,3243
Price: $15
Online filename: UPD8R-21.ZIP

WorldTime

Don't you sometimes wish that you had six clocks on the wall, each displaying the time in the time zones where your clients are located? We have something better. It's a pop-up Windows utility that you can customize to tell you the current time in the location of any long-distance customer, as shown in Figure 11-4.

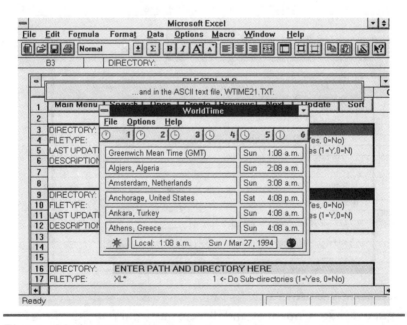

Figure 11-4 WorldTime will give you the correct time in any location you choose

WorldTime can give you the correct time for 170 locations around the world, including all the major cities from Stockholm to Beijing. It will even give you the correct time for locations in Antarctica. It is programmed to accommodate all the major time zones, and can even take into account local peculiarities in daylight savings policies. You can customize WorldTime so that at the click of a button it will display the time of six chosen customers or clients. It's indispensable for travelers with laptop computers, and anyone who does business across more than two time zones.

Pegasus Development
11900 Grant Place
St. Louis, MO 63131
Phone: 314/965-5630
Price: $16
Online filename: WTIM21.ZIP

Xtree

Straightening up your hard disk is more of a hassle than cleaning out the trunk of a car. Even the pathologically neat are often at a loss when it comes to rerouting stray TMP files from directories where they don't belong, and purging old word processing and spreadsheet files from bloated subdirectories. A thorough hard disk spring cleaning can eat up the better part of a day. Such time and effort doesn't need to be expended—not if you use Xtree.

Xtree is the ultimate hard disk management utility. Pop it up and it will display the directory structure of your entire hard disk as if it were a genealogical tree, as shown in Figure 11-5. Use its simple commands to delete, rename, and move files and directories. If you don't know what's in a file, Xtree will show you. You can move and delete large numbers of files at once. This is much easier than trying to use Windows' File Manager and any Windows add-on utilities. And it's infinitely easier than typing in all the commands yourself.

Executive Systems, Inc.
4330 Santa Fe Rd.
San Luis Obispo, CA 93401
Phone: 805/541-0604
Fax: 805/541-8935
Price: $25
Online filename: XTREE.ZIP

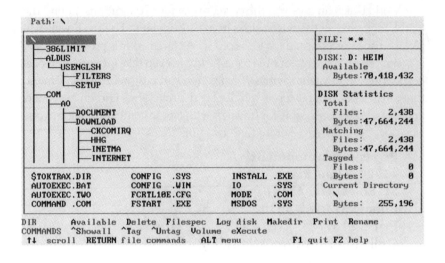

```
Path: \

                                            FILE: *.*
  ┌─386LIMIT
  ├─ALDUS                                   DISK: D: HEIM
  │  └─USENGLSH                               Available
  │     ├─FILTERS                             Bytes:70,418,432
  │     └─SETUP
  ├─COM                                     DISK Statistics
  │  ├─AO                                     Total
  │  │  ├─DOCUMENT                              Files:      2,438
  │  │  ├─DOWNLOAD                              Bytes:47,664,244
  │  │  │  ├─CKCOMIRQ                         Matching
  │  │  │  ├─HHG                                Files:      2,438
  │  │  │  ├─INETMA                             Bytes:47,664,244
  │  │  │  └─INTERNET                         Tagged
  │  │  │                                       Files:          0
  $TOKTRAX.DIR     CONFIG  .SYS    INSTALL .EXE   Bytes:          0
  AUTOEXEC.BAT     CONFIG  .WIN    IO      .SYS  Current Directory
  AUTOEXEC.TWO     FCRTL10E.CFG    MODE    .COM   \
  COMMAND .COM     FSTART  .EXE    MSDOS   .SYS   Bytes:    255,196

DIR       Available  Delete  Filespec  Log disk  Makedir  Print  Rename
COMMANDS  ^Showall   ^Tag   ^Untag   Volume  eXecute
  ↑↓  scroll  RETURN file commands   ALT menu         F1 quit F2 help
```

Figure 11-5 Xtree displays the directories on your hard
disk in genealogical tree-fashion

OMNIDay

Some of the most successful people in business, politics, and science keep personal journals. Diaries help us not only to sort out our ideas, but also to conduct our lives in a thoughtful way. OMNIDay is a personal electronic diary, shown in Figure 11-6, with a full supply of tools and pull-down menus. You'll never have to worry about your boss (or mom) snooping in it, because each time you exit it, your entry is automatically encrypted. You can only read entries with a password.

You use OMNIDay like a word processor, with the exception that entries are organized by date. When you start a new entry, the date and time are automatically added to it. The "Reminisce" feature lets you browse through entries by date and the first line of the entry. You can print single entries, or the entire journal.

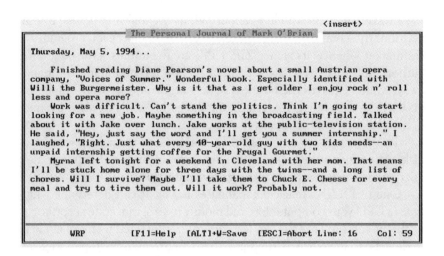

Figure 11-6 OMNIDay will store your innermost thoughts and ideas, and password protect them so no one can see

Unicorn Software Ltd.
P.O. Box 911
Wabash, IN 46991
Phone: 219/563-4663 (6 to 9 pm EST)
CompuServe ID: 70270,3317
Price: $29.95
Online filename: OMNIDAY*x*.ZIP (Windows);
ODAYWIN*x*.ZIP (DOS) or ODAY.ZIP

PKZIP

DOS

When you see a file on an online service with .ZIP at the end, you know it's been compressed in size with the online world standard compression program, PKZIP. A compression program is one that takes the air out of a file, so to speak, squeezing it down in size so that it takes up less disk space and is quicker to telecommunicate. If you plan to download files from online services, you're going to need this program.

PKZIP compresses a file to about half its original size, or less. It also performs this compression faster than any other compression program on the market—hence, its name, "ZIP." ("PK" are the initials of the program's author, Phil Katz, who has become a recluse, programming the night away, while he leaves the business of his burgeoning software empire to his business exec mom, Hildegard, to manage.) PKZIP can also be found in many commercial products, like Lotus.

The most recent version of PKZIP can be used to back up your hard disk, since it can store large archive files across multiple diskettes. It also encrypts and password-protects sensitive data files.

One of PKZIP's magical capabilities is that it can determine what type of CPU your computer has and modify its program code accordingly so that it can run faster. It can also run in 32-protected memory mode if it detects that your PC supports that. Consequently it performs at lightning speed when run under Windows or OS/2. It also clocks impressive speeds backing up network drives on Novell Networks.

You'll find PKZIP on the disks included with this book.

PKWare Inc.
9025 N. Deerwood Dr.
Brown Deer, WI 58228
Phone: 414/354-8699
Fax: 414/354-8559
BBS: 414/354-8670
Price: $47
Online filename: PKZ204G.EXE

List Plus

DOS

List Plus is an old-time favorite by one of the greatest programmers of all time, Vern Buerg. You can probably find it on most PCs in America. It's a simple little utility that lets you read text and program files and scroll through them on the screen. Through the years, List Plus has acquired more bells and whistles than a drill team in a mummer's parade. You can print files with it, or just portions of files. You can browse one or more related files with a single command and with split screens.

You can search through files, or search for files on your hard drive. You can view the contents of archive files. A built-in phone dialer lets you dial numbers in a text file. You can even edit, copy, delete, move, tag, and untag files on your system. It supports both networks and mice. Its many configurable options let you "clone" them so they're always available to you with just a keystroke. You can even configure the colors on your screen.

Vernon D. Buerg
139 White Oak Circle
Petaluma, CA 94952
Price: $30 (suggested)
Online filename: LISTXX.ZIP

Hot Computer Games

Every good management consultant knows that play is as important a part of formulating good ideas as work is. This book would not be complete without a word or two about shareware computer games. There are hundreds of *fantastic* computer games available as shareware. At this writing, the hottest one is Doom, an action-adventure game in which you play a Ramboesque Marine fighting your way through the Jungle of Doom with a high-tech arsenal and lots of brawn. (Look for two files named DOOM*xx*.ZIP online.) Second in popularity is Castle Wolfenstein 3-D in which you're a POW trapped in a Nazi castle prison and must fight your way out. (Look for 1WOLF-A.ZIP and 1WOLF-B.ZIP.) Another favorite is Xargon, an adventure-style game in which you guide the "very cool and muscular Malvineous through dangerous lands filled with hazardous enemies"—do we see a pattern here? (Look for XARGON.ZIP online.) For the sedentary at heart, there are the Commander Keen adventures. Commander Keen is a pint-sized tike in a football helmet who combats such atrocities as the vegetables on his plate. There are lots of Commander Keen games. Scan for KEEN when you're online. These are kid favorites, but adults like them too.

The best places to search for hot computer games are computer bulletin boards. Many BBSs have arrangements with shareware game vendors to let any caller download their games from their board for free. Exec-PC in Milwaukee offers the most free games for downloading (414/789-4210). General Electric's GEnie is another good place to look for games. (See Appendix A for more information on GEnie.) Generally, big information services like CompuServe are not so swell for game hunting. Games, with their cryptic names, tend to be hard to find. Also, since games are typically stored in multiple, whopper-sized files, downloading them gets expensive. PC-SIG's World of Games CD-ROM is a great buy, since it contains 550 games and you can play most of them on the disk without having to copy them to your PC first. Remember, though, you still have to pay your shareware registration for the games you like.

General Retail Operations Training (GROT)

DOS

If you want to integrate game-playing and the cutthroat world of retail business, here's your chance. GROT is a simulation game in which each player is the manager of a competing department store in the brutal retail empire of GROT INC. Players examine reports concerning inventory, sales, employee paychecks, store operating expenses, and past sale performance. Then they make decisions to do things like change profit margins, sell different goods, increase the number of sale items, and hire and fire employees.

A certain amount of cooperation among players is required because, with the vicissitudes of the retail world, all the stores are susceptible to sinking at once. The author denies that GROT, shown in Figure 11-7, is based upon some statistically precise model of retailing, but says that the point is that players learn all the different factors that can affect sales.

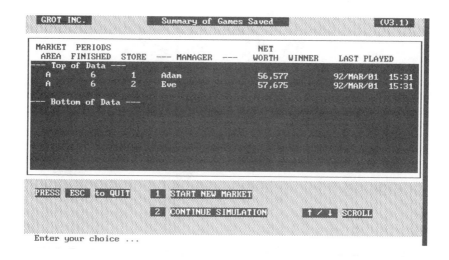

Figure 11-7   A playing screen from the retail simulation
game GROT

P.K. Winter
69 Summerhill Ave.
Toronto, Ontario M4T 1A9
Canada
CompuServe ID: 71213,1337
Price: $20; $60 for corporate site license
Online filename: GROT31.ZIP

FINANCE AND ACCOUNTING

3

CHAPTER 12

SOFTWARE FOR MAKING BUSINESS PLANS

hether you're waist-deep in the muck of a new business's startup travails or are impatient to start that mail order business that's still only a gleam in your eyes, there is shareware that can help you attain your entrepreneurial dreams. There are programs that can get you organized, programs that can help you write your first business proposal, programs that can advise you on the tax and licensing requirements of your state, and even programs that can help you apply for Small Business Administration loans and print out some of the forms for you.

Face it, no one is born an entrepreneur these days. The specialized knowledge that it takes to leap the hurdles of loan officers, state regulators, and Uncle Sam can be tough to come by. In this chapter you'll learn about a program designed by the Small Business Administration to help you in your quest for an SBA loan. You'll discover free and almost-free spreadsheet templates that will help you forecast your business's cash flow, anticipate the year's net sales, and even create a Form 1100 to apply for an SBA loan. You'll learn about several programs designed to help you write business proposals that will either win over your banker, or help you come to a correct decision about whether your future venture will actually earn money.

Starting a profitable business doesn't require an MBA, but if you avail yourself of the advice of some of these programs, no one will ever know you don't have one.

Small Business Adviser

It used to be that when you wanted to open a business, about all you had to do was hang a sign out in front of your house. Alas, things have gotten quite complex, what with tax forms, workers compensation laws, employee benefits plans, and state licensing requirements. Small Business Advisor will clue you in on how to maneuver some of the bureaucratic obstacles. Enter data about your new or planned venture into Small Business Adviser—where you live, what kind of business you're in, how many employees you have—and it will come up with a list of recommendations, advice, and checklists tailored specifically for your locale and enterprise.

It will tell you what the income and payroll tax requirements are for your state, as shown in Figure 12-1, as well as covering your state's worker compensation laws and what kind of insurance you're required to have, what you need to do to comply with state welfare plans, whether any licensing and incorporation requirements are applicable, plus what you need to do to comply with federal requirements like OSHA regulations and the Employees with Disabilities Act.

Pull-down menus offer further advice on filing forms and monies for FICA, and excise, sales, property, and self-employment taxes. In the Business Startup menu you'll find advice on getting venture capital, developing a business plan, marketing, hiring, and even buying an existing business or franchise. But the most advice-packed menu is one providing checklists on all the things you should do before you sign a business lease,

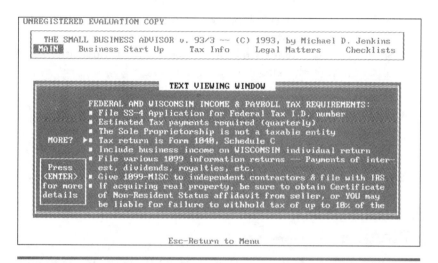

Figure 12-1   Small Business Adviser can clue you in on your state's income and payroll tax requirements

buy a business, hire employees and independent contractors, or buy a franchise, as shown in Figure 12-2. Lots of common sense precautions

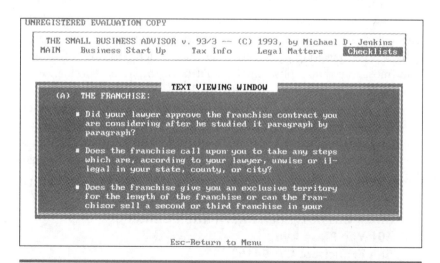

Figure 12-2   Small Business Adviser includes checklists, like this one for franchise-buying, to help you handle important business transactions

can be found in the Internal Financial Controls checklist, like "Do not let the same person handle cash receipts and also make bank deposits."

Small Business Adviser will prove invaluable to anyone with a small business, or anyone thinking of going into business.

> **Ronin Software**
> **3020 Issaquah-Pine Lake Rd., Suite 36**
> **Issaquah, WA 98027**
> **Price: $29.95, updated quarterly**
> **Online filename: SBA*xx-x*A.ZIP and SBA*xx-x*B.ZIP**

Small Business Administration Loan Planner

Financing your business through a Small Business Administration loan is a tricky affair. Maturity and interest rates on SBA loans are variable and dependent upon how you plan to use the borrowed funds. For instance, money used for inventory and working capital must be paid back in seven years or less. Loans for equipment and real estate, however, can be paid back over a longer period, but you'll be charged a much higher interest rate.

SBA Loan Planner, shown in Figure 12-3, quizzes you on all the particulars of your planned loan, then pieces together what your interest rates will be, how long you'll get to pay back which portions of the loan, and, most important, how much you'll have to pay on the loan each month. It can calculate the specifics of 7(a) Guaranty Loans, which are the most common type of SBA loans. It will also calculate loan origination costs and closing fees. You can use SBA Loan Planner to figure what-if scenarios that will help you decide how best to structure your SBA loan. Be aware, however, that the software's vendor, the Small Business Loan Information Center, is not affiliated with the Small Business Administration or any other government agency.

> **Small Business Loan Information Center**
> **601 Van Ness Ave.**
> **San Francisco, CA 94102**
> **Price: $20**
> **Online filename: SBAPLN.ZIP**

```
                         SBA LOAN PLANNER

   HOW THE LOAN FUNDS WILL BE USED:

   REAL ESTATE PURCHASE, IMPROVEMENT AND REFINANCING ─────────────
        Purchase of Real Estate for Business Use..............     $138,452
        Construction: Improvement of Real Estate Owned by the
             Business (or to be purchased with loan funds).....     $70,567
        Refinancing: Payoff of Existing Loans against
             Real Estate Owned by the Business................     $30,643

   PURCHASE AND REFINANCING OF OTHER FIXED ASSETS ───────────────
        Purchase of Machinery and Equipment...................     $257,892
        Purchase of Furniture and Fixtures....................     $10,454
        Construction: Leasehold Improvements..................          $0
        Refinancing of Existing Loans for Machinery, Equipment,
             Furniture, Fixtures or Leasehold Improvements.....          $0



                         Gathering Information                        READY
```

Figure 12-3   SBA Loan Planner shows how your loan will be structured and what your payment plan will be

Forecasting Cash Flow for Business Loans

DOS

The National Business Association together with the U.S. Small Business Administration have designed this handy (and free) utility to help the small business person forecast cash flow for the purpose of applying for loans. It's a simple program to use, much like a spreadsheet, with columns for estimated and actual income and expenses, as shown in Figure 12-4.

Enter financial particulars for your assets, such as cash on hand, receipts, sales, and collections, and for your outlays, such as wages and payments for services, supplies, repairs, and utilities. Then press a function key and the software displays your company's projected cash flow for the months ahead, as shown in Figure 12-5. Use the projection in conjunction with the spreadsheet template, discussed next, to simplify your preparations to apply for an SBA loan.

```
======= MONTHLY CASH FLOW PROJECTION =======
                   DORE ENTERPRISES
                 :      JAN     :      FEB     :     MARCH
    DESCRIPTION  :  EST : ACTUAL :  EST : ACTUAL :  EST : ACTUAL

 1. CASH ON HAND   64500   12000   63017   11100   60716   10199
 2. CASH RECEIPT       0       0       0       0       0       0
    CASH SALES       213     113     313     113     413     113
    COLLECTIONS      214     114     314     114     414     114
    LOANS, OTHER     215     115     315     115     415     115
 3. TOT CASH IN      642     342     942     342    1242     342
 4. TOT CASH AVL   65142   12342   63959   11442   61958   10541
 5. CASH PD OUT        0       0       0       0       0       0
    PURCHASES        319     118     319     119     419     119
    GROSS WAGES      220     120     320     120     420     120
    PAYROLL EXP.     221     121     321     121     421     121
    OUTSIDE SERV     222     122     322     122     422     122
    SUPPLIES         223     123     323     123     423     123
    REPAIRS & MT     224     124     324     124     424     124
    ADVERTISING      227     127     327     127     427     127

  F1  |   F2    |   F3    |  F4   |  F5  |   F6    |  F7  |   F8 KEY TO
 HELP | ADD AN  | DISPLAY | PRINT | EXIT |DELETE AN| EDIT |UPDATE TOTALS
      | ACCOUNT | TOTALS  | FORM  |      | ACCOUNT | CELL |ON SPREADSHEET
 ... Use Arrow Keys To Move About Spreadsheet ...
```

Figure 12-4   A cash flow spreadsheet for mythical Dore Enterprises in Forecasting Cash Flow for Business Loans program

```
========= TOTALS - CASH FLOW PROJECTION =========
                 :      JAN     :      FEB     :     MARCH
    DESCRIPTION  :  EST : ACTUAL :  EST : ACTUAL :  EST : ACTUAL

 1. CASH ON HAND   64500   12000   63017   11100   60716   10199
 3. TOT CASH IN      642     342     942     342    1242     342
 4. TOT CASH AVL   65142   12342   63959   11442   61958   10541
 6. TOT CASH OUT    2125    1242    3243    1243    4243    1243
 7. CASH POS'N.    63017   11100   60716   10199   57715    9298

        USE ( -> and <- ) ARROWS TO MOVE FROM MONTH TO MONTH
        PRESS 'ESC' KEY TO RETURN TO THE SPREADSHEET
```

Figure 12-5   Hit a function key and you'll go from the cash flow spreadsheet to this projection of future cash flow

National Business Association
P.O. Box 870728
Dallas, TX 75287
Phone: 800/456-0440
Fax: 214/960-9149
Price: Free
Online filename: CASH.EXE

Spreadsheet Template for Small Business Administration Loan Form 1100

Here's a nifty spreadsheet template that will prove invaluable to anyone applying for a Small Business Administration loan. Enter the financial data on your company—cash on hand, receipts, details of cash paid out, and operating expenses—and it will generate SBA Form 1100, Monthly Cash Flow Projections. It's designed for use in Lotus 1-2-3, but it works just fine in Microsoft Excel too, as shown in Figure 12-6. It

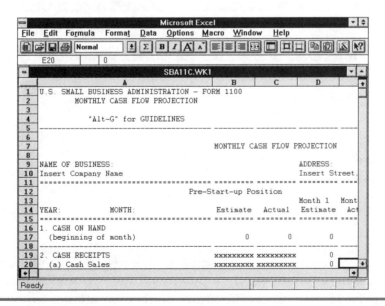

Figure 12-6   This free template for Lotus or Excel will automate creation of SBA Form 1100

includes the SBA's guidelines for filling out the form in a help file that you can refer to while you're working within the spreadsheet.

Tom Carnegie
CompuServe ID: 70267,2129
Price: Free
Online filename: SBA11C.WK1 or SBA11C.ZIP

Business Plan Master

The author of Business Plan Master is a firm believer in writing a business plan, even when you don't plan to apply for a loan. He should know. He's started several businesses himself and consults with business startups. He's created this selection of templates, one of which is shown in Figure 12-7, for use with Excel and Word for Windows to create what he calls a "no-nonsense" business proposal that is long on specifics but

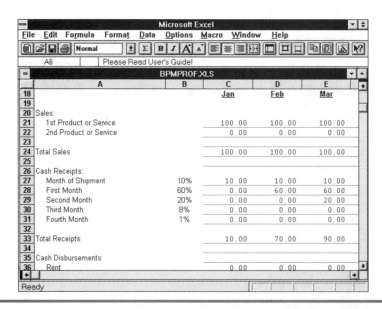

Figure 12-7   Business Plan Master includes spreadsheet templates for cash flow projections in Excel and business plans in Word for Windows

devoid of the kind of fluff that small business owners pad into proposals to impress their bankers.

Included in Business Plan Master is the outline of a business proposal that you can pull up in Word for Windows and edit to reflect the nature of your business. (There's also a version in plain text that you can use in any word processor.)

There are several spreadsheets that you can use to forecast cash flow and generate balance sheets, income statements, ratio analyses, financial comparisons, and historical statements on your finances. There's even a spreadsheet to help you determine your company's break-even point, and that may be the most important one of all. According to author David Works, too few entrepreneurs stop to carefully calculate whether the venture they're about to plunge into will make any money in the long run.

Grand Universal
Attn: David A. Works
P.O. Box 4118
Whitefish, MT 59937
Phone: 406/862-1280
CompuServe ID: 70400,153
Internet: david_works@cup.portal.com
America Online: davidw2959
Price: $34
Online filename: BIZPLN29.ZIP

B/Plan Developer

B/Plan Developer will take you step by step through the process of writing a winning business proposal. It's designed around a library of information files, each of which contains detailed explanations of how to write each section of a business proposal, from the management plan and details of manufacturing, shown in Figure 12-8, to the analysis of how the product or service fits into the market.

You can quickly toggle through the files and display sections of each in tiling or cascading windows. When writing a business proposal, you can never have too much advice. B/Plan Developer will help you write a

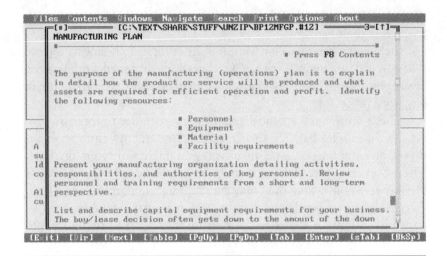

Figure 12-8 B/Plan Developer tells you how to write each section of your business proposal

proposal that's a realistic assessment of your venture—which will help sell the idea to investors.

Tom Welch Financial
6900 San Pedro Avenue, Suite 147
San Antonio, TX 78216
Phone: 210/737-7022
Price: $39 plus $5 shipping
Online filename: BPLN38A.ZIP

Business Forecasting

Windows

Here's a slick spreadsheet and calculation workbook that you use with Excel to forecast business stock and pricing data. As shown in Figure 12-9, it will analyze historical data that you either enter directly or import from another spreadsheet. It relies upon regressions, moving averages, and exponential smoothing calculations to forecast future performance. It can graph the results or give you just the numbers.

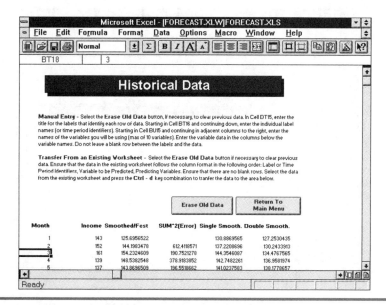

Figure 12-9 Use Business Forecasting to analyze historical pricing data in Excel

Innovations Consultants/Advanced Systems, Inc.
3304 Clearwood Ct.
Falls Church, VA 22042
Phone: 703/533-8414
Fax: 703/536-9115
Price: $39.95
Online filename: FORECAST.ZIP or FORECA.ZIP

MicroCast Sales Forecasting

Anticipate dips and highs in sales with this nicely designed spreadsheet that you can use in any version of Lotus as well as in Excel. A pop-up menu lets you enter data, view graphs, and forecast your sales' ebb and flow, as shown in Figure 12-10. A row of buttons on the bottom of the screen lets you draw pie and bar charts and run various calculations on the spreadsheet numbers. MicroCast is great for anticipating seasonal sales fluctuations.

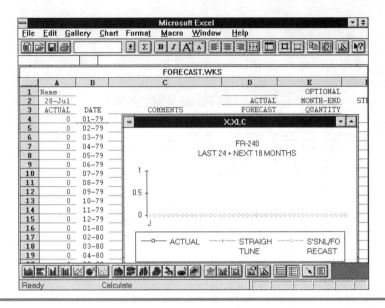

Figure 12-10   A MicroCast graph of projected sales with buttons on the bottom for drawing pie and bar charts and running calculations

CompuCast Software
5328 Fulton St.
San Francisco, CA 94121
Price: $25
Online filename: FORECAST.ARC or FORECA.ARC

CHAPTER 13

GENERAL LEDGER AND BOOKKEEPING SOFTWARE TO EASE YOUR ACCOUNTING HEADACHES

ou wouldn't expect first-rate accounting software to be sold as shareware. After all, aren't most shareware authors bedraggled 20-year-old hackers who burn the late-night oil to churn out games or other diversions for a few extra bucks? Not necessarily. One of the most successful shareware packages of all time is a series of accounting programs written and designed by a successful California CPA. In fact, accounting software itself is one of the most successful categories of shareware sold, even though the prices of these packages run up to $1,000. These high prices reflect the fact that an accounting software package is essentially a collection of integrated utilities—one for payroll, one for invoicing, one for accounts receivable, and so forth.

The people who are most apt to buy accounting software are computer consultants who license it for their clients. Everyone knows that the easiest way to please demanding customers is to give them a lot of choices, and it's easy to do that with shareware. A consultant can install shareware accounting programs on a client's PC for trial use. If the client doesn't like it, he or she can try a different package, or, in many cases, the source code can be obtained from the shareware author and modified to the client's needs.

The accounting software programs you'll find in this chapter are surprisingly versatile. At the low end, they range from simple bookkeeping programs for organizing a home business proprietor's shoe box of receipts to a basic accounting package for helping a small business get started. At the high end are powerhouse accounting packages that run on office networks and include sophisticated special-purpose modules to handle the most diverse accounting tasks. You'll find point-of-sale software that supports a variety of retail store hardware, including light pens, cash drawers, and bar code readers. There's software to manage the accounting needs of rental properties, restaurants, and temporary employment services. Are these just for small businesses? No way! One shareware accounting package is overseeing multimillion-dollar budgets at Disney World.

OWL Basic Bookkeeping

DOS

OWL Basic Bookkeeping is ideal for the lonely, struggling business owner who isn't interested in becoming a member of the Association of Certified Public Accountants, but needs a single-entry method of keeping track of income, expense, and profit that will pass muster with the IRS. This is perfect for anyone who runs a home business and needs to keep track of Schedule C expenses.

Basic Bookkeeping is the kind of software that requires zero setup time and no reading of the documentation. The main screen is beautifully simple, as shown in Figure 13-1. One pull-down menu lets you set up *accounts* (that's where you keep track of expenses—from advertising to cartons), and another lets you browse through and sort *expense* items. List *income* with a third pull-down menu and you can generate reports on

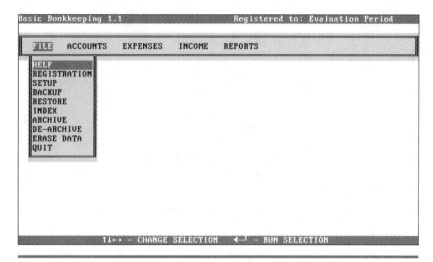

Figure 13-1   Basic Bookkeeping's main screen

profit, income, and your basic ledger. Throw away your spreadsheet, this is a heckuva lot more fun to use.

Otto-Williams Ltd.
P.O. Box 794
Lanham, MD 20703
Phone: 301/306-0409
Price: $39
Online filename: OBBKxx.ZIP

Medlin Accounting

DOS

Jerry Medlin's accounting software is terrific for small or medium-sized businesses that don't have inventory to track. In fact, over ten thousand small businesses use it. This industry classic (Jerry is the California CPA mentioned in the beginning of this chapter) includes five parts: the general ledger, the accounts receivable software, the accounts payable software, payroll software, and an invoice generator. Jerry has designed all with his usual fastidiousness, as demonstrated by the elegantly simple main menu shown in Figure 13-2. In fact, colleges and universities use these programs to teach basic accounting principles, and at least one book has been written on them.

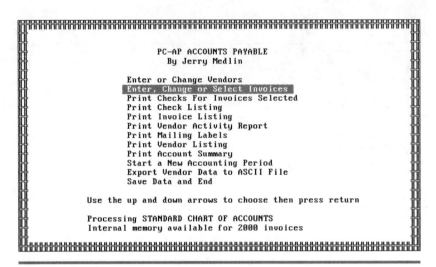

```
        PC-AP ACCOUNTS PAYABLE
            By Jerry Medlin

    Enter or Change Vendors
    Enter, Change or Select Invoices
    Print Checks For Invoices Selected
    Print Check Listing
    Print Invoice Listing
    Print Vendor Activity Report
    Print Mailing Labels
    Print Vendor Listing
    Print Account Summary
    Start a New Accounting Period
    Export Vendor Data to ASCII File
    Save Data and End

Use the up and down arrows to choose then press return

Processing STANDARD CHART OF ACCOUNTS
Internal memory available for 2000 invoices
```

Figure 13-2   Main screen of Medlin's Accounts Payable module

The *General Ledger* lets you enter as many as 800 items in the accounts chart. From the main menu you can enter or edit items in the accounts chart, shown in Figure 13-3, or print the chart transaction listing, the ledger, the income or balance statement, as well as an account summary.

```
Account    Prior   Account                          Balances
No.   Code   %      Description              Current        YTD
»»»»»»»»»»»»»»»»»»»»»»»»»»»»»»»»»»»»»»»»»»»»»»»»»»»»»»»»»»»»»»»»»»»»»»»»»»
965   71    0.00   GAIN ON SALES OF ASSETS      0.00         0.00
970   71    0.00   MISCELLANEOUS                0.00         0.00
979   72    0.00   TOTAL OTHER INCOME            *            *
980   81    0.00     OTHER EXPENSE              *            *
982   81    0.00   INTEREST PAID                0.00         0.00
983   81    0.00   LOSS ON SALES OF ASSETS      0.00         0.00
984   81    0.00   MISCELLANEOUS                0.00         0.00
990   82    0.00   TOTAL OTHER EXPENSE           *            *
999   96    0.00     NET PROFIT OR LOSS         *            *
=▶  ----                                                          ◀=

»»»»»»»»»»»»»»»»»»»»»»»»»»»»»»»»»»»»»»»»»»»»»»»»»»»»»»»»»»»»»»»»»»»»»»»»»»
Enter the ACCOUNT NUMBER
or Press <Esc> to go to the command mode.
```

Figure 13-3   Editing the accounts chart in Medlin's General
Ledger module

From the *Accounts Payable* main menu you enter names of vendors, enter invoices, print checks and mailing labels, and print vendor activity reports and account summaries. You can store information on up to 2,000 vendors. The *Accounts Receivable* software is set up similarly. The *Payroll* software is designed to let you print payroll checks, figure things like FICA, Social Security, and state taxes (it includes tables for most state taxes), and maintain records on employee payroll, taxes, and benefits, as shown in Figure 13-4. It also lets you generate numbers for employee W-2 forms.

A pop-up calculator is available in all the programs. All the modules use similar commands, so they're easy to learn. The only thing that's missing is a module to track inventory. The programs can also be integrated. The product was a recipient of a *Shareware Magazine* Editor's Choice Award as well as a 1992 Shareware Industry Award.

> **Medlin Accounting Shareware**
> **1461 Sproul Ave.**
> **Napa, CA 94559**
> **Phone: 707/255-4475**
> **Fax: 707/255-9266**
> **Price: $35 for each module except for invoicing module which is $25**
> **Online filename: MEDLIN.ZIP**

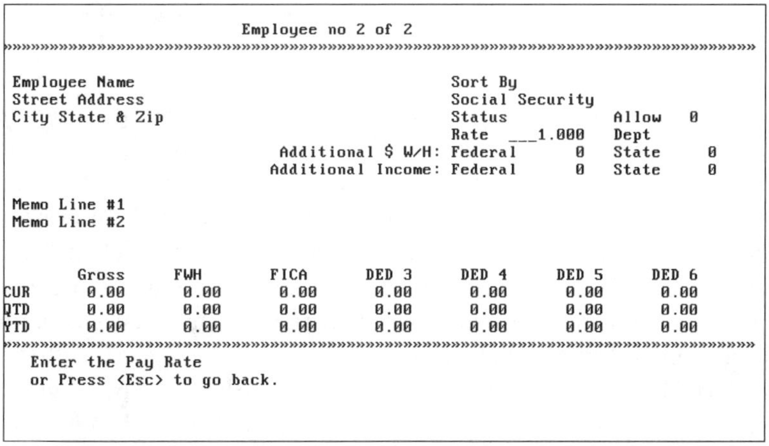

```
                        Employee no 2 of 2
>>>>>>>>>>>>>>>>>>>>>>>>>>>>>>>>>>>>>>>>>>>>>>>>>>>>>>>>>>>>>>>>>>>>>>>>>>>>>>>>>>>>

  Employee Name                           Sort By
  Street Address                          Social Security
  City State & Zip                        Status            Allow   0
                                          Rate   ___1.000   Dept
                       Additional $ W/H: Federal      0     State   0
                       Additional Income: Federal     0     State   0


  Memo Line #1
  Memo Line #2


        Gross     FWH      FICA     DED 3    DED 4    DED 5    DED 6
CUR     0.00      0.00     0.00     0.00     0.00     0.00     0.00
QTD     0.00      0.00     0.00     0.00     0.00     0.00     0.00
YTD     0.00      0.00     0.00     0.00     0.00     0.00     0.00
>>>>>>>>>>>>>>>>>>>>>>>>>>>>>>>>>>>>>>>>>>>>>>>>>>>>>>>>>>>>>>>>>>>>>>>>>>>>>>>>>>>>
    Enter the Pay Rate
    or Press <Esc> to go back.
```

Figure 13-4   Editing employee information in the Medlin Payroll module

Bottom Line Accounting

Bottom Line offers four times the features of Medlin, but stakes as its market niche small businesses without a lot of accounting savvy. Unlike Medlin, it's also ideal for retail operations that need to keep track of inventory and point-of-sale transactions. The point-of-sale module supports a variety of hardware including light pens, bar code scanners, and cash drawers. These features make it a favorite among Dairy Queen and Little Caesar stores. WindSoft claims that its product is installed in over 25,000 small businesses.

One of the things that make Bottom Line unique is that it lets you postdate or predate any transaction, and the transaction will still show up in the right place in your yearly accounts. This is nice for those of use who keep all our receipts in a shoe box and need to re-create a date-sorted list of business financial transactions at tax time. There's also no need with Bottom Line to close out accounts at the end of each month, something that's necessary with most accounting software. The general ledger module also lets you write checks on the fly in the ledger. WindSoft likes to brag: "Anything you can do with a piece of paper you can do with Bottom Line."

Payroll is a snap, and you don't need to understand the intricacies of debits and credits to do it. Just enter the number of hours an employee has worked, and the software does everything for you, including updating all associated records. Unlike Medlin and ZPay, Bottom Line's tax tables are user-defined so you don't have to buy new tax tables each year.

The eight modules available include one for a general ledger and others for accounts receivable, accounts payable, account reconciliation, and payroll. Many features make Bottom Line ideal for retail operations, including inventory and point-of-sale modules for handling retail receipts. The point-of-sale module supports a wide variety of retail hardware, including light pens, bar code scanners, and cash drawers. A module with financial utilities includes things like a calculator that performs loan analyses and figures bond returns. You'll find more functionality in these modules than you will in many commercial accounting packages intended for small businesses.

All tables are stored as Paradox tables, so if you have a copy of Paradox you can manipulate any data or export it to custom applications and databases. The software is menu-driven with pop-up help. It runs on Novell, Lantastic, and all NETBIOS compatible networks.

WindSoft International, Inc.
P.O. Box 590006
Orlando, FL 32859
Phone: 407/240-2300
Price: Packages range from $99.95 to $750. A
single-user 6-module accounting system is $349.95.
Online filename: 8 files range from BLA-0.EXE through
BLA-7.EXE

note

See Chapter 15, "Software That Manages Payroll and Tax Withholding,"
for more recommendations on payroll software.

Painless Accounting

Painless Accounting, which is geared to small and medium-sized
businesses, is the most customizable of the shareware accounting packages. It lets you customize all forms, checks, statements, invoices, and
reports. It also has powerful features that make it ideal for service
businesses, such as automatic billing and the ability to define invoices for
select groups of clients. It has some features for handling retail and
distribution accounting needs, but its point-of-sales features are not as
full-blown as those in Bottom Line or DAYO (discussed later in this chapter).

Painless Accounting's unique features include the ability to figure
sales representatives' commissions, generate finance charges, handle
multiple price levels, and automate recurring entries for receivables and
payables, as shown in Figure 13-5. It also supports first-in/first-out and
last-in/first-out accounting for inventory handling. It offers password
protection to restrict access to its databases.

Its modules include one for a general ledger, shown in Figure 13-6,
and others for billing, accounts receivable and payable, purchasing, file
maintenance, reports, closing, utilities, payroll, and beginning balance setup.
Painless Accounting runs on Novell, Lantastic, and any NETBIOS compatible network. The Windows and DOS versions are identical in features.

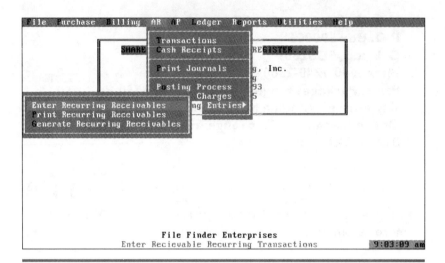

Figure 13-5 Working with receivables in Painless Accounting

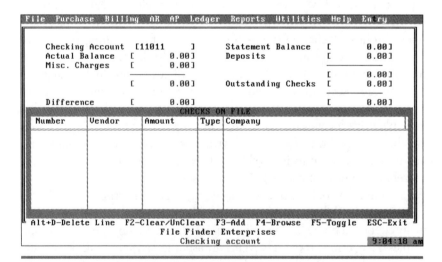

Figure 13-6 Reconciling checks with Painless Accounting's ledger module

Painless Accounting
4401 Birdsong
Plano, TX 75093
Phone: 800/788-0787 (orders) or 314/965-5630
Fax: 314/966-1833
Price: $175 for accounting; $125 for payroll; $250 for
both together
Online filename: Multiple files all listed as PA6_123.ZIP

DAYO

DAYO is king of high end accounting software. Its power, versatility, and wide variety of add-on modules have won it spots in the accounting departments of places like W.W. Grainger and Disney World. (One department at Disney uses it to keep track of the million-dollar Epcot Center budget for locks and keys.) TJS Lab provides add-on modules as specialized as one for managing commercial property, one for handling the accounting of a temporary employment agency, and one for handling restaurant receipts. The company does a brisk business in providing custom-made modules for businesses.

Shareware in Action

Product: DAYO
Company: Air Filter
Services

For all of its accounting needs, Air Filter Services of Sumter, South Carolina, uses DAYO. "Point of sale, general ledger—everything is tied into it," says Ruby McLendon, computer supervisor and South Carolina sales coordinator for this industrial filtration service company.

Among the features that appeal to her are DAYO's friendly user interface. "It's so easy," she says. "A noncomputer person can come in and easily use it"—an important feature when temporary help is needed or when staff changes occur.

She also likes the support that TJS Lab provides. Whenever changes or updates occur, Air Filter Services quickly gets out the word, says McLendon.

DAYO's modules include ones for tracking inventory, point-of-sale, back orders, accounts receivable and payable, payroll, materials-requirement planning, and more. All the products are multi-user and designed to work on Novell networks, although they can also work on a single PC. Utility modules are also available that provide password protection, end off a period, set the year and period to date, and index all modules.

The general ledger module, called DAYO GL, classifies all accounts as either an asset, liability, or proprietorship. It's a double-entry system requiring credit and debit posting for each transaction. DAYO stores its databases in dBASE format, making it easy to access with other accounting software and databases. This is not software for shoe box accountants.

DAYO
TJS Lab, Inc.
5104 North Orange Blossom Trail, Suite 200
Orlando, FL 32810
Phone: 407/291-3960
Price: Most modules are approximately $95.
Online filename: Many files—look for DAYOxx.EXE

CHAPTER 14

SOFTWARE TO TRACK BUDGETS, EXPENSES, AND BANK ACCOUNTS

ace it, the worst part of business accounting is keeping track of your own expenses. The IRS advises that small business owners keep a diary of their daily deductible expenses, but everyone knows that's the fast track to tax-time chaos.

Checking accounts can also get out of hand. Whether they're personal accounts, or business ones, it's easy for your checkbook ledger to deteriorate into a jumble of illegible scribbles and returned checks.

Office supply stores do a crisp business selling PC software to help you keep track of home office expenses and reimbursable business expenses. The products, like Quicken, are cheap (usually around $50) and they usually do the job. But how often have you purchased one of these on impulse in an office supply store only to take it home and discover it doesn't do *exactly* what you want it to do? With shareware, you can try the product first before you buy it, and with personal expense software, doing this is often essential.

SuperTraq

Keep track of your expenses with SuperTraq. It utilizes the Franklin Institute Day Planner system, which many corporate accounting departments use to record expenses and file receipts. SuperTraq lets you categorize expenses by project, employee, client, or custom-defined expense categories. You can group expenses by method of payment, including credit card, check, and cash. Each expense you list includes the expense date, description, tax status, daily entry number, amount, and daily total. SuperTraq will print daily, weekly, monthly, and annual reports for taxes, accounting, and project planning.

Hillary Neal Hooks
209 Scotts Valley
Hercules, CA 94547
Price: $49.95
Online filename: SPRTRAQ.ZIP

note

Home office entrepreneurs, check out OWL Basic Bookkeeping software reviewed in Chapter 13, "General Ledger and Bookkeeping Software to Ease Your Accounting Headaches," for an easy way to keep track of IRS Schedule C expenses.

CheckMate Plus

DOS

Using your PC to balance your checkbook might seem like a pretty prosaic task to assign to a $2K box with powerful microchips inside. Still, paying bills and tracking checking accounts are two of the most popular uses of PCs. CheckMate Plus is checkbook software, plus a little more. You can use it to track several hundred bank accounts if you need to (perish the thought). CheckMate will print out checks. It will attach explanations to transactions. It will even remind you to pay the mortgage on time. You can also use CheckMate just for reconciling your checking account each month and keeping track of deposits, withdrawals, and automatic-teller transactions. The software, shown in Figure 14-1, is extremely simple to use, with pull-down menus that work with a mouse.

A built-in financial calculator will help you track your loans and the interest on your bank accounts. It will even print out amortization schedules. Because CheckMate is a double-entry accounting system, you can use it to prepare balance sheets, income statements, and budget reports. You can export the numbers to any major-name spreadsheet. Password protection ensures that only you see what's going on inside your accounts.

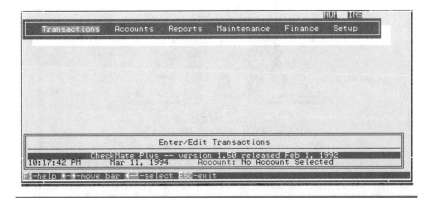

Figure 14-1 Checkmate is super-simple to use with pull-down menus and mouse support

Custom Technologies
P.O. Box 10551
Panama City, FL 32404
Phone: 800/541-6234 (orders only); 206/698-7754 (voice)
Price: $60 plus $5 shipping
Online filename: CMPLSxxx.ZIP

Banking Buddy

Don't we all wish we had a banking buddy? Banking Buddy is a basic budgeting system that will organize that swirling mass of banking and credit card statements on your desk. It will let you track the transactions in those accounts and print reports that will prove invaluable at tax time, as well as being useful in controlling budgets. Figure 14-2 shows Banking Buddy's opening menu.

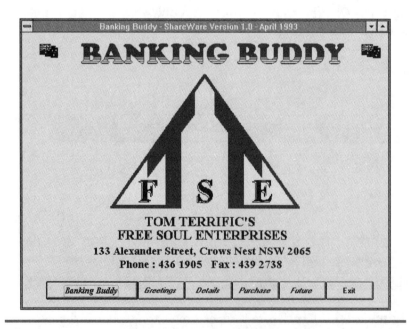

Figure 14-2 Banking Buddy makes banking easy with a visual interface that starts with this user-friendly menu

Reconciling your checkbook at the end of the month (or the end of the year for some of us) will become a breeze thanks to Banking Buddy's transaction reports, built-in budgeting features, plus end-of-the-year expense tallies for tax purposes.

Tom Terrific's Free Soul Enterprises
133 Alexander St.
Crows Nest
New South Wales 2065
Australia
Price: $25
Online filename: BNKBUDxx.ZIP

PC-Flow

DOS

PC-Flow, shown in Figure 14-3, will track your daily cash flow, both at home and in the office. You can record transactions individually, daily, weekly, or monthly, and categorize and sort them by group. The numbers you enter can be either exact costs or estimates, which are useful for forecasting expenses. PC-Flow will print reports on incoming and outgoing funds, transactions, and cash-flow. Reports can range from detailed breakdowns of daily expenses to summaries of periods of up to a year.

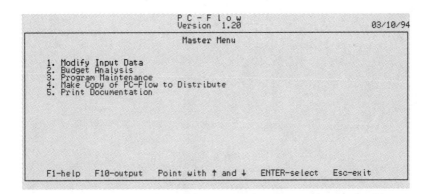

Figure 14-3   Use PC-Flow to track the transactions in your
home office or business

They can also be broken down by transaction classification. This is an excellent program for keeping track of where your project or department's money is going and for creating yearly budgets.

Daniel Comeau
603-1320 Richmond Rd.
Ottawa, Ontario
Canada K2B 8L3
Price: $40
Online filename: PCFL_xxx_.ZIP

For more information on tax-related expense-tracking software for vehicles and buildings, see Chapter 24, "Software to Help Maintain Cars, Trucks, and Buildings."

CHAPTER 15

SOFTWARE THAT MANAGES PAYROLL AND TAX WITHHOLDING

or a small business owner with a PC, payroll is the first task that should be automated. Why waste your time flipping through tax tables and hand-generating checks each month when you can do it with just a few mouse clicks with one of these programs? There are lots of great payroll want a program to automatically generate paychecks and keep track of employee benefits, or merely need a utility to generate W-2s and 1099-MISC forms and their mailing labels, you'll find a shareware solution. Shareware utiities can help even big corporate payroll departments by allowing bookkeepers to calculate answers "on the fly" to such tax-related questions as how an employee's number of claimed exemptions or participation in a pension program will affect take-home pay.

Of course, one of the best reasons for using these programs is that they'll make IRS inquiries a breeze should you ever be audited.

ZPAY 3

ZPAY, shown in Figure 15-1, is the most popular shareware payroll package, having been around since the early days of the CP/M operating system over 15 years ago. One reason for its longevity is its ease of use. It was designed in part to be used as an educational tool to help high school students in Chicago learn how to use a PC. Needless to say, you don't have to be an accountant to use ZPAY, although many accountants do use it.

ZPAY can handle multiple pay periods and figure payroll for employees in different classifications—like salaried workers, hourly workers, and those who work on commission. It can even generate payroll checks for employees who receive a salary plus commissions. It can take into account bonuses, tips, and different rates for overtime hours. Simple menus make

```
                     Page One of Six Pages
         Name of State Colorado      Abbreviation CO
         Maximum on wages to tax (Y/N) Y   Cut off amount    5000.00
         Limit of Unemployment      0.00  Rate  0.000 (Employer only)
         Is there SDI type Tax (Y/N)    State witholding (Y/N)
         Calculate by Table or Percent (T/P)
         Base on Gross or Tax (G/T)
         Amount or Percent on Standard Deduction (A/P)
         Single Standard Deduction      Percent     0.500 %
         Married Standard Deduction     Percent     0.500 %
         Head of House Std Deduct       Percent     0.500 %
         Minimum Standard Deduction     Amount      0.50
         Maximum Standard Deduction     Amount      0.50
         Standard Deduction Before or After Calculation (B/A)
         Single Personal Exemption      0.00
         Married Personal Exemption     0.00
         Head of House Pers Exempt      0.00
         Subtract Personal Exemption Before or After Calculation (B/A)
         Exemption Amount per Dependent     0.00
         Subtract Dependent Exemption Before or After Calculation (B/A)
         Deduct FICA (Y/N)    Deduct Federal W/H (Y/N)   All or Half (A/H)
         Deduct Before or After Calculation (B/A)
         PgUp for Previous Page, PgDn for Next Page, Up-Arrow for Previous,
         Down-Arrow or Return for Next, F1 for HELP, F10 to END
                                      Num-Lock              Overwrite
```

Figure 15-1   The main screen of ZPAY, the most popular shareware payroll package

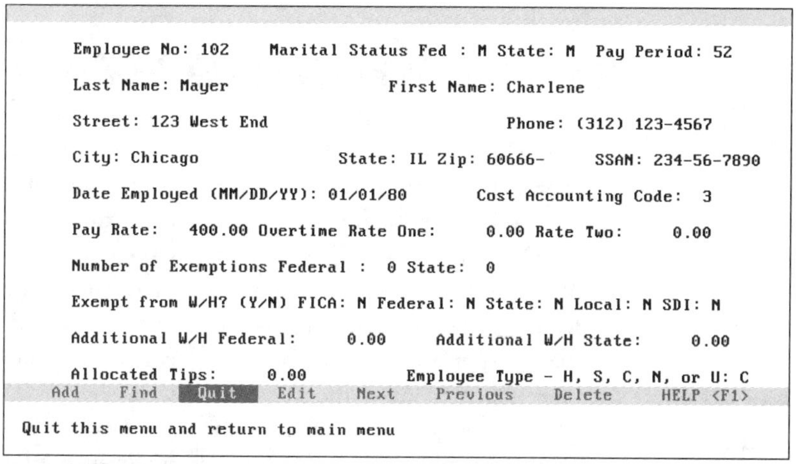

```
Employee No: 102    Marital Status Fed : M State: M  Pay Period: 52

Last Name: Mayer                First Name: Charlene

Street: 123 West End                    Phone: (312) 123-4567

City: Chicago           State: IL Zip: 60666-     SSAN: 234-56-7890

Date Employed (MM/DD/YY): 01/01/80      Cost Accounting Code:  3

Pay Rate:   400.00 Overtime Rate One:     0.00 Rate Two:     0.00

Number of Exemptions Federal :  0 State:  0

Exempt from W/H? (Y/N) FICA: N Federal: N State: N Local: N SDI: N

Additional W/H Federal:     0.00    Additional W/H State:     0.00

Allocated Tips:     0.00       Employee Type - H, S, C, N, or U: C
Add    Find    Quit    Edit    Next    Previous    Delete    HELP <F1>

Quit this menu and return to main menu
```

Figure 15-2   Editing an employee entry in ZPAY

it easy to edit an employee's entry, as shown in Figure 15-2. You can set up ZPAY to generate checks automatically at the end of each pay period. It will print checks, mailing and department labels, and even tax reports.

ZPAY's tax table editor lets you revise the built-in tax tables yourself, which means you don't have to buy new tax tables each year. Even better, ZPAY Payroll Systems runs a support forum on CompuServe where you can download for free new tax tables which ZPAY updates monthly. Such a deal!

Other ZPAY advantages include its ability to generate W-2 and 1099-MISC forms, plus their mailing labels, and the ability to track employee benefits including 401K and Section 125 cafeteria plans. It can even track and generate checks for employee reimbursement for things like auto expenses. Its drawbacks include its inability to import data from devices like time clocks, and although it will run on networks, it can't be shared by users. A well-deserved recipient of *Shareware Magazine's* Editor's Choice Award.

ZPAY Payroll Systems Inc.
2526 69th Ave., South
St. Petersburg, FL 33712
Phone: 813/866-8233 or 800/468-4188
Fax: 813/866-8034
Price: $69.95
Online filename: ZPAYxxx.ZIP

Shareware in Action

Product: ZPAY 3
Company: Forte Hotels,
Inc./TraveLodge chain

Forte Hotels, Inc. has a potential payroll nightmare on its hands trying to track the many employees who operate its hotels throughout the world. For its joint-venture with the TraveLodge chain in North America, the company uses ZPAY to keep track of payroll and report into corporate headquarters. More than 40 units of the chain now send identically formatted ZPAY reports, covering more than 400 employees, into corporate headquarters for posting to the main system. Eventually, the company plans to have the sites use ZPAY to report to the main system electronically.

"ZPAY is easy to use," said support services manager Donald Grisham. At each site, the manager simply needs to enter the hours for each employee; then "the program does the calculations, and they can send out the checks." It was difficult at first, said Grisham, to get managers to use any software. They had been preparing their reports by hand and were reluctant to change. "But when they saw how much time they saved—an hour or so a week, and the more employees, the more time they saved"—they not only embraced the program but convinced other units to use it as well.

One problem the company initially encountered with ZPAY was its inability to print in landscape mode on the dot-matrix printers used at most TraveLodge sites. A call to ZPAY Payroll Systems quickly provided a solution: Another shareware product, called On-Side (reviewed in Chapter 5), prints ZPAY reports in just the format the corporate office needs.

PayWindow

Generate payroll checks for all your employees with just two mouse clicks. Sound incredible? Get a copy of PayWindow, shown in Figure 15-3, and your payroll will become that simple. PayWindow is from the makers of ZPAY (described above) and it can do everything that that popular program can. Its straightforward screens make employee entries a breeze to edit, as shown in Figure 15-4. Plus, it runs under Windows. Not many payroll programs do that.

PayWindows also includes an extra feature we think is pretty neat, and that is a test drive mode that lets you give the software a trial spin without risking any of your own payroll data in the process. The test drive guides you through the payroll process step by step with example data so

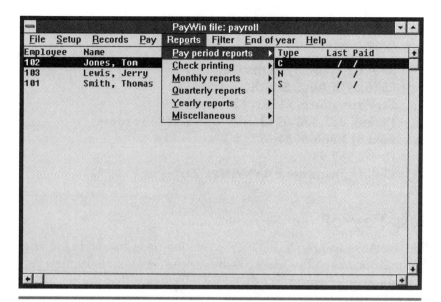

Figure 15-3 The main screen of PayWindow

Figure 15-4 Editing a tax table in PayWindow

you won't even have to crack open the manual to figure out how to generate payroll checks.

ZPAY Payroll Systems Inc.
2526 69th Ave., South
St. Petersburg, FL 33712
Phone: 813/866-8233 or 800/468-4188 (orders)
Fax: 813/866-8034
Price: $69.95
Online filename: PAYWINxx.ZIP

Painless Payroll

DOS

Windows

From the makers of Painless Accounting (see Chapter 13 for more information on the Painless Accounting programs), comes Painless Payroll, shown in Figure 15-5, a snazzy payroll package that works with the other Painless products.

It includes modules to do just about anything a small to medium-sized company needs done at payroll time, including generating tax liability reports, setting up payroll by departments, and closing at the end of the pay period. It accommodates employees paid by the hour, by salary, by commission, or by commission plus salary.

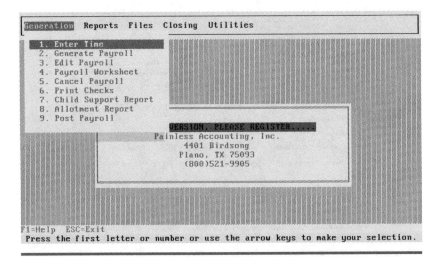

Figure 15-5   The main screen of Painless Payroll for DOS

It also lets you customize your check printing, a feature no other shareware payroll package has. One feature it does not have is the ability to track 401K and cafeteria employee benefit plans. It does, however, let you specify three different types of paycheck deductions, both before and after taxes. It won't accept imported data from other programs or devices like time clocks, but does store data in dBASE format so that it can be easily manipulated and exported.

It comes with withholding tables for all 50 states, plus federal withholding tables. You can buy upgrades for $35 per year, or modify the tables yourself. There's also a version for Canadian tax payers, plus one for businesses in New Guinea. It generates W-2 and 1099-MISC forms.

Painless Payroll will print mailing labels, employee lists, lists of pay codes, year-to-date reports, and tax liability reports. Keyboard macros further automate payroll procedures. Painless Payroll works on all NET-BIOS, Novell, and Lantastic networks. There are several versions available, so ask about them all before you buy.

Painless Accounting
4401 Birdsong
Plano, TX 75093
Phone: 800/788-0787 (orders) or 314/965-5630
Fax: 314/966-1833
Price: $75 plus $10 shipping and handling
Online filename: PPDxx.ZIP

TakeHome Payroll Program

TakeHome is not a full-blown payroll program, but a convenient utility for computing FICA and federal income tax withholding, plus the effects of the number of exemptions claimed and company 401K and Section 125 programs on an employee's paycheck. It's perfect for tiny businesses with just a few paychecks to generate, but also ideal for big company payroll departments that need to hand-generate a paycheck occasionally. It comes in handy when employees come to you and ask what the tax consequences on their paycheck will be if they claim more exemptions or choose to participate in a company pension program. It can handle hourly and salaried employees.

A handy W-4 and an IRS garnishment calculator are included and for $10 extra you can obtain state and local tax tables from TakeHome.

Updated yearly, TakeHome is used by the payroll departments of many Fortune 500 companies. It comes in both Windows and DOS versions.

TakeHome Software Products
P.O. Box 333
Barker, TX 77413
Price: $35 for DOS version, $50 for Windows version,
$10 for each state or locality tax table requested
Online filename: TAKEHO.EXE

Deduct! Payroll Processing

Deduct! is a tax withholding calculator similar to TakeHome for businesses that occasionally need to calculate and print a few paychecks by hand. It's also for payroll departments that need a fast way to figure the effects of exemptions and pension plan participation on an employee's salary. Enter all the data on the employee's W-2 and indicate what you want withheld, and Deduct! will give you the numbers. The version that you download includes tables for federal, New York State, City of New York, Yonkers, and FICA withholding taxes. Tax tables for other states are available at nominal cost. Deduct! prints continuous form checks on pin printers.

Marigold Computer Consultants
40 Douglas Road
Del Mar, NY 12054
Phone: 518/439-4845
Price: $29.95 plus tax

TaxForms

Use TaxForms to easily create, calculate, and print employee W-2 and 1099-MISC forms at tax time. This simple utility will even print the mailing labels for you to mail them out. Its only drawback is that you must key in the data yourself; you cannot import employee data from other payroll applications or databases. Still, it comes in handy for small businesses. There are both American and Canadian versions available.

Anthistle Systems & Programming Ltd.
563 Patricia Dr.
Oakville, Ontario
Canada L6K IM4
Phone: 905/845-7959
Price: $75
Online filename: TAXFRM.ZIP or TAXFORM.EXE

Tax94

Use this simple tax calculator to determine an employee's net pay after federal, Social Security, and Medicare withholding. Choose the pay period, the employee's marital status, the number of allowances, then enter their salary and Tax94 calculates all the tax withholding amounts for you. The program is updated annually (the name to look for online changes with the year), but lacks the ability to figure state and local taxes into the equation.

Stephen F. Procko
20205 N.E. 15th Court
Miami, FL 33179
Price: $35 suggested
Online filename: TAX94.ZIP (the last two numbers of the name will reflect the year)

CHAPTER 16

INVOICING SOFTWARE FOR BUSINESSES
BIG AND SMALL

There are probably thousands of shareware invoicing programs available online. Unfortunately, good ones are hard to find. Maybe it's because shareware authors rarely invoice anyone; they simply wait for the checks to roll in. The good invoicing programs—and there *are* some very good ones to be found—span from full-powered mega-accounting department billing packages with database capabilities to cutesy utilities for the home business.

Our favorite shareware invoicing system is a set of macros and templates for Microsoft Excel that works with your spreadsheet software to create a fully equipped invoicing system, complete with built-in faxing. At $35 it's a not-to-be-missed bargain. But an even better bargain can be found in one $9.95 invoicing package we discovered that, in terms of functionality and ease, is superior to many $100 commercial programs. At the high end, we were equally impressed by the imperishable DAYO billing system, which is full-featured enough to handle the invoicing needs of General Motors.

Personal Invoicer

Windows

Personal Invoicer is a series of really neat Microsoft Excel macros and templates that together create a full-featured customer invoicing system. You can use Personal Invoicer with your copy of Excel to create and print invoices, build and maintain a customer database, print customer accounting reports, and track sales data. One of its slickest features is its faxing: store clients' fax numbers in the customer database, then, when you want to invoice them by fax, click on the fax button in the invoice entry screen. It will load up your fax software and fire off the invoice.

Personal Invoicer is easy to set up. At its heart is a spreadsheet that serves as your customer database. Simply load it into Excel and you're ready to start generating invoices. Dialog boxes prompt you for the information to enter, as shown in Figure 16-1. Another very impressive feature about this program is the thoroughness of its built-in help (you usually don't find that with Excel macros). The maker's technical support can also be accessed through the main menu (something else you rarely find in either shareware or commercial software). Another nice touch that makes Personal Invoicer easy to use are buttons on the main invoice entry screen, which can be seen in Figure 16-2, that the user can link to any menu items so that they can be executed with a single mouse click.

Personal Invoicer's main template screen is a WYSIWIG invoice template. To create an invoice you simply fill in the fields and click the print button. You can bring up the customer list by clicking another button or just fill in the fields on the template if the customer isn't already in your database.

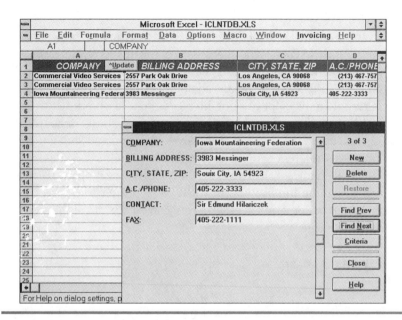

Figure 16-1   Personal Invoicer's customer maintenance dialog
box works with Excel

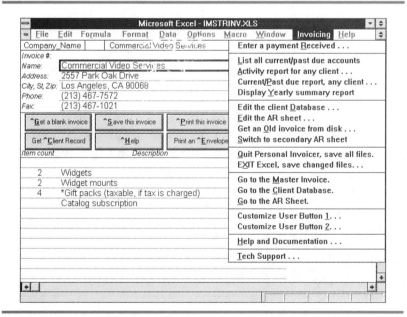

Figure 16-2   Personal Invoicer's main invoice entry screen with
the main menu pulled down

The nature of Personal Invoicer makes the invoice format easy to customize. You can change the appearance of the invoice by simply modifying the invoice template. You can change the fonts, add text, change the position of fields, and even add any additional fields you need this way.

Personal Invoicer prints out invoices on a laser printer that are incredibly cool. They include the payee's account status (amounts due 30-60 days, 60-90 days, and over 90 days), ordering and shipping information, terms, references numbers, Federal I.D. number, and description and notes on charges—all organized neatly with your company name and address across the top like a form you'd pay a printer to typeset. If you run a home business invoices like this can't help but enhance your professional image.

Shareware in Action

Product: Personal Invoicer
Company: VideoStill

VideoStill converts videotape to hard copy—mainly in the form of slides, but also as negatives, print, and Macintosh files—for advertising agencies, producers of television commercials, and film studios. The company generates 800 to 1,000 invoices a year, and until 1991, it had been generating them manually, using boilerplate text and a word processor. Then owner Rob Daly discovered Personal Invoicer.

"We use it," he said, "to invoice each client and keep track of accounts payable. The program fills in the billing information and prints the invoices and envelopes—and away they go."

To make entering information easy, he uses macros, created in Excel, to identify the 20 or so services VideoStill offers its clients. Personal Invoicer's large database easily manages all of his client information and keeps track of payments received.

Daly had seen other products before choosing Personal Invoicer, but "they offered way too much." A key reason this program is so well suited to the needs of a business like his, he says, is the program author's willingness to listen to suggestions and make changes. In the more than three years Daly has used the program, he has seen it evolve into a very versatile package that provides all the features he needs.

Commercial Video Services
2557 Park Oak Dr.
Los Angeles, CA 90068
Phone: 213/467-7572
Fax: 213/467-1021
CompuServe ID: 70741,116
Price: $35
Online filename: INVDEM.ZIP

Bob's Invoice Program

The casual name of this invoicing software is deceptive, for, make no mistake about it, this is serious billing software that can accommodate the needs of just about any size business. Plus, it's only $9.95! (After testing this program and discovering how terrific it was, we had to check that price three times because we were so astonished by it.) Bob's Invoice Program lets you track customer data, maintain a product and service database, and print invoices. Of all the programs we looked at, this one was the easiest to use.

Here's an example of how it works. When entering an invoice, you can call up the "customer look-up" table simply by leaving the customer field blank. Keys do what you would expect them to do—ESC gets you out of a function or data entry screen and ENTER puts you into a function or data entry screen. You're never guessing which key to press next. The user-interface is superb, as you can see in Figure 16-3. When printing an invoice, you can print a full page of half-sheet invoices as well as plain text or graphics characters. The invoice can be displayed, copied to a file, or printed.

There aren't a lot of extras in this program; it can't fax your invoice for you and it doesn't have a graphical user interface or mouse support. About the only perk is a customer address book that lets you look up names, addresses, and phone numbers quickly. To some degree, the simplicity is part of the program's charm. This is the invoicing software you've been searching for.

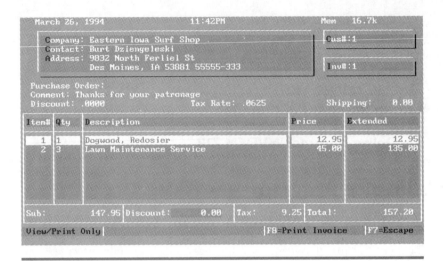

Figure 16-3   At $9.95, Bob's Invoice Program is a dynamite
package with all you need to generate invoices fast

Blue Moose Software
230 Old Turnpike Rd.
Barrington, NH 03825
Phone: 603/942-9917
CompuServe ID: 71240,460
Price: $9.95, plus $4 shipping
Online filename: INVOIC.EXE

Financial Freedom Billing Manager

Windows

Financial Freedom Billing Manager is an invoice-printing and cus-
tomer-billing system designed to give the small business owner as much
freedom as possible from the annoyances of financial chores. It has just
the right amounts of inventory-tracking features and accounts receivable
systems to make billing easy while including all the essentials. You can
print invoices, account-aging analysis reports, mailing labels, and even
delinquency letters.

When creating an invoice you enter billing codes, which resemble inventory item numbers. The description of the goods or services and the price are then automatically filled in, as shown in Figure 16-4. This pseudo-inventory method makes the software ideal for service companies or ones that sell items that never go out of stock. In addition to creating invoices using billing codes, you can also generate invoices with free-form entries. It doesn't appear that you can do both at once however.

You don't have to worry about forgetting billing codes, because whenever you are entering a reference to a code, a list of codes is displayed. You can use Billing Manager to maintain a mailing list of customers, and starting a mailing list is as easy as entering a new list name into the customer data entry screen. You can then print mailing labels for invoices and other customer mailings. Another convenience is that Billing Manager always gives you the option of either displaying a report on the screen or printing it.

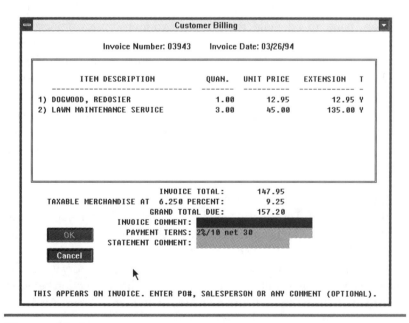

Figure 16-4   Enter services and goods by billing codes and Billing Manager inserts prices and descriptions

M & R Technologies, Inc.
P. O. Box 061298
Palm Bay, FL 32906
Phone: 407/951-2268
Price: $35
Online filename: FFBMGR.ZIP

DAYO Time and Billing

Here's another superb accounting product from TSJ Lab, maker of the DAYO accounting series. It's as robust an invoicing package as you'll find anywhere. You can use it to maintain customer and salesperson lists, handle cash receipts, print invoices and customer statements, maintain inventory, and generate account-aging statistics. It ties in with all the other DAYO accounting products. This is a product that everyone from a small mom-and-pop business to a corporate giant would find serviceable for all their invoicing needs.

At the main configuration menu you can set up everything from your company name to a default credit limit for your customers. You can also set up different printer ports for printing out your invoices, statements, cash receipts, and miscellaneous reports. Having multiple printer ports allows you to have one printer loaded with preprinted invoice forms while another has plain paper for normal reports.

DAYO Time and Billing stores data in dBASE-compatible files so it's easy to use with other accounting products, even those not sold by TSJ Lab. It also has features that give you direct access to the data, making it particularly easy to set up accounts.

To get DAYO Time and Billing working with other DAYO products, simply access the configuration menu and tell the program where the files for the other DAYO accounting modules are located. For instance, if you want to use DAYO Time and Billing with DAYO Inventory, bring up the configuration menu and select the [Inventory Location] item. The program will prompt you to enter the name of the subdirectory where the inventory module is installed. Once this is done, the connection between the products will be smooth and seamless, as you see in Figure 16-5.

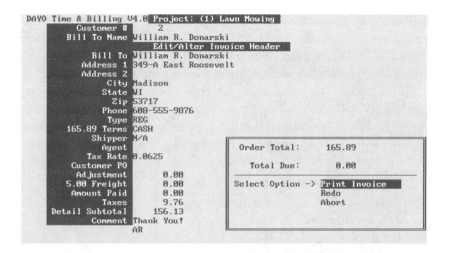

Figure 16-5 DAYO Time & Billing, the invoice creator, can be used with other DAYO accounting modules or as a stand-alone product

For more information about the DAYO series, see Chapters 13, 18, 20, and 25.

TSJ Lab, Inc.
P.O. Box 585366
Orlando, FL 32858
Phone: 407/292-4708
CompuServe ID: 76367,1401 or type GO DAYO
Price: $95
Online filename: DOTE.EXE and DOTD.EXE

General Invoice Sales Tracker

General Invoice Sales Tracker is a basic, easy-to-set-up invoice printing and customer tracking system for the small business, as shown

in Figure 16-6. General Invoice lets you add, change, and delete customer information, create and print invoices, and print customer and sales reports. It isn't as complete an invoicing system as the other packages in this chapter—it doesn't include any inventory functions, for instance—but its simplicity makes it ideal for consultants and home business entrepreneurs. It gives you eight sales categories in which you can enter amounts while invoicing and additional categories for shipping, handling, and discounts as well as a miscellaneous category. It can generate sales analysis reports showing the volume of sales in the different categories. General Invoice calculates the sales tax and invoice total for you.

Bob Keber
336 Swain Blvd.
Lake Worth, FL 33463
Phone: 407/969-3643
Price: $99
Online filename: GIST20.ZIP or GPP206.EXE

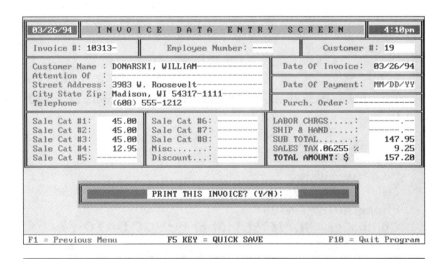

Figure 16-6 General Invoice Sales Tracker is a simple, self-explanatory program ideal for the occasional invoice generator

SALES AND MARKETING

CHAPTER 17

SOFTWARE FOR KEEPING TABS ON SALES PROSPECTS

f you're in sales, or in any type of business that requires you to keep in contact with clients as well as drum up new business, one piece of software you'll find indispensable is a prospect and customer contact tracker. *Contact trackers* (also called *contact managers*) record phone calls, remind you of meetings with clients, and store notes on the meetings. They will even help you generate follow-up letters with powerful mail merge features, snaring the customer's address from your phone book stored in the program and then popping it into a letter. These programs are particularly handy for the sales person or consultant on the road with a laptop. They'll store addresses, phone numbers, and just about anything else you want to remember about clients, including birthdays, favorite sports, and names of children. Plus, you can use contact managers to dial phone numbers for voice calls at the tap of a button (simply connect your phone to your modem or plug both modem and phone into the same phone jack, and the modem will dial the number for you). With the best of the contact management programs, when you call a client this way, the program will automatically update the client's records for you, making a note that you called.

There are dozens of customer contact managers available as shareware. We've sifted through them all to come up with the ones we think are most feature-packed, easiest to use, and most proficient at what they do. (Unfortunately, none of these programs will import data from databases or other phonebook programs.) Our favorite one is the most expensive, at $99. But we think it's well worth it because it includes extensive scheduling features, calendars, and a "tickler" to remind you of appointments. Get rid of those dog-eared spiral-bound calendars on your car seat and the bloated address books in your glove compartment. Get yourself a laptop and one of these programs and you'll never again find yourself pawing through business cards, looking for a client's phone number.

Contact Plus

Contact Plus is a complete sales prospect management system. It does just about everything you would want a sales prospect tracker to do. You can record all the standard information about customers and prospects like phone number, address, and so forth. But you can also use it for much more. You can keep track of calls you've placed and letters you've written. Contact Plus's tickler lets you record the time and place of future meetings, as in the six-month calendar shown in Figure 17-1. Unfortunately, it won't wake up and beep you to remind you of the meeting. You need to open up your schedule yourself and take a look at your appointments in order to be reminded. Contact Plus can also dial phone numbers for you and insert addresses from the address book into letters.

You can use Contact Plus's predefined record screen to record client particulars, but you can also create your own fields for extra information, like names of children and hobbies. Contact Plus lets you set up multiple

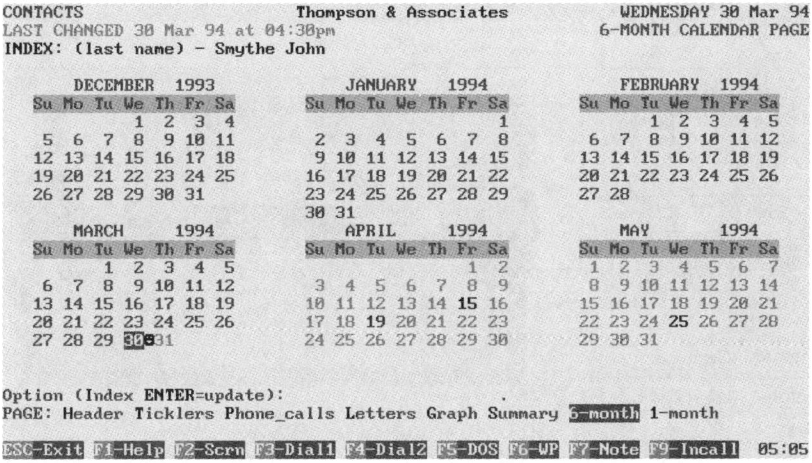

```
CONTACTS                    Thompson & Associates          WEDNESDAY 30 Mar 94
LAST CHANGED 30 Mar 94 at 04:30pm                          6-MONTH CALENDAR PAGE
INDEX: (last name) - Smythe John

        DECEMBER  1993            JANUARY   1994           FEBRUARY  1994
     Su Mo Tu We Th Fr Sa      Su Mo Tu We Th Fr Sa     Su Mo Tu We Th Fr Sa
              1  2  3  4                         1                1  2  3  4  5
      5  6  7  8  9 10 11       2  3  4  5  6  7  8      6  7  8  9 10 11 12
     12 13 14 15 16 17 18       9 10 11 12 13 14 15     13 14 15 16 17 18 19
     19 20 21 22 23 24 25      16 17 18 19 20 21 22     20 21 22 23 24 25 26
     26 27 28 29 30 31         23 24 25 26 27 28 29     27 28
                               30 31

        MARCH    1994            APRIL     1994            MAY      1994
     Su Mo Tu We Th Fr Sa      Su Mo Tu We Th Fr Sa     Su Mo Tu We Th Fr Sa
              1  2  3  4  5                      1  2      1  2  3  4  5  6  7
      6  7  8  9 10 11 12       3  4  5  6  7  8  9       8  9 10 11 12 13 14
     13 14 15 16 17 18 19      10 11 12 13 14 15 16     15 16 17 18 19 20 21
     20 21 22 23 24 25 26      17 18 19 20 21 22 23     22 23 24 25 26 27 28
     27 28 29 30 31            24 25 26 27 28 29 30     29 30 31


Option (Index ENTER=update):                    .
PAGE: Header Ticklers Phone_calls Letters Graph Summary 6-month 1-month

ESC-Exit F1-Help F2-Scrn F3-Dial1 F4-Dial2 F5-DOS F6-WP F7-Note F9-Incall  05:05
```

Figure 17-1   The six-month calendar in Contact Plus highlights
days with appointments

customer and contact databases, which can each have its own configu-
rations and screens if you choose. The tickler will display a list of past and
pending contacts for each prospect. There are also six-month and one-
month calendars that highlight days on which you contacted the client.
Contact Plus can also display vibrant graphs with color-coded bars
showing contacts, when you called them, when you met with them in
person, when you wrote them, and other similar data.

You can run it as a normal program, or load it as a memory-resident
one to keep running all the time and pop up over other applications. Use
the autodialer to call a client with the tap of a key, and, as shown in Figure
17-2, Contact Plus will record the time and date of the call in the client
database. Similarly, the mail merge feature, which works with WordPerfect and WordStar documents, also automatically records in the client
database the fact that you've sent a client a letter. You can tell the tickler
to remind you to follow up phone calls with letters.

Contact Plus has too many bells and whistles to mention here. Suffice
it to say that if you're in sales, you'd be smart to download a copy of
this—and pay the $99 registration. It's worth the price.

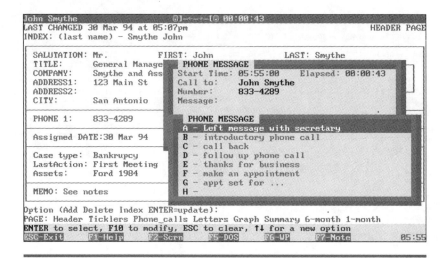

Figure 17-2   Contact Plus automatically records phone calls when you use its autodialer to phone customers or prospects

Contact Plus Corp.
P.O. Box 372577
Satellite Beach, FL 32937
Phone: 407/779-4900 or 800/366-9876 (orders only)
Fax: 407/779-3311
BBS: 407/779-4422
Price: $99
Online filename: CPLUS25.EXE

KBS: People Management System

Windows

If you'd like a prospect tracker like Contact Plus but prefer one that runs under Windows, take a look at KBS: People Management System. KBS includes many of the features that Contact Plus does, including automatic tracking of contacts with customers, sales prospects, and professional contacts; an autodialer; and mail merge that works with Word for Windows and Word Perfect documents. Like a database program, it lets you query your contact database by searching for things like a particular area code or company name. As shown in Figure 17-3, the

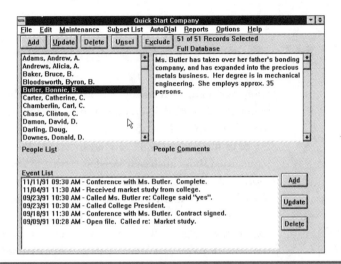

Figure 17-3   KBS: People Management System is a friendly and
fun prospect tracker that works under Windows

database lets you include "people comments" to help you remember all
the important details about your clients.

KBS is super-easy to use—easier than Contact Plus. It displays a list
of your clients in one window, while a list of your contacts with a
highlighted client is displayed in another. To see another client's records,
just click on the client's name. When you call the client with the
autodialer, KBS records the call in the contact record for that client.

You can store client names and records in up to 20 different categories
that you create yourself. You can create categories like "trade show
contacts" or "prospective clients" or "esteemed customers." It's KBS's
search capability that really sets it apart from the other prospect trackers
in this chapter. Say you want a list of all the CPAs listed in your database.
Just click on the CPA box on the query screen and KBS starts the search.
It will display a subset of the records of CPAs that it's found, and you can
print reports from those records only.

Shareware in Action

Product: KBS: People Management System
Companies: Corning Asahi and Commercial Crystal Laboratories

As information services business manager of Corning Asahi Video Products Company, a joint venture between Corning Glassworks and Asahi, in Japan, Scott Patterson is responsible for providing information technology and services to potentially hundreds of internal customers as well as some external customers. To do this, he relies on scores of internal and external service providers. "I am in constant dialog with my customers and suppliers," he said. "With this many demanding customers coupled with the sometimes tough-to-pin-down suppliers, it was getting difficult to keep track of who said what to whom, what was agreed on, when it was to be delivered, and so on." Concerned about the possibility of losing control and even more concerned about customer satisfaction declining, he decided to give People Management System a try. Although in the past he had tried contract manager software with no real success, he was delighted to discover that PMS was exactly what he was looking for.

"PMS enables me to quickly capture key information during or immediately after a conversation and easily retrieve it when I need it. This enables me to follow up more effectively and efficiently to meet my customers' needs. I can also react to a phone call equipped with an audit trail of all of the latest and greatest information from previous dialogs with that individual." With its intuitive user interface, excellent documentation, reliability, and flexibility, he added, People Management System is clearly "designed with the business professional in mind."

Michael Urbanik, president of Commercial Crystal Laboratories, agrees. He was originally skeptical of using shareware for operations so critical to his business, but after using PMS for about a year, he had this to say about the program:

"As a sales tool, PMS provides an excellent way to monitor the success ratio of bid quotations on a customer-by-customer and product-by-product basis. PMS also allows us to view price trends so that we do not over- or underprice our products. We have PMS set up to provide a log of technical discussions and interactions between our staff and our customers. This allows us to respond quickly to a customer request for repeat orders."

Urbanik also likes that PMS allows them to recall information necessary to make new decisions based on historical data. "Easy retrieval of archival information is extremely important to our operation," he said. "This information consists of recent as well as decades-old quotations, purchase orders, and engineering comments. I have not found a commercially available product that can produce the results that PMS provides."

KBS Systems
1089 Ruppert Rd.
Marco Island, FL 33937
Phone: 813/394-9359
Fax: 813/394-5965,,,,62
CompuServe ID: 70062,3526
Price: $79
Online filename: KBSPMS.EXE

Impulse!

Impulse! is a customer and prospect tracker that includes all the basics, such as a customer database, contact logging, autodialer, and mail merge capabilities—but it also offers a built-in word processor for writing follow-up letters without having to skip out of the program to load your own word processor. Another great feature is that it lets you create up to 36 additional data fields for each customer record so that you can record a host of particulars, like information on the customer's site or order preferences. (Figure 17-4 shows two custom fields.) These specialized fields can consist of characters, numbers, dates, or even true/false entries.

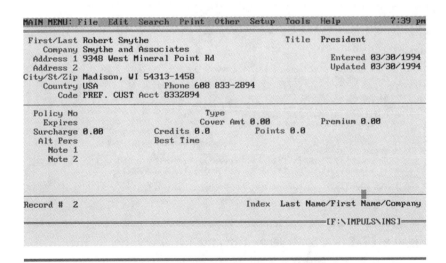

Figure 17-4   The Impulse! client contact data entry screen with two custom fields: POLICY NO and NOTE 2

When you define new fields for a your customer database, Impulse! automatically adds them to all the customer records in the database.

Impulse! includes a report writer that you can use in mail merges. For instance, when you fire up the report writer, Impulse! displays a form with many of the predefined fields from the database, like name, title, and address, already set up for a mail merge (a sample screen is shown in Figure 17-5). All you have to do is specify those fields in the body of your letter and Impulse! will generate customized letters with the appropriate additions. There is no limit to the number of contact records you can store in Impulse! You can also create multiple customer databases.

International Solutions, Inc.
52 Tolman St.
Canton, MA 02021
Phone: 617/575-0290
Fax: 617/821-4487
Price: $69; professional version $199; sales version $299
Online filename: IMPULSE.ZIP

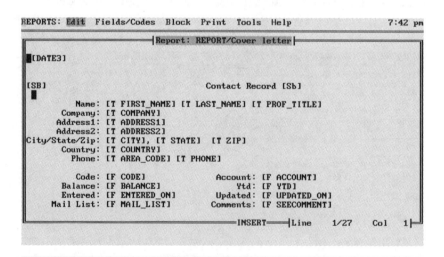

Figure 17-5   A cover letter from the Impulse! report writer used with mail merge for fast and easy follow-up letters to customer contacts

InContact!

Windows

InContact! is a pleasant and proficient prospect tracker that Windows aficionados will appreciate. It offers features that only a contact tracker that works under Windows can, like an edit menu for copying information into the Windows clipboard for use in other applications like your word processor. Its Attached Files feature is similar to the Windows File Manager launch feature. It lets you load another Windows application by just clicking on the file name. InContact! lets you add your word processor (as well as other items) to its own main menu so that you don't have to skip around Windows each time you want to fire it up and write a follow-up letter.

Beyond this, InContact! is a bit humbler in scope than the other prospect trackers covered by this chapter. It lets you record work and home addresses for each client, as well as six different phone numbers, and includes an autodialer for calling them, but it doesn't automatically update its records whenever you call numbers, as the other prospect trackers do. You must type in phone call results manually, as shown in Figure 17-6. It offers mail merge capabilities for sending out follow-up letters, but again, it doesn't record in the customer database that you've sent them.

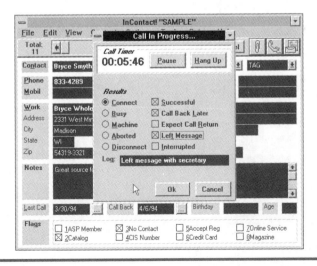

Figure 17-6   Recording the result of a phone call with InContact!

It does have a slick feature that lets you search out and select subsets of customer records, so that, for instance, you can retrieve records of customers you want to call on a particular day. InContact! even lets you retrieve from your database a list of all the customers with birthdays during a given week. There are many fields in customer records that users can define for themselves. InContact! is a capable program that any Windows-equipped salesperson will appreciate.

Serious Shareware
P.O. Box 5523
Arlington, TX 76005
CompuServe ID: 70404,3014
Price: $20, an extra $20 for manual and 30 days support
Online filename: INCT*xx*.ZIP

CHAPTER 18

SOFTWARE FOR MERCHANTS, CASH REGISTERS, AND CONTRACT BIDS

f you're just starting out in the retail business and not ready to splurge on a pricey, high-tech system, you'd be smart to check out some of these shareware programs designed for retail stores. They range from $50 to $125 in price, and sometimes that price includes licenses for more than one store. They may not be the most whizbang, feature-stuffed software on the market, but if they can get your startup operation going, heck, they're worth a look. Anyway, it takes no longer than 30 minutes to download one of these programs to see if it's for you.

On the other hand, if you're in a business that requires you to formulate price estimates for contracts, there are several shareware packages that can provide assistance in this area. One of the packages we talk about below is ideal to take along to the job site on a laptop. Another will tell you your profit margin (or lack thereof) on each listed material and labor cost included in the bid. It will even figure in the cost of shipping parts that you'll need for the job and tell you the amount of lead time you'll need for ordering items.

Point-of-Sale Software

Good point-of-sale (POS) software is hard to find in the shareware world. That's a pity because a good commercial point-of-sale system can cost a merchant thousands of dollars. If you're new to the retail business, you may not want to take that kind of plunge until you can see that your store is actually going to generate sales. The best shareware point-of-sale program is DAYO Point of Sale. For under $100 this will get your registers up and running fast. Since it ties in with the many other quality DAYO accounting packages, like its general ledger and inventory modules, you can outfit yourself with all the software you need to get your retail business going, and for a pittance.

Sophisticated inventory tracking features are among the attractions of shareware point-of-sale software. As they record sales, they'll update your inventory not just at one store, but at multiple locations. They'll print out records of weekly or monthly sales statistics, tracking sales by product, customer, and location. They'll print price tags, bar codes, and shipping labels. They'll print purchase orders and track vendors. Some will let you export data to other database applications.

DAYO Point of Sale

DOS

DAYO Point of Sale is your best choice if you're looking for low-cost POS software that interfaces with a cash drawer. In addition to cash register control, it offers invoice entry and printing, and customer and inventory databases. Although you can use it as a stand-alone product, it ties in with the other DAYO accounting software packages so that you can have a complete, integrated accounting, invoicing, and inventory system for under $1,000. (See Chapters 13, 16, 20, and 25 for information about other DAYO products.)

Point of Sale lets you open up to six cash registers, as shown in Figure 18-1. When you run the program, you pick a cash drawer to open and enter the amount of cash originally in the drawer. As invoices are entered, DAYO keeps a running total of the amount of cash in the drawer so that employees can justify the total at the end of the day. You can also use the software to literally open a cash drawer by hooking it up to your PC's communications port.

DAYO Point of Sale will print invoices on a different printer than it does the rest of its reports so you can keep one printer loaded with preprinted forms. It allows you to configure invoice printing in several different ways, including a receipt style that prints 40-column condensed print to fit on a cash register roll, as shown in Figure 18-2.

Adding customers and inventory items on the fly is easy. When you're entering an invoice or a cash register receipt, a single key stroke lets you add a new customer or inventory item to the database.

The main difference between DAYO Point of Sale and TJS's Time and Billing program (see Chapter 16) is the cash register features that can be found in the former. Point of Sale also includes some cash

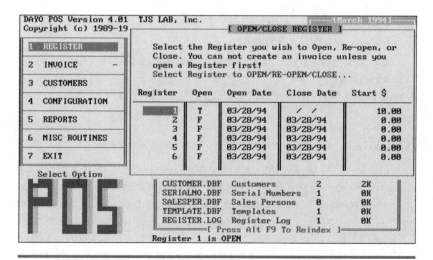

Figure 18-1   Opening a cash register in DAYO Point of Sale

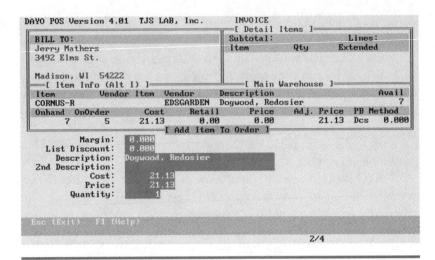

```
DAYO POS Version 4.01  TJS LAB, Inc.      INVOICE
                                        ┌─[ Detail Items ]──────────────────┐
  ┌─BILL TO:──────────────────────────┐ Subtotal:              Lines:
  │ Jerry Mathers                     │ Item         Qty       Extended
  │ 3492 Elms St.                     │
  │                                   │
  │ Madison, WI  54222                │
  └─[ Item Info (Alt I) ]──────────── └──[ Main Warehouse ]─────────────────
  Item         Vendor Item  Vendor    Description                      Avail
  CORNUS-R                  EDSGARDEN  Dogwood, Redosier                    7
  Onhand  OnOrder       Cost    Retail     Price   Adj. Price  PB Method
      7        5       21.13      0.00      0.00       21.13   Dcs     0.000
                          ─[ Add Item To Order ]─
          Margin:  │0.000
    List Discount:  │0.000
      Description:  │Dogwood, Redosier
  2nd Description:
             Cost:        21.13
            Price:        21.13
         Quantity:            1

  Esc (Exit)   F1 (Help)

                                                  2/4
```

Figure 18-2   DAYO Point of Sale is about to print a cash register receipt

register-specific reports, but lacks some of the accounts receivable aging reports that can be found in Time and Billing.

TJS Lab, Inc.
P.O. Box 585366
Orlando, FL 32858
Phone: 407/292-4708
CompuServe ID: 76367,1401 or type GO DAYO
Price: $95
Online filename: DAYOPD.ZIP or DAYOPD.EXE

The Retailer

DOS

The Retailer is point-of-sale software designed for small stores with up to five locations. While you can use it to generate purchase orders and post sales transactions, it excels at inventory control, giving the retailer easy access to comparative performance data on how the same items sell at different stores. The Retailer is extremely easy to set up, learn, and use, with pull-down menus and easily understood prompts at each step of the way.

The care that went into this program cannot be overstated. At the danger of sounding maudlin, we quote from author Gary McNutt's eloquent opening to the manual: "The Retailer is dedicated to the memory of my father who was a retailer all his life. I still have a mental image of him laboring over his order forms and inventory books. Many times, I saw him with his head down on a stack of order forms, cat-napping." That's the philosophy of this program: it strives to spare the new retailer from all the tedium of retail record-keeping, the sorts of things that cause your head to drop to the page in exhaustion.

RetailWare
2107 W. Britton Rd.
Oklahoma City, OK 73120
Phone: 405/749-1763
Fax: 405/751-5629
CompuServe ID: 72331,53
Price: $49
Online filename: RET405.ZIP

The Invoice Store

The Invoice Store is an invoicing and billing program designed especially for mail order companies, but it's suitable for any small retail business. Its multiple modules let you maintain a customer database with essentials on orders, credit, and billing. An inventory database tracks the flow of products through your doors. Invoicing and receivables modules let you print out invoices and keep track of company finances. Other built-in databases include one for vendors and another for sales people. It includes an appointment scheduler and also has the ability to print mailing labels and even issue form letters.

Software Store Products, Inc.
P.O. Box 562
Oakdale, NY 11769
Price: $95
Online filename: INVOIC.EXE

TRAXX Point of Sale

DOS

TRAXX Point of Sale is a powerful software program that updates inventory records with each sale. It's designed to let the small retailer use PCs—including old 8086s and XTs as well as modern 486s—as low-cost point-of-sale hardware and skip the expense of pricey special purpose retail hardware. You simply hook an electronic cash drawer up to a PC. To enter a sale, all your clerks have to do is enter the product number. TRAXX will tally the price, figure the tax (there's also a Canadian version available that will tabulate the GST and provincial taxes), print the receipt, and open the cash drawer. It's designed to make ringing up a sale as simple and automated for the clerk as scanning a bar code.

It takes care of all recordkeeping for point-of-sale transactions, including recording sales tax by date range. Besides figuring costs for consignment sales, at the end of the day TRAXX will even do your cash drawer reconciliation. It conducts extensive inventory analysis, as shown in Figure 18-3, and automatically generates reorders when inventory levels are low. It prints sales receipts, price labels, and checks for suppliers. It can track inventory and sales at multiple locations, assuming the locations are hooked up by a network. You designate one PC as the

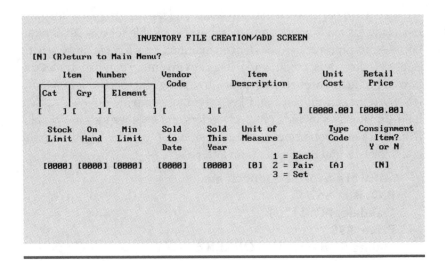

Figure 18-3   An inventory monitoring screen in TRAXX Point of Sale software

"master" to store all the latest sales and inventory data. You run TRAXX's update program once, or several times a day to update data on all the other PCs. TRAXX is used by lots of small stores on the West Coast and in Canada, including antique and computer stores.

Financial $oftware Engineering
14015 N.E. 87th St.
Redmond, WA 98052
Phone: 206/881-1968
Price: $95
Online filename: TRAXX.ZIP

Retail Plus

Retail Plus is also designed for small stores with multiple locations. It was originally designed and commissioned by Canadian franchisees of Body Shop stores, and is an extremely popular point-of-sale program among stores in Canada and the United States. It was designed to be easy to use, with pull-down and pop-up menus, but still offer powerful point-of-sale features like the ability to read in sales data from electronic downloading cash drawers.

One unique feature is its ability to easily handle record-keeping for stock transfers between stores. Not only does it track sales and inventory data for all store locations, but it can also track sales by product, client, or store department. For instance, it includes a daily sales log which lets you look up the date, time, and sales clerk for any item sold, as well as the price and any discounts. You can also generate equally detailed weekly and monthly sales reports for individual departments. You can analyze the sales performance of a particular product or product catagory. You can generate a list of overstocked items, or create inventory auditing reports that will satisfy your accountants. The program is set up in such a way that you can access daily, weekly, and monthly sales data at any time with the touch of a key. Password protection gives employees three different levels of access to the system—security that store owners can easily turn on, off, and reconfigure at any time.

Printing price tags, bin labels, and shipping labels with bar codes is no problem with Retail Plus. It can print sales slips and handle all point-of-sale recordkeeping. It can print monthly or weekly reports on sales figures for each item. You can export sales data from Retail Plus into

Shareware in Action

Mike Snyder, general manager of the Triangle Shooting Club in Raleigh, North Carolina, recently installed Retail Plus at his indoor shooting range and store. He now uses the program to manage the cash register system, inventory, and client database. He hadn't used a computerized point-of-sale system before, but he did survey other products before the store owner pulled Retail Plus off of CompuServe and gave it to him to try. Compared to similar programs, he said, Retail Plus, with its menu-driven screens, is easy to use. "It's simple. That's why I like it."

Product: Retail Plus
Company: Triangle Shooting Club

---

many word processors and database applications. Retail Plus can also generate purchase order and vendor lists.

> **K. Egger**
> **Adelaide Box 423**
> **36 Adelaide St. East**
> **Toronto, Canada M5C 2J5**
> **Phone: 416/961-7810**
> **Price: $125 for unlimited locations and a manual**
> **Online filename: PLUS41.ZIP**

Micro Register

Micro Register is a point-of-sale invoice printing program. It's ideal for the small business that needs to print out a receipt and log in-person sales every once in an azure moon, but not for the storefront that anticipates mobs of customers. It doesn't support cash drawers or light pens for reading bar codes, but it does come equipped with a *super* user-friendly interface.

While you're in Micro Register's sales menus all you need to do to reach the customer database is press a function key. If you need to get into the inventory database, you press another function key. Micro

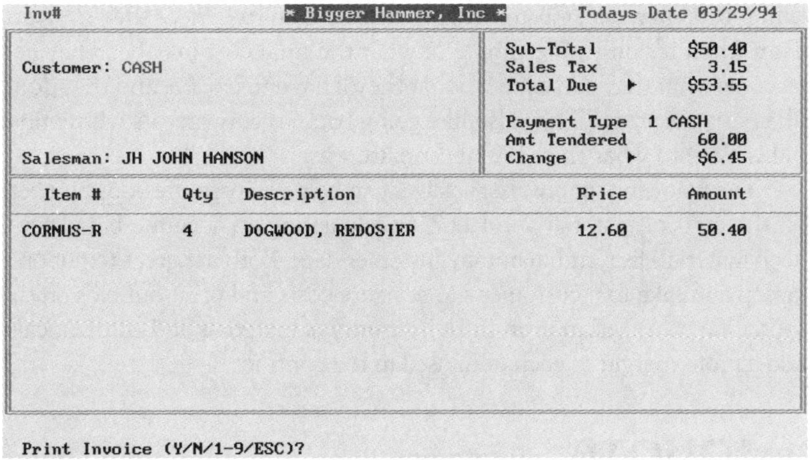

```
Inv#                    * Bigger Hammer, Inc *      Todays Date 03/29/94
                                               Sub-Total        $50.40
   Customer: CASH                              Sales Tax          3.15
                                               Total Due    ▶   $53.55

                                               Payment Type  1 CASH
                                               Amt Tendered      60.00
   Salesman: JH JOHN HANSON                    Change       ▶    $6.45

    Item #        Qty   Description                   Price      Amount

   CORNUS-R        4    DOGWOOD, REDOSIER             12.60       50.40




   Print Invoice (Y/N/1-9/ESC)?
```

Figure 18-4   Entering a cash transaction in Micro Register

Register can print multiple copies of the receipt and is designed to handle cash, check, and credit card transactions only (in other words, no billing). It will even calculate the correct change that a customer should receive, as shown in Figure 18-4. Most of the fields have default values that allow you to move quickly through the invoice generating process. MicroRegister is complete enough so that you won't need another billing system if your customer tracking and inventory needs aren't overly complicated.

> **Micro Methods**
> **P.O. Box 2027**
> **Evansville, IN 47728**
> **Phone: 812/476-0999**
> **Price: $75**
> **Online filename: MICROREG.ZIP**

Price Estimating Software

One of the best ways to send a potential customer shopping elsewhere is to give them a contract bid full of numbers that look like they were pulled from a hat. Far-ranging guestimates on the price of materials, vague references to additional costs scattered throughout the bid sheet, all these things can kill a sale. Customers like precision in the prices they're given, even when it's only an estimate of what the final cost may be. They like to know what they can expect, what they'll have to pay for, and they don't like nasty surprises. They also like going back to contractors whose final bill is close to what their initial estimate was.

The following shareware packages can help you organize your numbers on the costs of material and labor for calculating an accurate bid. They'll keep materials lists and maintain customer data. Both are great to put on a laptop and take to a customer site to figure costs and print out bids on the spot. One package can even track inventory of materials and automatically add a profit margin to each item used in the contract.

ProDev*QUOTE

ProDev*QUOTE will help you assemble the information you need to make accurate price quotes for customers when bidding on contracts or preparing cost estimates. You enter individual lists of the different materials and labor categories that might appear on the quote, then pick which items will appear on the printed quote. ProDev*QUOTE's major advantage over the usual invoice-style estimating program is that it can be set up to automatically add a profit margin to each item.

The materials and labor master lists that you create are rather like inventory files. Instead of keeping count of the number of items in stock, you record things like the number of days of lead time you need for ordering the item. ProDev*QUOTE even lets you automatically account for shipping charges on items you'll need to order if the bid is accepted. You can also include in the equation rental items, insurance, and discounts on the bids. Labor can be charged either by the hour or by some other unit, like per foot for jobs like laying cable. Quotes are easily modified, as shown in Figure 18-5. This is a much easier and more thorough method of writing bids than scribbling notes on a legal pad and "guestimating" how much profit you'll earn.

PRO DEV Software
545 Grover Rd.
Muskegon, MI 49442
Phone: 616/788-2243
Price: $65 plus $5 shipping
Online filename: PDQUOT.ZIP

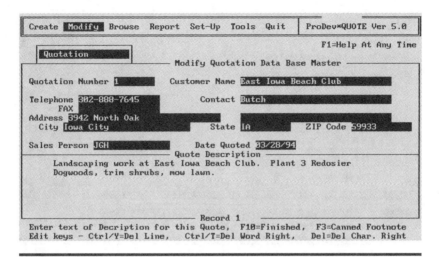

Figure 18-5   Entering a quote description while modifying a
quote in ProDev*QUOTE

Dyna-Quote

Dyna-Quote is another program to help you estimate prices to bid contracts. It's a much simpler program than ProDev*QUOTE, described above. It's similar to an invoicing program in its layout, in fact. That and the fact that it takes up less memory make it easier to send out to the customer site with an employee with a laptop. It will store a materials price list and a customer database. As you're formulating a price quote, you can easily create new customer records.

To formulate a quote, the first thing you do is enter the applicable customer information and add it to your database. You can also look up a customer entry in the database and Dyna-Quote will fill in your bid with all the pertinent customer information. After that, Dyna-Quote pops you into the materials list, shown in Figure 18-6, so that you can choose which items will appear on the quote. Next, you're given a chance to enter additional miscellaneous charges, discounts, and comments.

One nice feature is the ability to add notes and comments to the end of your estimates. Dyna-Quote will shell you out to your favorite text editor so that you can write and edit the text and insert it in the bid.

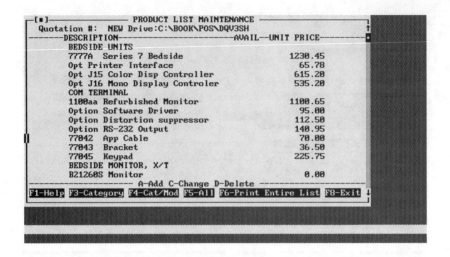

```
-[■]————————— PRODUCT LIST MAINTENANCE ————————————┐
  Quotation #:   NEW Drive:C:\BOOK\POS\DQV3SH                      ↑
————————DESCRIPTION—————————————————————AVAIL——UNIT PRICE————————▐
       BEDSIDE UNITS
       7777A  Series 7 Bedside                     1230.45
       Opt Printer Interface                         65.78
       Opt J15 Color Disp Controller                615.20
       Opt J16 Mono Display Controler               535.20
       COM TERMINAL
       1100aa Refurbished Monitor                  1100.65
       Option Software Driver                         95.00
       Option Distortion suppressor                 112.50
       Option RS-232 Output                         140.95
       77042  App Cable                              70.00
       77043  Bracket                                36.50
       77045  Keypad                                225.75
       BEDSIDE MONITOR, X/T
       B21260S Monitor                                0.00
————————————————— A-Add C-Change D-Delete ——————————————————
F1-Help F3-Category F4-Cat/Mod F5-All F6-Print Entire List F8-Exit ↓
```

Figure 18-6 Dyna-Quote's categorized materials list makes it easy to generate quotes

Dynamacs, Inc.
639 Sedgefield
Bloomfield, MI 48304
Phone: 800/755-2616 (orders only)
Price: $19.95
Online filename: DQV3SH.ZIP

CHAPTER 19

SOFTWARE FOR MAILING

Doing a mass-mailing can be one of the most labor-intensive, aggravation-fraught undertakings of any small business. Mailings are a great way to reel in customers, so it is often one of the first things you do when you start a business. But thanks to the gods of inexperience, that first mailing invariably becomes a higgledy-piggledy affair with endless trips to the post office, mailing permits improperly applied for, and address labels printed upside down. Then there is the cost. To mail a one-ounce, black-and-white brochure to everyone on a mailing list of 20,000 potential customers, you're talking $30K in postage, paper, and printing bills. With an investment like that, mass-mailings are not something to undertake without careful planning. You want to be sure to save costs wherever you can.

You'll find that information services have literally hundreds of low-cost shareware packages designed to help you organize mass-mailings. There are envelope printers, label printers, and programs to print bulk rate stamps and postal service delivery bar codes. There are programs to keep track of your mailing list and even your responses. And there are programs to help you track Federal Express and United Parcel mailings. These programs will not guarantee you a smooth mass-mailing campaign. But used in conjunction with a heavy-hitting commercial database like Paradox or FoxPro, they may shave a few hours off your labor costs, and a few pennies off your unit postage costs by helping you print discount-garnering bar codes and nine-digit ZIP codes. When you're doing mass-mailing, savings like that can really add up.

DMAIL

DMAIL is a robust mailing list manager with easy-to-use, easily navigated pull-down menus. It can store and search for names, addresses, titles, ZIP codes, home and work phone numbers, and date of last mailing. You can also establish a user-defined field in addition to those that are predefined. With DMAIL you can append notes of up to 100 lines to each record, and you can easily toggle from full-record to table mode, in which records are summarized one to a line. DMAIL will also conduct searches for duplicate records. Subsets of the database can be selected for printing envelopes or labels, and U.S. Postal Service PostNet bar codes can be printed if you have a Laserjet printer. DMAIL can also print Rolodex cards and create mail-merge files for WordPerfect and Word. Data is stored in dBASE format and can, therefore, be easily exported to other database applications. The shareware also includes a handy backup and restore feature.

K. Egger
Adelaide P. O. Box 423
36 Adelaide St. East
Toronto, Ontario
Canada
Fax: 416/862-3420
Price: $35 for up to two PCs
Online filename: DMAIL.ZIP

Label Master

DOS

Label Master, shown in Figure 19-1, was chosen as *PC Magazine's* Editor's Choice mailing list program a few years back. It prints labels of any size, plus PostNet bar codes, and carrier route numbers for bulk mailers. Since it's CASS-certified by the U.S. Postal Service, you can qualify for postal discounts from the Postal Service if you use it to print bar codes on your mail.

Label Master can store an unlimited number of records, imported from any dBASE format database or plain text word processor. These records can be searched, and the results of the search can be saved for future use. Although slightly more expensive than DMAIL, Label Master offers several advantages. Its search features are more flexible than DMAIL's, and Label Master lets you print on any type of label (although the parameters of labels can be hard to configure) while DMAIL limits you to five types of labels.

Label Master can work all sorts of ZIP code magic. It will convert your entire database of 5-digit ZIP codes to 9-digit ones (something the post office will like). It can check for duplicate records plus verify that the ZIP code assigned to each address is one of the ones assigned to that state. It also includes built-in PostNet bar codes.

It also includes a form letter writer, a report generator, an auto-dialer to dial any phone number in your customer database, plus a pop-up calendar.

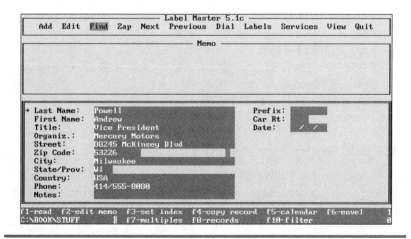

Figure 19-1   Printing labels is easy with Label Master

Shareware in Action

Product: Label Master
Company: Acudata

Acudata is a mailing house which provides lists of potential clients to small businesses, stock brokers, and other companies. During the past four years, Acudata has also provided clients with copies of Label Master.

Customers use the program not only for label printing but also for "custom selection of data segments," says Acudata's manager, Alan Edwards. "Some use it for telemarketing, as a simple contact manager," which allows them to make use of its built-in dialer.

Acudata chose Label Master for very specific reasons:

▷ The record size is manageable.

▷ Because the program is menu driven, it is easy to use, even for people with no computer experience.

▷ The program is flexible and so meets the needs of Acudata's diverse group of customers.

▷ The program offers dBASE compatibility.

"We've sent out five or six hundred copies," said Edwards, "and the response has been 99 percent positive."

RKS Software, Inc.
3820 N. Dittmar Rd.
Arlington, VA 22207
Phone: 703/534-1726
Fax: 703/534-4358
BBS: 703/534-7812
Price: $39
Online filename: LM51C.ZIP

Pony Express

Pony Express is a nifty pop-up utility that can tell you whether it will be cheaper to send your package by U.S. Mail, United Parcel, or Federal Express. Simply enter your ZIP and the particulars on sending the package, including whether you want a return receipt, insurance, and what type of delivery. Then enter the weight of the package and the declared value and Pony

Express will tell you the cheapest way to send it with a price chart and estimated time of arrival. Melisco Marketing updates Pony Express whenever one of the carriers changes their prices. You can buy an extra scale interface from the company so Pony Express will read data from your shipping department scale. It's network compatible.

Melisco Marketing, Inc.
9719 Ensley Lane
Leawood, KS 66206
Price: $50; or $150 with postal scale interface and cable
Online filename: PONY20.ZIP

WunderBar

WunderBar is a pop-up program that prints PostNet bar codes on envelopes or labels. It will work with any word processor, mailing list software, or database program. It will even work with Windows applications like Word. The shareware version comes packed with a primer on making your addressing comply with postal regulations, and hence qualify for lower postal rates. It works with Laserjet, Epson, and Proprinter, and compatible printers.

Binary Systems
P.O. Box 1621
Brandon, FL 33509
Price: $35
Online filename: WUNBAR.ZIP

Envelopes Plus

Envelopes Plus is an easy-to-use envelope printer that will also print labels and Rolodex cards, as shown in Figure 19-2. It will maintain an address book of names, addresses, and phone numbers that can be searched by name, state, address, phone number, or any text fragment. You can mark records for batch printing, and a pop-up dialer will dial any phone number on the screen for you—an easy way to make voice or data calls. Its menus make it easy to pick the size of envelope, labels, or card you want to print and to quickly insert salutations into letters. Envelopes Plus also prints bulk rate imprint stamps and includes a calculator.

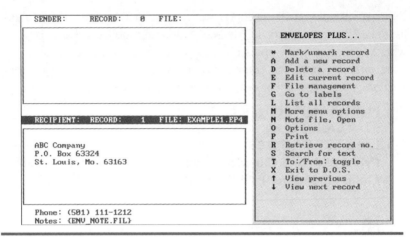

Figure 19-2   Simple menus let you create envelope formatting in Envelopes Plus

Philip Kapusta
P.O. Box 5423
Falmouth, VA 22403
Price: $16.95
Online filename: ENV403.ZIP

Winvelope

Windows

Here's a Windows envelope printer that can give your envelopes sizzle by printing your logo on them. You don't have a company logo? Design one in Windows' Paint, or any other paint program. Winvelope will print it on the envelope along with your return address. It can also print any address pasted into the program from any other Windows applications, as shown in Figure 19-3, and can print in batches any addresses stored in Windows' Cardfile. It will print messages such as "Please Hand Stamp" or "First Class Mail," and if you have a laser printer, it can also print PostNet bar codes. This is not something to use for a major mass-mailing, but it does come in handy for printing envelopes for the day's batch of business letters.

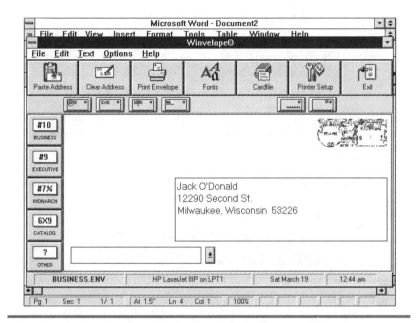

Figure 19-3   Winvelope pops up over any Windows application
so you can paste in addresses

J. E. McCullum
P. O. Box 1145
Jenkins, KY 41537
Phone: 606/832-2493 (6:00-9:00 p.m. EST M-F)
BBS: 606/832-4029
Price: $20
Online filename: WNVLOP43.ZIP; on CompuServe,
look for WENV43.ZIP

GRAB Plus

DOS

Windows

GRAB Plus is an all-purpose envelope addresser. It captures addresses from any application screen and prints them onto envelopes or labels with the fonts you specify. It also prints graphics logos and PostNet bar codes. The DOS version of the program is called GRAB Plus. You'll

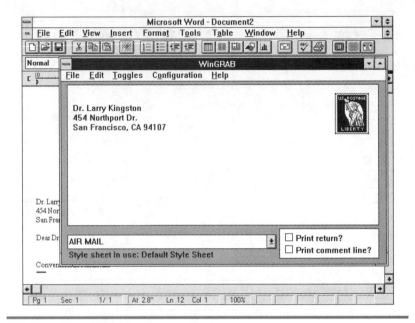

Figure 19-4 WinGrab makes it easy to cut and paste addresses from letters onto envelopes

also find online, either packed with GRAB Plus or floating around separately, its Windows module, called WinGrab.

A common use of GRAB Plus is to pop it up over a letter you're typing in a word processor and instruct it to print an envelope for the address at the top of the letter, as shown in Figure 19-4. You can edit the address prior to printing. GRAB Plus also stores two standard return addresses.

GRAB Plus includes a built-in address book that you can pop up over any application to look up addresses and phone numbers and then use to print envelopes. You can import into GRAB Plus any addresses stored in comma-delimited text form or dBASE format. GRAB Plus prints many Avery label sizes, but you can also configure it for other label styles.

ZPAY Payroll Systems
2526 69th Ave. South
St. Petersburg, FL 33712
Phone: 813/866-8233 or 800/468-4188
Fax: 813/866-8034

CompuServe ID: 70040,645
Price: $39.95 for DOS GRAB Plus, $49.95 for DOS
GRAB Plus with WinGrab
Online filename: GRAP.ZIP for DOS version;
WINGRA.ZIP for Windows version

ZIPKey

Type a ZIP code and ZIPKey injects into your document—whether it be a word processing or database file—the city and state associated with it. You can also use it to look up individual ZIP codes by entering a city and/or state into its pop-up menu. In addition, it will provide telephone area codes for ZIP codes, cities, and states. It's a memory resident program that can also be customized to inject into documents boilerplate text, such as your own mailing address. When you hit the hotkey, ZIPKey can pop up a menu for you, or operate invisibly for less obtrusive operation.

Eric Isaacson Software
416 E. University Ave.
Bloomington, IN 47401
Phone: 812/339-1811
Price: $30; $25 for annual update disk
Online filename: ZIPKEY.ZIP

CHAPTER 20

SOFTWARE FOR INVENTORY CONTROL, SHIPPING, AND RECEIVING

Whether you're a newcomer to the retail business with a small mail-order company that you run out of your home, or a retail store magnate with a half-dozen shops spread out across a wide geographic area, you'll find something for you among the many shareware inventory control packages that can be downloaded from online services. At the high end are the DAYO accounting and inventory control packages, which manage the budgets and inventories of a variety of businesses ranging from convenience stores to Disney's Epcot Center. At the entry level are packages like Easy Inventory that supply all the basics in an easy-to-use format. If your business is a startup, it's especially important to try out a range of inventory control products so you know what you want in this software as well as what you and your employees feel most comfortable with. Shareware gives you that opportunity in a way that commercial software doesn't.

DAYO Inventory

DAYO Inventory is a total inventory control system from TSJ Lab, the maker of a full line of wonderfully designed accounting software programs, all of which are sold as shareware. DAYO Inventory neatly ties together inventory tracking, vendor entry, receiving, and purchase order generation. There's absolutely no inventory information you'll need to store that DAYO can't handle in its default record structure. For instance, the inventory item record lets you store six different prices for volume discounts. Like any good inventory system, DAYO allows you to record a minimum on-hand quantity, but it also lets you store a maximum quantity. The records for vendors and purchase orders are equally complete (a sample purchase order is shown in Figure 20-1). DAYO offers 17 reports, including ones for purchase orders (the whole purchase order, or just the headers), inventory adjustments, inventory reorders, and a neat little bar graph of your top 10 vendors.

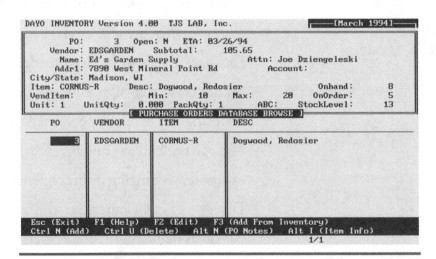

Figure 20-1 Entering a purchase order in DAYO Inventory is easy

One of the most attractive features of DAYO Inventory is that it can share data with the other DAYO accounting packages, which have a similarly complete line of features. (See Chapter 13 for more information about DAYO products.) DAYO Inventory tracks your inventory from purchase orders through receiving. TSJ Labs also markets a sales module that links in nicely with the inventory software.

One unique feature of DAYO Inventory is the capability of direct access to the database tables. DAYO Inventory data tables are dBASE compatible, so you can import and export data easily between DAYO Inventory and other leading software products. The program includes a host of utilities and features for working directly with the DAYO Inventory data. You can browse the data itself, export it, and even change the lengths of the fields in the files.

Other important features include the ability to look up and add vendors and inventory items from the purchase order entry screen. DAYO Inventory works on all major networks.

TSJ Lab, Inc.
P.O. Box 585366
Orlando, FL 32858
Phone: 407/292-4708
CompuServe ID: 76367,1401
Price: $95
Online filename: DAYOIE.EXE

Easy Inventory

Just like the name implies, Easy Inventory is an extremely easy inventory system to set up and use. While not as comprehensive as DAYO Inventory, Easy Inventory is also not quite as complicated. We were able to get Easy Inventory up and running reports in about five minutes—try that with a commercial package!

The program has five sections: purchases, sales, inventory, locations, and suppliers, with the ability to generate reports on all these things. Data entry screens make extensive use of functions keys and lookup tables. We found the interface to be very intuitive and were able to enter inventory items and suppliers (as shown in Figure 20-2), generate purchase and sales transactions (which in turn affect the inventory items), and generate period sales reports without ever referring to the manual.

```
                        INVENTORY ITEMS
      CORNUS-R          Dogwood, Redosier              1

                        INVENTORY ITEM
                     Record will be Changed

      Number         CORNUS-R
      Description    Dogwood, Redosier        Unit       1
      Price              12.950               Location  DOTY ST

      On hand        11.0000   Total Cost       96.71      8.7917  1
      On order        0.0000   Minimum          15.0000
      Supplier   EDNURS        Last Cost         9.250

                     PERIOD                         TO DATE

      PURCHASES     5.0000   $      46.25      5.0000   $      46.25

      SALES         7.0000   $      90.65      7.0000   $      90.65

      COSTS                  $      61.54               $      61.54
```

Figure 20-2   Updating an inventory item with Easy Inventory

It has few bells and whistles (except for a screen saver program), but all the basics are there. If your inventory control needs are simple and you want a program that's easy to set up and use, Easy Inventory is the one for you.

I. J. Smith
9795 Rustling Oaks
Baton Rouge, LA 70818
Price: $35
Online filename: EASYINV.ZIP

Inventory Control Program

Inventory Control Program is a complete and fully configurable inventory system that includes sections for tracking inventory, purchasing, orders, receiving, and a vendor list. It can be configured to use LIFO, FIFO, or a weighted average for item costing. It can be set up to track inventory at multiple locations. For security reasons, you can configure it in a read-only mode.

The menus are a little terse, but that allows you to speed through them faster once you get to know what they're all about. For example, there's an item on the main menu labeled SOR. That takes you into the

Sell-Order-Receive portion of the program. Who but an inventory pro would have guessed it? Obviously, you'll want to read the manual thoroughly before you start entering inventory figures. A sample screen for ordering an inventory item is shown in Figure 20-3.

The nicest feature of Inventory Control is that many of the steps in controlling inventory are automatic: Items that fall below the minimum on-hand quantity can be automatically added to the purchase order report, all items on a purchase order can be automatically added to inventory, and so on. Another pleasant feature is that you can preview many of the reports on your PC screen before sending them to the printer. The program will also send reports to a file that you can pull up in a word processor later on.

Spirit7 Software, Ltd.
P.O. Box 777
Waynesboro, VA 22980
Phone: 703/943-4635
Price: $65
Online filename: ICPxx.ZIP

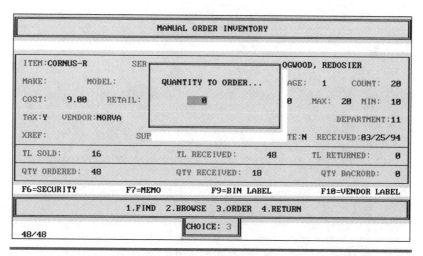

Figure 20-3   This is how you set up an order for an inventory item in Inventory Control

PC-Inventory

PC-Inventory is a simple, easy-to-use inventory control system ideal for the budding retail entrepreneur. All activities in PC-Inventory center around entries for an inventory item. There are no sales, purchase order, or vendor records to keep track of. Sales, for example, are entered by modifying the item record and updating the stock portion of the record. To indicate that you've sold some items you simply update the quantity on hand and the quantity sold fields, as shown in Figure 20-4. The new values you enter will be reflected in PC-Inventory's reports.

PC-Inventory doesn't print purchase orders or vendor listings. It *does* print a sales report and a list of items for which the quantity on hand is low. PC-Inventory's main selling point is its simplicity. To some degree it achieves this by leaving out some major features.

If you're running a large company with thousands of items and dozens of employees, PC-Inventory is not for you. If you're just getting started and you just want to make sure that you're not selling stuff for less than what you paid, PC-Inventory might work just fine for you.

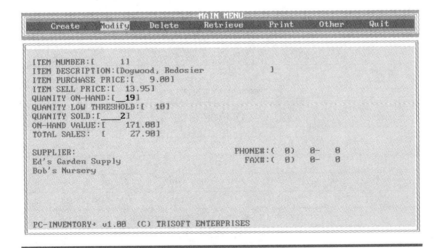

Figure 20-4 Updating the quantity of an item on hand in PC-Inventory

Trisoft Enterprises
5666 Hamstead Crossing Dr.
Raleigh, NC 27612
Price: $25 (plus $10 for disks)
Online filename: PCINV.ZIP

SPC Inventory

SPC Inventory is a product by the same folks who created Easy Inventory, described above. SPC Inventory has many of the features of commercial inventory systems, including the grouping of inventory items based on the first few characters of the item number, and the use of transaction sets for both the purchases and the sales functions, which you post only after you're sure they're correct.

Like Easy Inventory, SPC Inventory has a very intuitive user inter-face. Updating inventory items is easy, as shown in Figure 20-5. The main differences are that SPC Inventory provides for multiple prices to reflect quantity discounts and that it uses the BTRIEVE database, a very fast

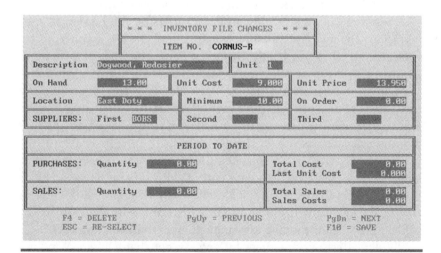

Figure 20-5   You'll never waste time trying to unriddle menus
with the straightforward inventory update ability in
SPC Inventory

and reliable database manipulation utility that's found in many software packages.

SPC Inventory's only fault is that it's a stand-alone product. There is no general ledger or accounts receivable module that you can link it with as you can with DAYO, described previously. It does offer other advantages, though, like the use of BTRIEVE for handling database functions.

I. J. Smith
9795 Rustling Oaks
Baton Rouge, LA 70818
Price: $50
Online filename: SPCINV.ZIP

Track-It

Track-It is full-featured inventory control software that includes inventory tracking, vendor tracking, customer tracking, order entry, receiving, and invoice printing. Data entry is made easy through simple and self-explanatory screens, such as the customer entry screen shown in Figure 20-6. It even lets you run tabs for your customers.

From the sales menu you can enter orders or else head right into invoicing. The inventory menu lets you "clone" entries; in other words, you can copy entries with only the item number changed. This comes in handy if your inventory contains many similar items (or if you stock the same item at different locations). Track-It's many reports include the usual stock report, price list, and reorder report, as well as an overstock report, customer reports sorted by name and zip code, and daily and monthly sales reports.

Track-It's pull-down menus make for a true user-friendly interface. You can click anywhere on a data entry field with your mouse to place the cursor there, or you can double-click on a field and all the text in that field is highlighted. Adding to its ease of use is its ability to accept wildcard characters for inventory item numbers and vendor codes.

If all of this sounds perfect for you, except that you're a Windows user, take heart. Millennium Software has announced that it will soon be releasing a Windows version of Track-It.

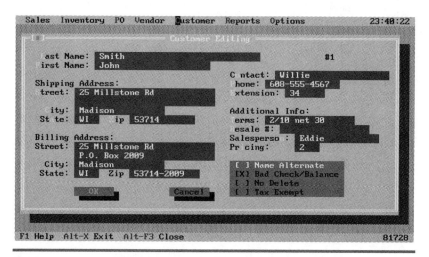

Figure 20-6   Use Track-It to track customers and their orders, then print a variety of sales reports tracking daily and monthly sales

Millennium Software
P.O. Box 2209
Dublin, CA 94568
Phone: 510/828-5892
BBS: 510/828-4153
CompuServe ID: 72560,2466
Price: $149 plus $5 shipping
Online filename: TRKIT309.ZIP

ADMINISTRATION AND GENERAL MANAGEMENT

5

CHAPTER 21

FORM TEMPLATES AND GENERATORS TO MAKE YOUR BUSINESS LOOK GOOD

ust as clothes don't make the man (despite the old saying), forms don't make the business—but both can go a long way towards making a good impression. Whether they're for receipts, purchase orders, or "While You Were Out" notes, nicely designed forms can make you look good, as well as go miles in keeping you organized. Take invoices, for example. Think of how many times you've spotted one of those dull, gray-lined invoices ripped from a cheap office store pad and thought to yourself that it must be from a home business. Why spend big bucks for custom pre-printed forms, especially if you run a small company, when you can use your PC and laser printer to print your own for much less?

These days, many word processors like Microsoft Word 6.0 come with form wizards that generate forms for you, but they run unpardonably slow on PCs that have an internal processor slower than that of a 486 (they'll run snail-like on a 386, and probably won't even run on a 286). Plus, creating new forms and automating their use is not exactly intuitive. Shareware offers some easy solutions for those who'd rather not tussle with a slow and obtuse word processor forms generator, but still want professional-looking forms. You'll even find pre-designed legal forms available as shareware, including rental leases and conditions of credit. Both lawyers and business people alike will find them extremely useful in helping to get everything in writing.

Form Generators and General Business Forms

It's easy to create customized business and legal forms on your PC with the following shareware programs. Use their paint program-like features to draw lines, boxes, and even checkboxes. Add your own text, and voila! You have your own business forms. You can create custom invoices, work orders, even accounting record forms. You can fill them in on your PC, or print them out on a dot-matrix or laser printer so that employees can fill them out by hand. If you don't want to design your own forms from scratch, use the templates or pre-designed forms that come with some of the packages. You can use them as-is or customize them to your needs.

Dr. Form

DOS

As a business form generator, Dr. Form is a bit more basic in features than some of the other form generators discussed in this chapter. But it does give you a dazzling screen with simple menu choices through which you can create forms. Plus, it includes built-in features for filling out the forms on your PC screen. What it doesn't offer are half-tone screens or a selection of fonts. But, if you need an easy-to-use program that will help you quickly create a simple invoice, look no further!

To create a form, you begin by telling Dr. Form what size you want the form to be, issuing commands via keyboard or mouse as in Figure 21-1. You can draw single lines or double ones. An erase function lets you remove any mistakes. When you enter text, it can be double-width, italic, double-height, condensed, bold, underlined, superscript, or subscript.

You can move your check boxes around the page with the move command, create columns, or fill an area with any character you want. If you want to create a form that's a list of small check boxes, create your check box and then use the copy command to regenerate it. Dr. Form comes with form templates, one of which is shown in Figure 21-2, that you can modify to create your own forms. You can start filling in forms immediately after you create them with the Fill-In-a-Form option.

Dr. Form comes with pre-designed forms that include an 80-column daily planner, an order form, a weekly schedule, a contract template, a template for Federal Express air bills, a purchase order, a sales order, a monthly planner, a salary review form, and a service invoice. When you register the program you get 50 more forms. Dr. Form works with a wide variety of printers including six varieties of Epson printers, Deskjets, HP LaserJets, Paint Jets, and five different IBM printers.

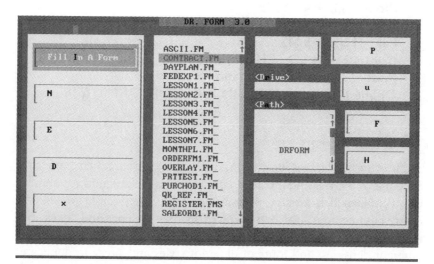

Figure 21-1 This is where you start when creating a form with Dr. Form

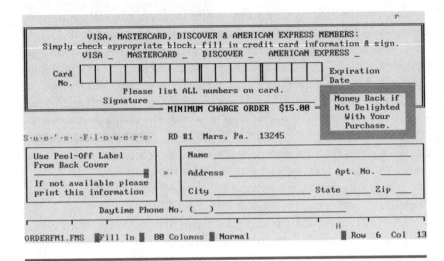

Figure 21-2 This is one of the pre-made forms that comes with Dr. Form

IrwinWare
113 Beechmont Ave.
Pittsburgh, PA 15229
Phone: 412/ 931-9577 or 800/242-4775 (orders only)
Fax: 412/931-8442
CompuServe I.D.: 71045,222
Price: $39 plus shipping and handling
Online filename: DRFORM.ZIP or DRFORM31.ZIP

FormGen II

DOS

If you want fancier effects and don't mind working a bit harder to generate your forms and invoices, FormGen II is the program you should use. FormGen II is a paint program-like form generator in which you create business forms, such as invoices, by drawing lines and boxes and typing in text. You can create forms with half-tone screens, lines of different densities, and fonts of different styles and sizes. To duplicate segments of the screen, you mark blocks of the form with a mouse and copy and move them. Blocks can be moved and text inserted wherever you want in the form. Figure 21-3 shows an invoice being created in

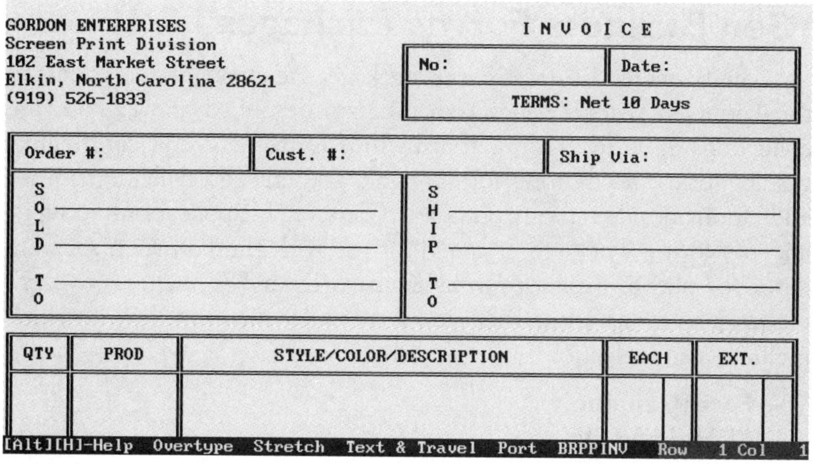

```
GORDON ENTERPRISES                              I N V O I C E
Screen Print Division
102 East Market Street         ┌──────────────┬──────────────┐
Elkin, North Carolina 28621    │ No:          │ Date:        │
(919) 526-1833                 ├──────────────┴──────────────┤
                               │      TERMS: Net 10 Days     │
                               └─────────────────────────────┘

┌─────────────────────┬────────────────────┬──────────────────┐
│ Order #:            │ Cust. #:           │ Ship Via:        │
├─────────────────────┴──────────┬─────────┴──────────────────┤
│ S                              │ S                          │
│ O  _____           │ H  _____       │
│ L  _____           │ I  _____       │
│ D  _____           │ P  _____       │
│                                │                            │
│ T  _____           │ T  _____       │
│ O                              │ O                          │
├──────┬───────┬─────────────────┴──────┬─────────┬───────────┤
│ QTY  │ PROD  │ STYLE/COLOR/DESCRIPTION │  EACH   │   EXT.    │
├──────┼───────┼────────────────────────┼─────────┼───────────┤
│      │       │                        │         │           │
└──────┴───────┴────────────────────────┴─────────┴───────────┘
[Alt][H]-Help  Overtype  Stretch  Text & Travel  Port  BRPPINV   Row   1 Col   1
```

Figure 21-3   An invoice in FormGen II

FormGen II. Other forms included are fax cover sheets, message forms, ledger forms, and invoicing and mileage record forms.

To fill in forms on your PC screen, you should ideally use the $49 FormGen Fill program described below. However, you can easily export forms to ASCII format and fill them in in any word processor, but you'll lose some of the printing effects. You don't need FormGen Fill to print out forms. FormGen supports a wide variety of laser and dot-matrix printers. It's not surprising that it's become one of the most popular form drawing software packages in the world. FormGen's vendor markets other variations of this package, so contact the company before you send in your money.

FormGen, Inc.
11 Holland Dr.
Bolton, Ontario
Canada L7E1G7
Phone: 905/857-4141
Fax: 905/857-4531
Price: $49
Online filename: FORM.ZIP

FormGen Business Forms Packages I & II

The FormGen Business Forms Packages are companion products to the FormGen II form generation program described above. Both are collections of business forms that include forms for credit card billing, cashier forms, accounting forms, bank account reconciliation forms, audit forms, accident forms, purchase orders, credit applications, receipts, and pay forms. They are designed for use with the FormGen software described above. Business Forms Package II for $89 includes over 70 predesigned forms, while Package I is a smaller subset for $49.95 which includes just a selection.

FormGen, Inc.
11 Holland Dr.
Bolton, Ontario
Canada L7E1G7
Phone: 905/857-4141
Fax: 905/857-4531
Price: Package I $49.95, Package II $89
Online filename: FG-BUSII.ZIP or FG-BUS.ZIP

FormGen Fill

This is another companion product to the FormGen II form generation program described above. You can use this software for quickly filling in business forms designed with FormGen, such as the credit application shown in Figure 21-4. Display the forms on your PC screen and just type the information you want entered. FormGen Fill will not only align your numbers, but also calculate them like a mini-spreadsheet and automatically fill in time and date entries. It will also let you define dollar and decimal entries. Once you're done, just press a key to print.

FormGen, Inc.
11 Holland Dr.
Bolton, Ontario
Canada L7E1G7
Phone: 905/857-4141
Fax: 905/857-4531
Price: $49
Online filename: FGFx-xx.ZIP

```
                         YOUR COMPANY

        ┌─────────────────────────┐  Account #  78902-472
                CREDIT APPLICATION     Date Business Started 06/03/72
        └─────────────────────────┘
        Advertiser: Paul Brown             Phone: · · · · · · · · · · · · · ·

        Agency:     Stanley & Winkleman    Phone: · · · · · · · · · · · · · ·

        Address:

        City/State/Zip: · · · · · · · · · · · · · · · · · · · · · · · · · · · · · · · · · · · ·

                    Names of Owners, Partners or Officers
FormGen Fill   [F10]-Print   [Alt][X]-Exit                   Row  18 Col  15
```

Figure 21-4   Filling out a credit application in FormGen Fill

PCForm

PCForm lets you create custom business forms, just as with FormGen, but what makes it unique is that it lets you organize your forms into a catalog that's easy to search and reference. It's also a whole bunch cheaper than FormGen, and just as good in the effects that it lets you create. To load a form all you need to do is pick its name from a list and the form appears, as shown in Figure 21-5. Use PCForm's pull-down menus to create forms with full capability to cut, paste, copy, and move screen segments. PCForm prompts you for input when it needs information you've forgotten to enter.

CareWare
307 Gracie Rd.
Nevada City, CA 95959
Phone: 916/265-8704
Price: $25
Online filename: PCFxxx.ZIP

307

Frm: DAILYAPP.FRM Pth: C:		Dir:	Sub:	Pg 1 of 1 PCForm

```
>>>>>>>>>>>>>>>>>>>>>>>    Daily  Appointments    <<<<<<<<<<<<<<<<<<<<<<<<
```

For			Date	

Time	Morning	Time	Afternoon
6:00		12:00	Lunch with Andrew B.
6:15		12:15	-----
6:30		12:30	-----
6:45		12:45	-----
7:00		1:00	-----
7:15		1:15	-----
7:30	Drive Sue to Dentist	1:30	Appointment with Xargon Cor.

```
Alt+ Sgle Dble Char Again Line Box Undo Menu Title Ruler Help      11   R:22 C:47
```

Figure 21-5 An appointment form designed in PCForm

PC-Forms

DOS

PC-Forms stores boilerplate text that's used again and again in legal and business documents and provides an easy way to import text from major word processors, like WordPerfect and Microsoft Word. When you load the program, PC-Forms lists the forms that are available to you (a menu of the corporate form library is shown in Figure 21-6). You choose one, or create a form of your own, then add to it the associated boilerplate text. You can tell PC-Forms to prompt you for things like names and addresses to include in the text.

If you link PC-Forms to your word processor, any completed PC-Forms documents will be loaded into the word processor. PC-Forms relies on plain ASCII text, so you'll have to go through some machinations to format it in your word processor the way you want. Authored by a retired Texas lawyer, PC-Forms comes with a special library of boilerplate text for legal documents. It's a very popular program.

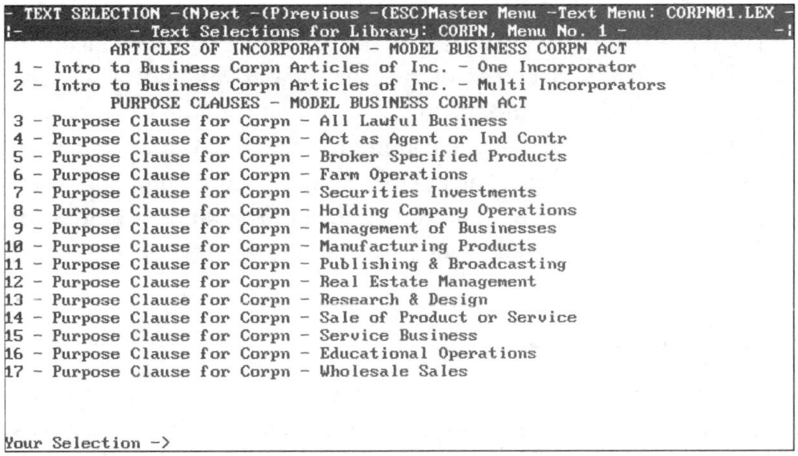

```
- TEXT SELECTION -(N)ext -(P)revious -(ESC)Master Menu -Text Menu: CORPN01.LEX -
:-        - Text Selections for Library: CORPN, Menu No. 1 -          -:
            ARTICLES OF INCORPORATION - MODEL BUSINESS CORPN ACT
 1 - Intro to Business Corpn Articles of Inc. - One Incorporator
 2 - Intro to Business Corpn Articles of Inc. - Multi Incorporators
            PURPOSE CLAUSES - MODEL BUSINESS CORPN ACT
 3 - Purpose Clause for Corpn - All Lawful Business
 4 - Purpose Clause for Corpn - Act as Agent or Ind Contr
 5 - Purpose Clause for Corpn - Broker Specified Products
 6 - Purpose Clause for Corpn - Farm Operations
 7 - Purpose Clause for Corpn - Securities Investments
 8 - Purpose Clause for Corpn - Holding Company Operations
 9 - Purpose Clause for Corpn - Management of Businesses
10 - Purpose Clause for Corpn - Manufacturing Products
11 - Purpose Clause for Corpn - Publishing & Broadcasting
12 - Purpose Clause for Corpn - Real Estate Management
13 - Purpose Clause for Corpn - Research & Design
14 - Purpose Clause for Corpn - Sale of Product or Service
15 - Purpose Clause for Corpn - Service Business
16 - Purpose Clause for Corpn - Educational Operations
17 - Purpose Clause for Corpn - Wholesale Sales


Your Selection ->
```

Figure 21-6 The menu of the corporate form library in PC-Forms

William W. Blackledge
The Warwick, #151
2400 Arrowhead Dr.
Abilene, TX 79606
Phone: 915/692-9105
Price: $35
Online filename: PCFMS1.EXE, PCFMS2.EXE, and
PCFMS3.EXE

Legal Forms and Templates

Law firms often pay thousands of dollars to rent collections of legal forms that they can use with their word processing software. These forms contain boilerplate text for things like pleadings, wording in wills, and standard paragraphs in contracts. There are many legal forms that are available as shareware—or can even be downloaded and used for free. Of course, these forms must often be customized to comply with the statutes of specific states, but the overall wording is often fairly generic and since the forms are in ASCII it's easy to customize them. They can be used with any word processor.

Legal forms are also invaluable to businesses. For instance, if you're a landlord, you'll find copies of standard leases and rental renewal agreements available online for free. If you grant credit to customers, you'll find forms spelling out the conditions of credit. While we'd never suggest that you go without the advice of an attorney completely, these forms will, at the very least, give you an idea of the kinds of things you need to get in writing to help your business run smoothly.

LegalDOC

This collection of over a hundred commonly used legal form letters is free. You'll find forms for powers of attorney, lease renewal agreements, libel releases, affidavits of no lien, equipment maintenance agreements, bills of sale, letters of credit, and lots more. The forms can be used in any word processor since they're written in ASCII text. All you need to do is insert the particulars in the blanks. Business owners will find legal forms of interest in here to help them draft out forms like rental agreements.

Online filename: LGLDOC.COM

Legal Forms

Here's another free collection of over a hundred commonly used legal forms and letters, from photo releases and releases for minors, to employment agreements, escrow receipts, and bids for purchase of property. The business owner will probably find more forms here than in any other similar collection to handle minor legal matters like issuing credit and selling or purchasing property. As with LegalDOC, these forms are all in ASCII text and can be used in any word processor.

Online filename: LEGAL.LZH

PC-Forms Legal Forms

Use this collection of over fifty common basic legal forms covering titles, sales, wills, licenses, and settlements with the PC-Forms Document

Assembly System reviewed in the section "Form Generators and General Business Forms" earlier in this chapter.

William W. Blackledge
The Warwick, #151
2400 Arrowhead Dr.
Abilene, TX 79606
Phone: 915/692-9105
Price: Free if you register PC-Forms
Online filename: PCFMS2.ZIP

Legal Eagle

Legal Eagle is a collection of over 600 legal forms designed for non-lawyers. They include promissory notes, notices of default, notices of delinquent accounts being turned over to a collection agency, and much more that a small business owner will find useful. They can be displayed with Windows Write, the word processor that's built into Windows. Sorry, no other word processor is supported.

Eagle Software
Rt. 1, Box 121
Washington, NC 27889
Phone: 800/447-5757 (orders only)
CompuServe I.D.: 71355,470
Price: $39.95
Online filename: EAGLEPAK.EXE

CHAPTER 22

PERSONAL AND PROJECT SCHEDULERS TO PLAN EVERY DETAIL OF YOUR BUSY LIFE

Americans are obsessed with scheduling. We schedule our work days as rigorously as a Marine drill, and even our free time is often held to the mercy of plans scribbled on a calendar. Maybe it all started when Dr. Spock advised new mothers to hold their infants to strict eating and napping schedules. In the computer world, you will find no end to software schedulers. The most popular type of schedulers are personal information managers, or PIMs.

Think of a personal information manager, or PIM, as an electronic Filofax. You store all the bits of information in it that a business executive of yore would carry in his spiral-ring day-planner: reminders of appointments, a tiny calendar, phone messages, phone numbers, notes about meetings, a notepad perhaps, and even an inspirational quote or two. PIM software takes all these functions and gives them an electronic spin. In addition to built-in address books and scheduling calendars, PIMs include pop-up calculators, reminders, envelope printers, and links to your spreadsheet and word-processing software. You can even dial phone numbers by clicking your mouse on a number in their pop-up phone book.

Some PIM programs link your phone book entries to calendar and notebook functions so that you can see at a glance all your appointments, past and future, with a particular client and note what you discussed. Other PIMs help you prioritize your day's activities, even taking into account your long-range goals. Some PIMs are good at scheduling. They'll help you block off the time you need to accomplish certain chores and make sure that you don't overbook yourself. Still other PIMs excel at keeping track of those random bits of information—client phone numbers, items you've promised to follow-up on, things you need to remind yourself of each day, and gems of inspiration.

There's a shareware PIM described in this chapter for every one of these functions. We'll tell you about one, which is used by dozens of Fortune 500 companies on their office networks, that can scan the personal schedules of everyone in the office and find the best time slots to schedule meetings. We'll tell you about another that was designed by the Franklin Day Book people to help busy executives manage their limited time resources and make sure they accomplish their life's ambitions.

Project planners are another popular scheduler. They help you juggle the myriad of details of a project, from the deadlines to the employees to the supplies. Use them to track simple projects or labyrinthine ones. One of the planners we've included lets you track the work of hundreds of employees as well as manage all the tangible and intangible resources (like time and labor) that the project requires. Most people expect project trackers to be some sort of database software with Rolodex-like records that you riffle through. That's not the case. Think of project trackers as EKG machines that record the heart beats, the breaths, and the stutters of your project as it progresses to completion. Some are like project diaries and scheduling calendars built into one. They're also highly visual in nature, with charts that let you zero in on deadlines and tasks that need to be completed. Commercial project planners run from around $300 up to several thousand dollars. Most of our shareware ones cost about $30 and offer comparable functionality to the commercial ones. Some even let you organize projects with Gantt charts which let you plot activities in a time-line fashion together with their relation to other steps in the project. Once you use one of these packages, you'll wonder how the pyramids were built without them.

Personal Information Managers

If you log on to information services like America Online and CompuServe you'll find that some of the most impassioned online debates among business PC users concern PIMs. Everyone has a favorite. The choice of a PIM program is as personal a decision as the choice of a briefcase. The market leaders among commercial software packages include PackRat, Lotus Agenda, and Instant Recall. But in these discussions the names of many of the shareware packages listed in this chapter pop up with equal frequency. Naturally, all the best PIM software requires Windows because Windows' graphical interface lends itself well to the layering of reminders, notes, and schedules on the screen. If you don't have Windows and you plan to use a PIM, by all means get yourself a copy of Windows. When you get a look at these programs you'll see why PIMs have become one of the most popular high-tech tools in the office.

Time & Chaos

Windows

Here's a personal information manager that includes all the essentials of a phone and address book, a multi-view calendar, daily schedules and to-do lists, and a notepad. Locating information in Time & Chaos is a snap because everything fits on the screen, as you can see in Figure 22-1. You can also easily click between elements and find the data you need.

Time & Chaos includes dynamic links between its elements that makes it an especially powerful PIM. For instance, open the address book and click on a person's name and you can pull up a list of appointments with that individual as well as notes on their outcome. Or you can link your to-do list to appointments and names. You can also link data to Excel spreadsheets or to your word processor. For instance, when you write a

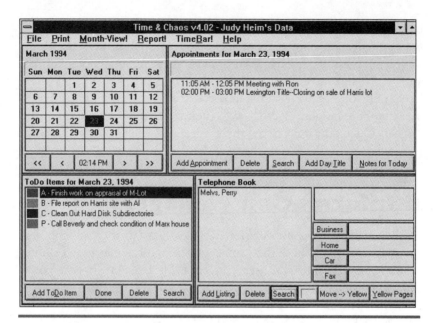

Figure 22-1   With its simple format, Time & Chaos brings order to numbers, names, and notes

letter in your favorite word processor, simply pull the address out of the Time & Chaos address book with but a few mouse clicks for use in the letter. Time & Chaos will also print the envelope for you. You can also import and export ASCII data so that you can use any information stored in the program with other applications.

The calendar lets you view your schedule in daily, weekly, monthly, and yearly allotments. New appointments are easy to enter; this is not a PIM you're going to have to devote a Saturday afternoon to learning how to use. The telephone and address book is nicely designed, with slots in which you can enter business, home, car, and fax phone numbers—most PIMs just give you one telephone number slot in each entry. You can use the phone book to dial voice calls or shuffle phone numbers off to your fax software.

When you create your to-do list, you can rank items as Important, Critical, Work It In, and Pending. This is a much more realistic ranking system than what some PIMs give you, requiring you to rank items on a scale of 1 to 10 in importance and making your day into a bureaucratic headache before you even start it. The program uses a unique Rolodex card-like format for storing and displaying information. Shuffling through your address book, notes, and to-do list is like shuffling through a stack of cards on the screen.

You can print out any of the data stored in Time & Chaos. You can also use it to write custom reports on how you spend your time. Time & Chaos gets our vote for the most functional (and fun) PIM for the person in quest of ultimate desktop organization.

**iSBiSTER International
1314 Cardigan St.
Garland, TX 75040
Fax: 214/530-6566
BBS: 214/530-2762
CompuServe ID: 74017,3424
Price: $29.95; $6 for manual
Online filename: TC402P.EXE**

Above & Beyond

Windows

Above & Beyond, which is included on the disks packaged with this book, is one of the most sophisticated time schedulers you'll find among PIM software, either commercial or shareware. While Time & Chaos is ideal for the individual, Above & Beyond is the sort of thing you give to everyone in your office. Then, teach your assistants to use it so that they can juggle schedules, plan meetings, and keep projects moving smoothly. It's used by an impressive list of Fortune 500 companies, investment firms, and government agencies, including NASA, Hewlett-Packard, Arthur Anderson, Kidder Peabody, Siemens AG, Merrill Lynch, and DuPont.

While Above & Beyond includes a pop-up calculator, a phone book (a very simple one with a single entry for phone numbers), a notepad feature, and the ability to print reports, the program's heart is its scheduling and time management features, as you can see in Figure 22-2. Type in the name of an appointment or chore, then move it around on the calendar with your mouse to the desired day and time slot. Above & Beyond will automatically juggle the other items on your schedule, ask you how much time you plan to spend on the task, and make sure you don't overextend yourself on the calendar.

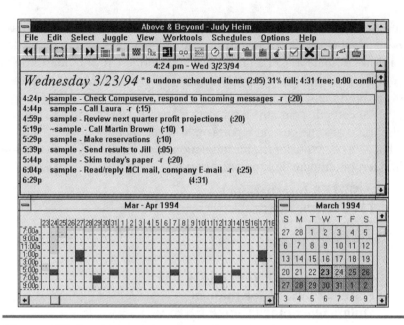

Figure 22-2   Above & Beyond will check other employees'
schedulers for meeting conflicts

Like other PIMs, it lets you see your week-at-a-glance and month-at-a-glance. It also includes a priority list, but it doesn't include a to-do list. Above & Beyond, its documentation explains, doesn't believe in to-do lists. It prefers to give you a more realistic approach, organizing chores by priority and the amount of time you have.

Above & Beyond has some amazing workgroup features. For instance, if you install it on an office network (you don't have to, but you can), you can use its Meeting Maker to scan the schedules of other Above & Beyond users on the network, locate time slots when everyone—or at least a majority of people—are available, and adjust everyone's computerized schedules accordingly to plan the meeting. Assistants can use it to post e-mail and phone messages into notes in the schedules of busy executives. They can also check the status of projects. Password protection ensures that even on a company network you afford access to your schedule only to the people you want to have access to it.

Shareware in Action

Product: Above & Beyond
Company: Bausch & Lomb

At the corporate headquarters of Bausch & Lomb, network administrator Lee Stoddard has used Above & Beyond for more than two years. He and the 35 or so other people on his file server use Above & Beyond to manage their time and tasks. They consult their colleagues' calendars to schedule meetings and meeting rooms and consult their own calendars to see where they stand in completing their tasks. Stoddard also uses Above & Beyond to schedule and run backfiles when performing system maintenance; a backfile runs and then is automatically crossed off the list so he knows it is completed. He also uses Above & Beyond to see how much space he has left on volumes.

Other programs Stoddard looked at were too full of features and relied on to-do lists. "I'm not a to-do list person," he said. He prefers Above & Beyond's pop-up memos. He also likes the way the program lets him append notes to items, bring items forward, and check his log to see whether a task has been completed. Another that appealed to Stoddard was Above & Beyond's warning feature: "If a meeting was scheduled for 8 o'clock and I show up at the office at 9 o'clock, the program beeps as soon as I turn it on to tell me that I missed the meeting. The program also tells me if my schedule is full." His favorite description of the program, though, is a single word: "simple"—which, for managing a busy person's schedule, is exactly what such a program should be.

This is an absolutely dazzling program. Anyone who needs to coordinate their day with the schedules of lots of other busy people will love it.

1Soft Corp.
P.O. Box 1320
Middleton, CA 95461
Phone: 707/987-0256
Fax: 707/987-3150
Price: $99
Online filename: AB.ZIP

Ascend

Ascend is a personal information manager of a slightly different bent. It organizes your phone numbers and schedule, but it's designed primarily to keep you focused on your goals, short-term as well as life-long ones. It's a product of time management specialist Franklin Quest Co., creator of the Franklin Day Planner with its trademark red tabs on the pages. Ascend's central asset, according to the literature, is its pyramid icon, as shown in Figure 22-3. Click on it and the program will display a list of Values and Goals: what you want to accomplish today, this week, this year, in this lifetime. Ascend asks you to assign numeric values to your daily tasks indicating the degree they help you reach these goals. It then helps you design your day's schedule as effectively as possible.

Other things you will find in this program that you won't find elsewhere include an icon you can click on to display your favorite inspirational quotes. Click on the Focus icon and Ascend will display the name of the highest priority list task for the day—to keep you focused. Click on the Turbo File icon and you can store e-mail, stories, and articles that don't as yet belong to any file folder or project, but that you just want to save for curiosity's sake. Click on the clever Back Burner icon and you'll get a list a things you want to do someday—you know, all those

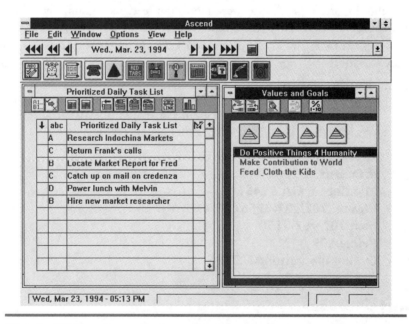

Figure 22-3   Ascend helps prioritize your day's activities to meet long-term goals

projects you put off for retirement or a two-month lull in work. Doing this can certainly give one food for thought. There's also a journal for recording your day's thoughts and activities in Doogie Howser, M.D.-fashion.

Ascend has many of the features of other PIMs, including an appointment scheduler, an address book, and a daily to-do list. It also runs on office networks. But you won't use the program just for those features. This is a program to help prioritize the often jumbled state of our affairs according to the things that are really important to each of us.

Franklin Quest Co.
2550 S. Decker Lake Blvd.
Salt Lake City, UT 84119
Phone: 800/877-1814 or 801/975-9992
Fax: 801/975-9995
Price: $149.95
Online filename: ASCNEV.ZIP

Almanac

Windows

Almanac is a delightful scheduler with a built-in phone book, a to-do list, and a notepad. This is a personal information manager for someone who wants nothing but the basics. You can tile or arrange your calendar, phone book, and other accessories on the screen and click between them, as shown in Figure 22-4. Click on the Day View option for a list of the day's appointments—what time they start, what time they end. Or click on the Month View for the month at a glance. You can also bring up a year's calendar, although without, mercifully, all your appointments added to it.

The to-do list lets you rank projects by Should Be Complete, Must Be Complete, and Would Be Nice. You set the date for when they should be done. The phone book lets you store office phone, fax, and addresses. It's a rudimentary phone book, but you can copy the items to Windows' clipboard for inclusion in other documents, like word processing ones.

Impact Software
12140 Central Ave., Suite 133
Chino, CA 91710
Phone: 909/590-8522
BBS: 909/590-0500
Price: $49.95 plus $2 shipping
Online filename: ALMxxx.ZIP

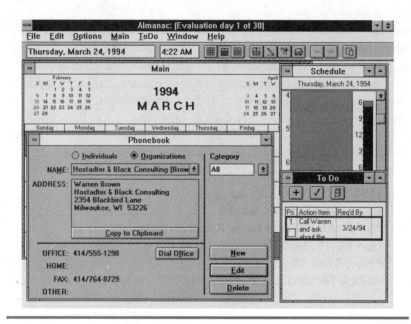

Figure 22-4   Almanac organizes personal information in a
simple, easy to search format

TickleX

DOS

Here's an old-time shareware favorite for DOS users. TickleX is a
personal scheduler with the ability to set schedules for other employees
too—up to 200. It's a personal reminder program (or *tickler* program, the
term has now become generic) with the ability to serve double-duty as a
project scheduler.

As a scheduler, its capabilities are not as whiz-bang, and its interface
not as glossy as its Windows peers, but it is highly functional nonetheless.
It will keep your appointments, beep reminders for you to do things, keep
notes, and attack your day with a to-do list. It can also link recurring
events like appointments with particular projects.

Its abilities to organize projects and deadlines will prove invaluable
in tackling Cecil B. deMille-scale productions. You can assign employees
to tasks, give them deadlines, track their progress, and even keep a
schedule of their trips and vacations so you'll know when key people will
be out of town.

This program has lots of hidden goodies, like a city time table so that you'll always know the local time of the business associate you're calling long-distance. You can password protect TickleX so that employees can access only their schedules and no one else's. TickleX can also log personal expenses for tax purposes and run automatic backups of its data.

> **Integra Computing**
> **910 Cobb Place Manor Dr.**
> **Marietta, GA 30066**
> **Phone: 404/426-5735**
> **Price: $60**
> **Online filename: TICKLE.ZIP (note: you may find lots of files named TICKLE.ZIP, since "tickler" has become a generic term for a reminder program)**

Appointment Book

Keep track of the day's appointments in your office with this elegantly simple appointment book which can track the day's appointments for up to ten staff members in each of its folders. Search appointments by patient, doctor, day, time, and other variables. Hit a function key for the day's appointments at a glance, or yesterday's or tomorrow's. You can also bring up a chart that will graphically display the day's appointment activity and any open time slots. Appointments can be scheduled in ten-minute increments.

> **Silicon Systems**
> **5217 Millsprings Dr.**
> **Arlington, TX 76017**
> **Price: $50**
> **Online filename: APT.EXE or APPTBO.ZIP**

Project Planners and Trackers

Whether your project is one that requires the man-hours of one of the Seven Wonders of the World or is one more humble in scope, such as leading a team to research a new market, project planning software can be an invaluable ally. It will help you break tasks down into small do-able segments, then allocate the time, employees, and funds needed to accomplish them. You can track your project's progress through schematics or Gantt charts, which depict a project's progress in relation to time by plotting events, the time required to complete them, and their relation to other events. If your project veers off-course, you'll be able to spot it. If it goes over budget or requires more employee hours, you'll be the first to know.

We've sorted through over a dozen shareware project managers and come up with the three prize-winners. What impresses us the most about this category of shareware is that the prices of the products are so low (usually around $30), and the packages do so much.

A Project/Event Planner (APLANR)

A Project/Event Planner or APLANR is our favorite project planner. You can devise schedules for complex projects that require hundreds of jobs or events. Unlike the other shareware packages we've looked at, APLANR lets you assign several resources, like employees and funding, to a single event, as shown in Figure 22-5. You can have APLANR divide

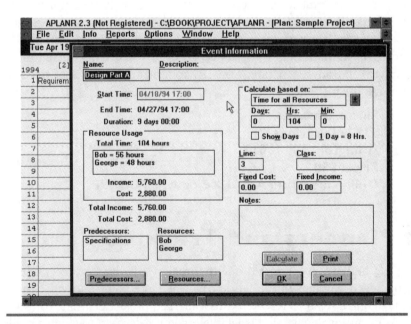

Figure 22-5   APLANR lets you schedule tasks for multiple employees and resources

the workload between resources. You can assign each resource its own work calendar, so if the resource is an employee, for example, you could exclude from the calendar evenings and weekends.

You can specify that the length of the task is its duration, or the amount of time you have available for all resources, or the length of available time for individual resources. You would specify *duration* for fixed-length events, like waiting for a part to be delivered. You would use *time-for-all resources* for tasks that would be speeded up if they were given more resources, such as man-hours. APLANR would take the amount of time you allocated for the job and divide it between the people assigned to it. You would use *time-for-each-resource* for projects that include tasks like training; assigning more people to a training program doesn't shorten or lengthen its duration, but the total number of hours worked is increased.

If this seems to you extremely technical, fear not. APLANR gives you an easy way to plan complex jobs that require great investments of man-hours, time, and tangible resources. It gives you a nice drag-and-drop interface. A box on the schedule represents each event. Lengthening the time that a task will require for completion is as easy as clicking on the right edge of the box and dragging it to the right. A status window at the top of the screen informs you of the new length of the event. The Windows environment makes your planning very visual, with a schematic-like view, as you can see in Figure 22-6. It's easy to see if your project is on track and staying within its budget. At $29, this is a bargain that can't be beat. We've included it on the disks packaged with this book because we think it's so wonderful.

Sapphire Software, Inc.
6650 Hawaii Kai Dr., Suite 219
Honolulu, HI 96825
Phone: 808/395-5587 (voice)
CompuServe ID: 71223,3653
Price: $29
Online filename: APLANR.ZIP

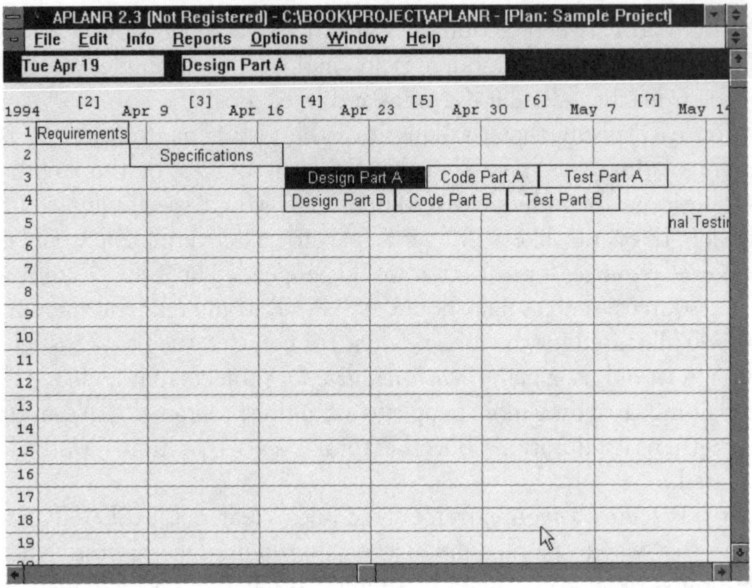

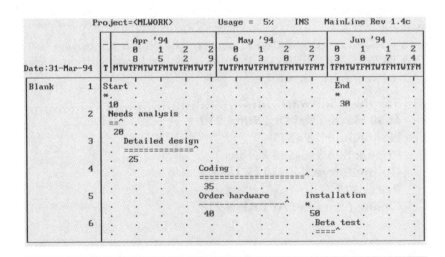

Figure 22-6 A sample project schedule in the highly intuitive and productive APLANR

Figure 22-7 A sample Gantt chart designed in MainLine to track a software design project

Shareware in Action

Product: APLANR
Companies: Special District
Risk Management
Authority and Integra, Inc.

The Special District Risk Management Authority provides risk management services for a variety of California state government agencies. When Stephen Putman, a database developer and LAN administrator at SDRMA, began evaluating project management software, he quickly discovered the benefits of shareware.

"We currently use a well-known commercial scheduler program in our office. However, our company needed software that would allow us to plan projects with a broader, office-wide perspective. Shopping around, I found that I could easily pay $500 for a new scheduler program that had lots of features that we didn't need and wouldn't use. I turned to shareware. I downloaded a few programs from CompuServe and spent a few weeks testing them out. I found that APLANR was everything we needed—high functionality at a cost well below its commercial competitors. Although we'll continue to use a commercial product for personal scheduling, we will use APLANR for our mission-critical office-wide scheduling needs."

For the detailed scheduling, precise allocation of staff and resources, and complex budgeting he requires in writing grant proposals for scientific projects, research scientist Bill McCown of Integra, Inc. also turned to APLANR. This software, says Dr. McCown, "makes it easy to develop the details of time lines and figure costs per hour." Its features, he adds, also make it handy for calculating the cost of value-added products and, for subcontractors, submitting bids. And unlike most commercial products, APLANR is easy to learn. "I had it up and running in a minute and a half," he says. "There was no learning curve."

MainLine

MainLine is a project planner that lets you build a Gantt chart by defining task dependencies and durations in your project, as shown in Figure 22-7. You can specify a start date for a task and, if you specify a task that must precede it, MainLine will calculate the start date for you. MainLine will also calculate the end date if you specify a task's duration.

You can enter task durations in units of days or weeks. You can specify a wait-time before a task is to begin. For instance, if you're designing a software system for a client, and you want to wait a few days after the specifications for the system are finished before ordering the computer hardware, you can depict that in a MainLine chart.

MainLine finds the critical path in your schedule and displays it with double dashed line. Items off the critical path are displayed with single dashed lines.

You can move around easily within charts. For example, there's a key that follows the critical path from one event to the next. The registered version of MainLine contains functions to allow you to re-sequence events. Because MainLine always saves its reports to a disk file, you'll have an extra step in printing them out. However, this does make it easier to pull up a Gantt chart into your word processor.

> **Minuteman Systems**
> **P.O. Box 152**
> **Belmont, MA 02178**
> **Price: $29.95**
> **Online filename: MAINLI.ZIP**

ProTracs Professional Project Management

ProTracs is an extremely simple to use project scheduler. It doesn't do everything the other project managers discussed in this chapter do, but its simplicity puts it in the winner's circle. To enter events into ProTracs' scheduler, all you have to do is enter the information on the screen: a task description, a start date, and an end date, as shown in Figure 22-8. If you also enter task duration, ProTracs will calculate the end date for you. Unfortunately, ProTracs doesn't let you enter conditions, such as requiring that one task finish before another starts, the way you can with the other programs.

You can assign a three-character responsibility code and a single-character priority code to each task. ProTracs displays and prints Gantt charts with the tasks grouped by responsibility code, priority, or chronology, as shown in Figure 22-9. The Gantt charts show the estimated start and end dates with dashed lines and the actual start and end dates with X's.

ProTrac's slickest feature is "Gun Sights." You use this feature to change the estimated start and end dates of a task when you're viewing a Gantt chart on your screen. Press a key and ProTracs gives you a set of cross hairs that you can move around the calendar. Center the gun sights

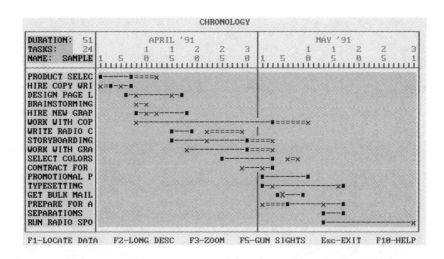

ACT NO.	USER FLD	ACTIVITY DESCRIPTION	PTY CDE	RSP	SCHEDULE START	SCHEDULE END	ACTUAL START	ACTUAL END
-1-	-2-	------3------	-4-	-5-	---6---	---7---	---8---	---9---
1		PRODUCT SELECTION	A	RFS	04/01/91	04/07/91	03/29/91	04/12/91
2		HIRE COPY WRITING FIRM	B	DEM	04/03/91	04/07/91	04/01/91	04/05/91
3		DESIGN PAGE LAYOUTS	A	DEM	04/06/91	04/17/91	04/08/91	04/15/91
4		BRAINSTORMING - SLOGANS	B	DEM	04/08/91	04/10/91	04/08/91	04/10/91
5		STORYBOARDING	A	DR	04/15/91	04/30/91	04/22/91	05/03/91
6		WORK WITH COPY WRITERS	B	RFS	04/08/91	05/03/91	04/08/91	05/10/91
7		HIRE NEW GRAPHIC ARTIST	B	DEM	04/08/91	04/18/91	04/10/91	04/12/91
8		WRITE RADIO COMMERCIALS	A	DEM	04/15/91	04/19/91	04/22/91	04/29/91
9		CONTRACT FOR RADIO SPOTS	A	DEM	04/29/91	05/03/91	04/29/91	05/01/91
10		RUN RADIO SPOTS			05/13/91	05/31/91	05/31/91	
11		PROMOTIONAL PHOTOS	A	RFS	05/01/91	05/18/91		
12		SEPARATIONS	A	RFS	05/13/91	05/17/91		
13		LAYOUT PAGES - GREEKED	B	RFS	05/15/91	05/22/91		

```
MAXIMUM TASKS:    30      SAMPLE                      MARCH '94
CURRENT TASKS:    24                          S    M    T    W    T    F    S
                                                             1    2    3    4    5
F1-FILE           F6-STATUS REPORTS           6    7    8    9    10   11   12
F2-TASK           F7-GANTT CHARTS             13   14   15   16   17   18   19
F3-ADD BELOW      F8-PROJECT DEFINITIONS      20   21   22   23   24   25   26
F4-DEL/UNDEL      F9-DEFAULT DEFINITIONS      27   28   29   30   31
F5-UTILITIES      F10-HELP                                          REL. 1.10
```

Figure 22-8   Schedule tasks and track their progress with ProTracs

Figure 22-9   ProTrac displays a Gantt chart mapping planned accomplishments for each stage of the project on the new estimated end date for a task, press a key and the end date is changed. It's almost as good as playing Castle Wolfenstein 3-D.

Another swell feature is the easy way that ProTracs lets you configure your printer. It displays a table in which you enter your printer's escape codes (found in your printer manual) for things like condensed mode and landscape mode. This ensures flawless printing. ProTracs prints impressive professional-looking reports.

Applied MicroSystems, Inc.
425 Crossville Rd., Suite 101
Roswell, GA 30075
Phone: 404/552-9000
BBS: 404/552-1257
Price: $89.95
Online filename: PROTDEMO.ZIP

CHAPTER 23

SOFTWARE TO KEEP TRACK OF EMPLOYEES AND THEIR NEEDS

n many small businesses, employee work schedules are penciled haphazardly onto a clipboard hanging from the back of a supply closet door. Employee information, like emergency numbers and work history, is often stored in a bedraggled ring-binder in the bottom drawer of someone's desk. Such an arrangement may be serviceable for awhile, but it eventually evolves into chaos. There's no excuse for not computerizing your personnel information and employee schedules, no matter how small a business yours may be. This chapter will introduce you to some excellent scheduling and personnel management software, with an average price of $30.

Medical practices have special employee scheduling needs. The scheduling of patients is directly tied to which personnel, be they doctors or nurses, are working at any given time. There are several shareware products designed specifically for managing medical offices and they include, in addition to straightforward employee scheduling features, calendars to schedule patients and even databases to track insurance billing.

Personnel Schedulers

Scheduling software will line up available employees with the hours you need them to work, plus keep track of vacation and sick leave. One program will tell you the hours when a part-time employee absolutely cannot work (ideal if you employ students). It can even keep track of schedules in multiple departments. There is also a $35 personnel management program in which you can store personal data, like phone numbers and Social Security numbers, plus use to manage employee reviews. Whether you have two employees or 5,000, you can be guaranteed of finding at least one program in this chapter that will help you or your personnel manager more efficiently keep track of employees.

Scheduler 4000

Windows

Scheduler 4000 is a calendar-based program for scheduling employee shifts. You can schedule employees by listing the hours that each employee is working each day so if your business is one in which it doesn't matter who or how many employees are scheduled at any given time, work scheduling can be centered around the employee rather than by the time slots. Or, you can set up time slots and type in the name of the employee who is working each slot if your business is one that, like a restaurant, requires that certain jobs be filled and certain employees be working at certain times. Scheduler 4000 is fairly easy to use. You first define the shifts; for instance, if you're scheduling a help desk where employees work in one-hour shifts, you'd set the shifts to one-hour intervals. You're not limited to scheduling work in regular hourly shifts like you are with most scheduling programs and that gives you a lot of flexibility. You can set up odd schedules as well as change the shifts on a day-to-day basis.

The next step is to assign an employee to each time slot. As you can see in Figure 23-1, Scheduler 4000 gives you a pop-up list of the names of all your employees, so you don't have to type the name each time, just the first time you schedule them. You can also add notes of up to three lines to each of your schedules. Once the day's schedule is complete, you can easily duplicate it, or a particular shift, with a feature that allows copying up to ten days forward. You can print schedules for individual employees, for all employees, for a specific day or month, or up to six selected weeks.

Number Six Productions
1733 13th Ave. S.W.
Calgary, Alberta T3C 0V1
Canada
Price: $20
Online filename: SCED40.ZIP

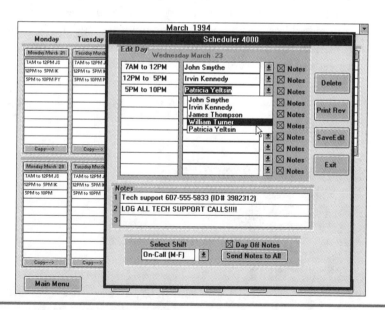

Figure 23-1   Scheduling an employee for a particular time slot in
                   Scheduler 4000

Personnel Supervisor

Personnel Supervisor is just what its name implies: software to help a personnel supervisor manage an employee roster. Use it to record personal information about employees as in Figure 23-2, like date of birth, salary, marital and veteran status, and emergency phone numbers. Keep track of accumulated vacation days, as shown in Figure 23-3. You can track sick leave by entering employee absence records and letting Personnel Supervisor automatically deduct the number of days from the appropriate leave type. You can also keep a log of OSHA-reportable injuries.

You can also use Personnel Supervisor to manage employee reviews. With just a few key strokes, you can display a list of all the employees who have reviews coming up in the weeks ahead. You can then record and print the results of the review. The software has built-in functions to record and issue employee commendations and warnings which you can create to your own specifications, which is helpful in keeping a paper trail on employees' performances. You can display and print out plenty of reports, including compensation and attendance histories for an employee, a home address and phone list of employees, and a salary totals report. Personnel Supervisor offers just about everything your personnel manager needs to keep organized.

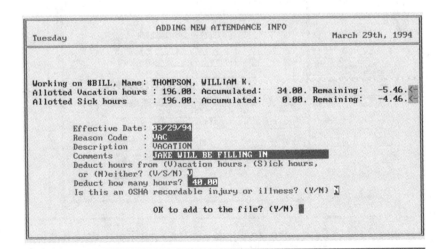

Figure 23-2   Update employee data through a straightforward database system in Personnel Supervisor

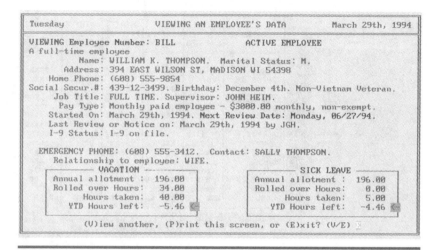

```
Tuesday                VIEWING AN EMPLOYEE'S DATA        March 29th, 1994

VIEWING Employee Number: BILL                    ACTIVE EMPLOYEE
A full-time employee
         Name: WILLIAM K. THOMPSON.  Marital Status: M.
      Address: 394 EAST WILSON ST, MADISON WI 54398
   Home Phone: (608) 555-9854
Social Secur.#: 439-12-3499.  Birthday: December 4th.  Non-Vietnam Veteran.
    Job Title: FULL TIME.  Supervisor: JOHN HEIM.
     Pay Type: Monthly paid employee - $3000.00 monthly, non-exempt.
   Started On: March 29th, 1994.  Next Review Date: Monday, 06/27/94.
   Last Review or Notice on: March 29th, 1994 by JGH.
   I-9 Status: I-9 on file.

  EMERGENCY PHONE: (608) 555-3412.  Contact: SALLY THOMPSON.
     Relationship to employee: WIFE.
    ┌─── VACATION ─────┐          ┌─── SICK LEAVE ──────┐
    Annual allotment :   196.00    Annual allotment :   196.00
    Rolled over Hours:    34.00    Rolled over Hours:     0.00
          Hours taken:    40.00          Hours taken:     5.00
         YTD Hours left:  -5.46          YTD Hours left:  -4.46

          (V)iew another, (P)rint this screen, or (E)xit? (V/E)
```

Figure 23-3   This is how you enter an employee's vacation time
in Personnel Supervisor

MST Software
Mortgage Service Tools, Inc.
25541 Indian Hill Lane, #Q
Laguna Hills, CA 92653
Phone: 714/837-3664
Fax: 714/768-0736
Price: $35, plus $4 shipping
Online filename: PSUPER.ZIP

WhoWorks

Create work schedules for up to 32 employees in the grid-like design
of WhoWorks, as shown in Figure 23-4. Begin by entering the names of
your employees along one side of the screen and the times and dates
across the top. Then, block out the daily schedule of the employees on
the grid. You can configure WhoWorks to make the grid area from 1 to
11 spaces, as the example in Figure 23-5 demonstrates. A grid with just
one space would be used to enter a character that indicates whether the
employee is working on a certain date. With 11 spaces, you can enter
complete shift information, like "23:00-8:00."

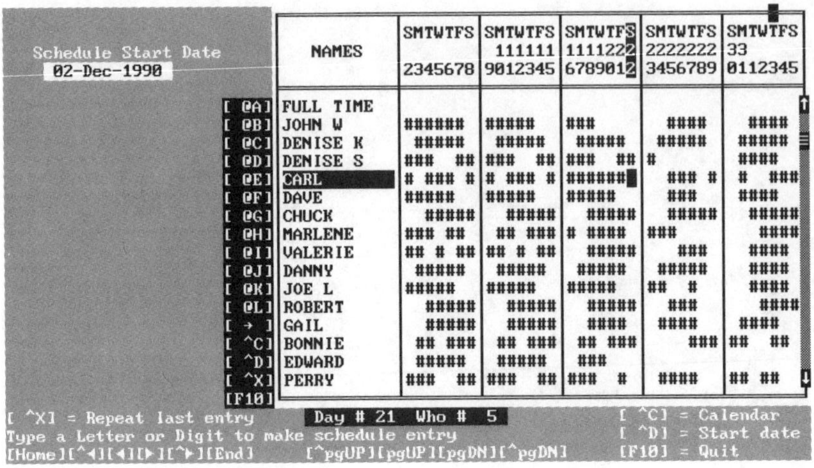

Figure 23-4   Employee schedules set up in WhoWorks

Macros make entering shift information easy. For instance, you can set up the program to enter an employee in the "23:00-8:00" time slot when you press ALT-A. You can configure up to a dozen such keys. You can print a master

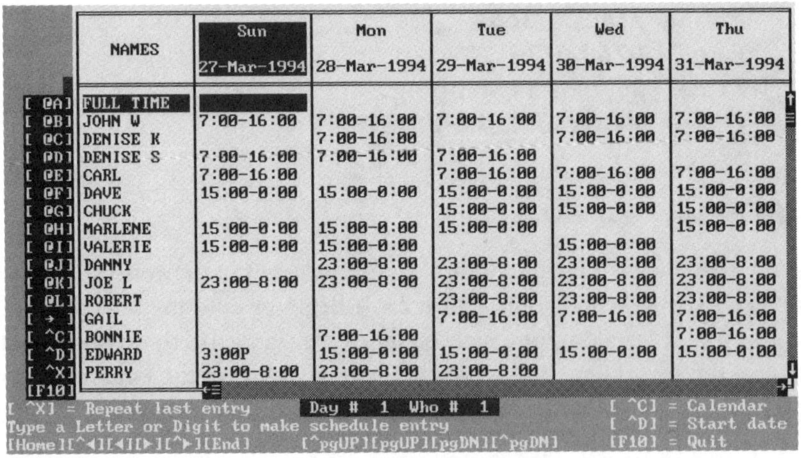

Figure 23-5   WhoWorks employee schedules with column width set to eight

schedule showing the work schedules for all employees, or print work schedules for individual employees. You can create headers and footers for the schedules. There are numerous built-in functions for managing employee schedules, letting you list, erase, and rename schedules.

C. Kenneth Curtis
46 Woodland Dr.
Califon, NJ 07830
Price: $50
Online filename: WHWK21.ZIP

EZ-Staff

EZ-Staff is a simple, but comprehensive personnel scheduling program that will handle any number of employees and shifts. It has lots of nice extras not found in other employee scheduling programs, including a feature that allows you to set up a schedule of hours when a particular employee is not available for work. If you inadvertently schedule the employee for one of these time slots, a subtle message—no annoying beeps or message boxes—appears in the upper-right corner of the screen. This feature, which is demonstrated in Figure 23-6, is handy if you have part-time employees with school or other work commitments.

Another convenient feature is a status bar at the bottom of the screen that tells you how many employees are scheduled for each hour of a particular day, either for your entire organization or for the specific department of the employee whose schedule you are currently viewing. This feature can help you determine whether the department will be understaffed if you don't schedule an employee for a particular time.

Scheduling an employee for a particular time-slot is as simple as typing in the starting time. EZ-Staff calculates the ending time from information you enter into the employee's profile. From there you can add to or subtract hours from the employee's daily schedule with a minimum of keystrokes. The program will display the schedule of an employee for four weeks at a time, and you have as many as six types of leave codes that you can schedule. You can assign leave codes to things like jury duty, National Guard duty, sick leave, and personal days.

You can print individual employee schedules, or master schedules for the entire company. You can also print a daily report showing what time

```
Year   94                        Bigger Hammer, Inc      Conflict-Press F4 for Help
Employee Name ROGERS GEORGE                              (608)555-4587
Department      Full time
              Sun       M  This chart shows hours that an employee cannot work.   w  t  f  s
                           Press spaceber to restore screen.
                                           1 1 1 1 1 1 1 1 1 1 2 2 2 2
40    3/27    3            8HOURS 1 2 3 4 5 6 7 8 9 0 1 2 3 4 5 6 7 8 9 0 1 2 3 4   8  8  8
      off     7
31    4/3     4    Sun  * * * * * * * * * * * * * * * * * * * * * * * *             5  5  5
      off     7
                   Mon  * * * * * *             * * * * * * * * * *                 8  8  8
40    4/10    4
      off     Va   Tue  * * * * * *             * * * * * * * * * *
40    4/17    4    Wed  * * * * * *             * * * * * * * * * *                 8  8  8
      off     7
                   Thu  * * * * * *             * * * * * * * * * *
39    4/24    4                                                                    7  5  5
  →   8-16    7    Fri  * * * * * *             * * * * * * * * * *
   30  = on        Sat  * * * * * * * * * * * * * * * * * * * * * * * *           Day off
   31  =                                                                         Start shift
   22 23 24 1  2                                                                 21 22 23
   0  0  0  0  0  0  0  0  0  0  1 1 1 1 1 1 1 1 0 0 0 0 0 0 0 0 0
   0  0  0  0  0  0  0  0  0  0  1 1 1 1 1 1 1 1 0 0 0 0 0 0 0 0 0
   F3 Change Emp.    F5 Hour-   F6 Hour+   F7 Block→   F8 Block←   F9 Paste  F10 Save
```

Figure 23-6   A schedule of when an employee can't work
overlaid on the regular 4-week schedule in EZ-Staff

slots are covered. EZ-Staff will also tell you how many employees are
scheduled for a particular time. Reports can be sent to a printer or a file.

K Ballif Inc.
P.O. Box 3367
Conroe, TX 77305
Price: $30
Online filename: EZSTAF.ZIP

Specialized Schedulers

While online services are laden with software and macros for law
offices, there's not a lot available online for medical practices. That's
probably because the number of doctor/computer jocks is few (most
doctors will tell you they prefer dealing with people instead of computers),
and those few are probably too busy healing the sick to have time to write
elegant Excel macros. However, there are still a few shareware programs
available for scheduling patients and appointments. If you're a dentist,
doctor, or optician just starting out in a solo practice you can't afford not

to give some of these programs a try. They'll not only help you schedule office help, but also provide assistance in keeping track of patient records, billing, and insurance forms.

Physician's Office Management System

Schedule appointments, keep patient records, and bill insurance companies with this all-in-one medical office management system. Pull-down menus store all the information in an easy-to-find-and-enter format, as in the Service Menu, shown in Figure 23-7. You can do invoices, issue receipts, store all pertinent insurance and guarantor information, as well as apply service diagnostic codes and maintain records of services provided to patients. A daily journal feature lets you see the day's activity in the office at a glance, plus accounting features let you generate annual financial records. This is ideal for the small practice that's just starting up. The only drawback to POMS is that you can't customize the format of database records. You must use the record format that is included.

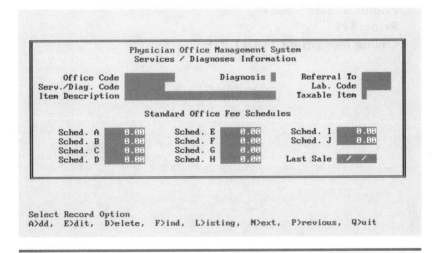

Figure 23-7   The Service Menu of the Physician's Office
                 Management System

K. R. Plossl & Co.
P.O. Box 669681
Marietta, GA 30066
Phone: 404/973-6361
Price: $250
Online filename: POMS1A.ZIP

Nurse's Aid Charting System

Use this convenient calendar program to schedule nurses' shifts. Individual full-screen calendars display the month's scheduling for evening, morning, and afternoon shifts. Nurses can also track admissions with a database that includes such essentials as the patient's name, allergies, TB screening status, and insurance information. Author Fred Small has other innovative health care programs (like simulation software that tests the competence of emergency technicians), so when you call him about Nurse's Aid Charting System, ask him about his other programs.

Fred Small
P.O. Box 57621
Los Angeles, CA 90057
CompuServe ID: 70742,2473
Phone: 213/387-0887
Price: $99
Online filename: CHART.ZIP

CHAPTER 24

SOFTWARE TO HELP MAINTAIN CARS, TRUCKS, AND BUILDINGS

Think how much simpler life would be if we didn't have to keep track of the maintenance on our buildings and cars. If your business owns real estate, whether it be a shopping strip or a string of apartment buildings, you'll find the shareware packages discussed in this chapter useful for keeping track of everything from doorknob repairs to floor buffing. Both of the facilities maintenance tracking packages detailed below were designed by facilities-maintenance managers with decades of experience in overseeing the maintenance of sprawling business and hospital complexes. Their software will help you generate work orders, make sure that the work gets done on time, prepare daily schedules for your maintenance engineers, and record which departments or accounts should be billed for the work. The programs will also let you track the spare parts inventory and the maintenance schedules on equipment.

For businesses with company cars to track, there are many shareware products available for recording mileage, maintenance, and repairs. One will even record information on the driving records of the employees you lend the cars to and remind you when their licenses are about to expire. If you take deductions for car mileage on your taxes, you'll also find these programs indispensable for justifying car-related expenses to the IRS.

Building Maintenance Software

My father ran a small janitorial company. He would schedule maintenance procedures at the handful of shabby office buildings he cleaned with the precision of an admiral in charge of a fleet. Light ballasts and fluorescent bulbs were removed from the ceiling and cleaned the first weekend in June when the weather was nice enough that they could be taken outside and hosed. Floors were waxed on sweltering Saturdays in July and August when the whole family could help move furniture, and also enjoy the building's air conditioning, or in December—just before company Christmas parties. Floors were buffed on a bi-weekly basis. Ashtrays were emptied two nights a week. Employees' coffee mugs were removed from their desks and washed three nights a week. His desk was a sea of neatly filled-in calendars and schedules. I can't help but think that some of this software might have been a big time-saver for him.

Facilitate, Jr.

DOS

Facilitate, Jr. is an elaborate database system for tracking maintenance on equipment and buildings. It was designed for use in the biomedical and facilities-management departments of a major medical center. It is intended as an intermediate-level facilities-management software package, straddling the middle road between the products that cost thousands of dollars and include lots of often unnecessary frills and the cheap packages that provide nothing more than basic equipment and work order tracking.

Facilitate, Jr. includes forms for generating work orders with fields that range from the name of the individual and department requesting the service to the planned completion date, priority level, and department that is to be billed for the work. You can also append to work orders history on equipment, labor information, notes on the materials used, and other information. You can print and display work orders by priority level, service group, employee and account codes, location code, due date, and work order type.

Facilitate, Jr. can track maintenance contracts, equipment servicing history, and performance and safety verifications. You can use it to generate daily and weekly maintenance schedules, and then print work orders from the schedules. You can print any number of maintenance and scheduling reports. You can establish up to four levels of password security for accessing different portions of the system. Facilitate, Jr. uses R:Base so you or your programmers can modify the program to suit your needs. Facilitate, Jr. works on DOS-based office networks, including Novell.

Facilitate, Inc.
1268 Halifax Rd.
Knoxville, TN 37922
Fax: 615/544-8888 ATTN: Harry Herrmann or Al Kuntz
Price: $395
Online filename: FJRVI I.ZIP

PC Mechanic

PC Mechanic is billed as basic, low-cost software for generating work orders and tracking building and equipment maintenance. Designed for use in the hotel industry, it incorporates simple pull-down menus, like the one shown in Figure 24-1, along with mini-databases of maintenance records, work orders, spare parts, and even particulars on maintenance employees, like date of birth and emergency phone numbers. It can print out work orders on form-feed forms but only on a dot matrix printer.

You can generate work orders that describe the work, provide the name of the individual requesting the work, and identify the relevant department, location, and account. The schedule database tracks maintenance tasks and their frequency. Through the equipment database you can log and issue receipts, track vendors, issue purchase orders, and print reports on parts and other inventory-related matters. The employee

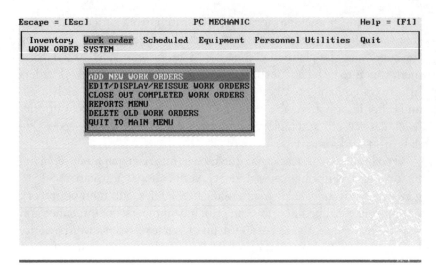

Figure 24-1   PC Mechanic's simple pull-down menus make it easy to track maintenance and generate work orders

database includes the basics: employee's name, ID, Social Security number, pay rate, last review, and home phone number. Unlike Facilitate, Jr., it doesn't offer any password protection.

PC Mechanic is a simple system that's ideal for tracking equipment and maintenance in a single building with just a few maintenance personnel. It's also perfect for anyone who runs a small building maintenance business and wants to keep track of repairs and repair expenditures that are out of the ordinary.

Michael R. Busman
18306 Mansel Ave.
Redondo Beach, CA 90278
Phone: 310/542-7330 (evenings)
CompuServe ID: 71121,2014
Price: $70
Online filename: PCMECH*xx*.ZIP

Shareware In Action

**Product: PC Mechanic
Companies: Allstate
Insurance Company and
Pepsi Cola International**

Expensive commercial products offered no extra benefits to Michael Gilbert, building engineer for Allstate Insurance Company. With PC Mechanic, he can easily plan building maintenance, set up work orders for engineers, and schedule preventive maintenance. If a piece of equipment breaks down frequently, he uses this shareware to spot trends. Some other products, he said, provided more bells and whistles, "such as fancier graphics," but he didn't need them, and they made the software more difficult to use. They also added up to a price tag of $1,000 or more. PC Mechanic, he said, meets all his needs, it's simple to use—and the price is right.

PC Mechanic's user friendliness also appealed to Rafael Ramos, director of manufacturing for Pepsi Cola International. When the manufacturing operation decided to computerize its maintenance procedures, Ramos wanted a program that was uncomplicated and that related to what his staff was already doing manually. PC Mechanic offered these features and more. "PC Mechanic is easy to configure," he said, "and setting it up has made the entire maintenance operation more organized."

Car and Truck Maintenance and Mileage Trackers

Hundreds of shareware programs are available for tracking the mileage and maintenance of cars. If anything, this is a reflection of how devoted PC users are to the other inscrutable chunks of metal in their lives. Weeding through these programs, we looked for ones that could track maintenance on multiple vehicles, could store information on the cars' drivers (like their license numbers and insurance information), and also included adequate space to record details of visits to mechanics. You can use these programs to track mileage and maintenance on company cars, but you can also use them to track, for tax purposes, mileage you rack up on your own car in the course of doing business.

Chris's Automobile Recorder

Chris's Automobile Recorder is ideal for tracking expenses on a company fleet of cars. What makes this program special is that it stores all the relevant details in an easy-to-view format, shown in Figure 24-2, plus it's fun to use. From its colorful screens to its no-brainer interface, it makes recording mileage, maintenance, and insurance costs as simple as typing **CAR** at the PC prompt.

With Chris's Automobile Recorder you can tabulate details on fuel and oil costs, track the cost and age of tires, keep an eye on repairs, and be reminded of preventive maintenance procedures and monthly inspec-

```
1981 Clunkmobile (sample file)          Est. Odometer 111,878 for today  3/28/94
┌────────┬────────┬─────────────────────────────────────────────┬──────────┐
│  DATE  │ MILES  │ DESCRIPTION                       1:54:08 AM │ COST   $ │
├────────┼────────┼─────────────────────────────────────────────┼──────────┤
│08/08/91│ 78,249 │ 15000 MILE INSPECTION                        │          │
│08/13/91│ 78,439 │ FUEL:  10.4 Gallons @ $0.999  Gas R Us FU: 22.9 MPG │ 10.39 │
│08/14/91│        │ INSURANCE PAYMENT: 8/7/91                    │   395.12 │
│08/20/91│ 78,654 │ FUEL:   8.4 Gallons @ $0.999  Gas R Us FU: 25.6 MPG │  8.39 │
│08/27/91│ 78,904 │ FUEL:  10.8 Gallons @ $0.999  Gas R Us FU: 23.1 MPG │ 10.79 │
│08/27/91│ 78,914 │ OTHER: Log Started                           │          │
│09/03/91│        │ FUEL:   8.0 Gallons @ $0.999  Gas R Us       │     7.99 │
│09/05/91│ 79,130 │ TIRES: Replaced All                          │   208.95 │
│09/05/91│ 79,130 │ PM: ROTATE & BALANCE TIRES                   │          │
│09/05/91│ 79,143 │ MONTHLY INSPECTION                           │     6.99 │
│09/05/91│        │ SPEEDING TICKETS: Harshman Road              │    10.00 │
│09/10/91│ 79,323 │ FUEL:   9.8 Gallons @ $0.999  Gas R Us FU: 23.5 MPG │  9.79 │
│09/17/91│ 79,563 │ OIL: 0.5 Quart Wesson                        │     1.49 │
│09/17/91│ 79,563 │ FUEL:  10.2 Gallons @ $0.999  Gas R Us FU: 23.5 MPG │ 10.19 │
│09/17/91│        │ PARKING TICKETS: Downtown                    │    12.50 │
│09/26/91│ 79,880 │ REPAIR: Replaced Muffler Bearings            │   165.49 │
│10/01/91│ 80,138 │ FUEL:  13.6 Gallons @ $0.999  Gas R Us FU:   │    13.59 │
│10/01/91│ 80,145 │ MONTHLY INSPECTION                           │          │
│10/08/91│ 80,366 │ FUEL:   9.9 Gallons @ $0.999  Gas R Us FU: 23.0 MPG │  9.89 │
└────────┴────────┴─────────────────────────────────────────────┴──────────┘
Add View Edit Delete   Locate Sort   PMdue Report Form   Misc Help   Xfer Quit
```

Figure 24-2 Chris's Automobile Recorder puts all the pertinent information about the fleet of company cars at your fingertips tions. You can also record speeding and parking ticket costs (no small expense for some of us). You can view all the entries in log format, sort through them, and generate reports on things like miles-per-gallon, inspections, usage, and repair costs. You can record expenses for as many cars as you want. The only thing that Automobile Recorder lacks that similar programs have is a database on drivers. Chris doesn't require that you send in the registration to use his Automobile Recorder, but do it anyway. It's worth it.

> **Cooney Applied Technology**
> **P.O. Box 292039**
> **Kettering, OH 45429**
> **Price: $79; $40 for nonprofit organizations**
> **Online filename: CAR132.ZIP**

TBS! Vehicle Maintenance

TBS! Vehicle Maintenance is a fairly thorough vehicle expense recorder for any business with a fleet of cars. As with Chris's Automobile Recorder, you can use it to keep track of expenses on one or more vehicles, recording insurance, repair, maintenance, and gas costs. You can generate reports on fuel usage, the vehicle's operating costs over the course of its lifetime, and the car's maintenance history. It will remind you when the car's insurance policy is about to expire, and when it's time for an oil change.

One of the things that distinguishes TBS! Vehicle Maintenance from its peers is the thorough information you can store on the cars' drivers. Things like when their driver's licenses expire, what their insurance policies are, their accident records, and how many miles they've driven the cars. TBS! Vehicle Maintenance also gives you lots of comment space in the records in which repairs are recorded, and that's important for keeping thorough notes on what the repair shop told you and how it planned to do the repair.

Taylor Business Software
16835 Algonquin, Suite 180
Huntington Beach, CA 92649
Phone: 714/840-5021
BBS: 714/840-3767
Price: $25
Online filename: TBSVM1.ZIP

Vehicle

Vehicle is a unique expense database that lets you track all expenses related to a car including purchase, repair, service, mileage, fuel, and all other running costs. A surprisingly detailed and sophisticated database, Vehicle can be used to log business use of one car or a fleet of cars. Perfect for anyone who uses a company car, or who takes car deductions on taxes. Vehicle would even be great for a company that rents cars—it's that good.

Graham Ferguson
3 Cristata Ave.
Endeavor Hills, Vic 3802
Australia
Phone: (03)700-3764
Price: $35
Online filename: VEHICL.ZIP

COMPUTER AND
NETWORK OPERATIONS

6

CHAPTER 25

UTILITIES THAT HELP YOU KEEP YOUR NETWORK RUNNING SMOOTHLY

Think of your office computer network as part of the urban infrastructure of your company. When it fails, if it suffers a breakdown, when memos or e-mail messages aren't transported to the department where they're destined, your company can be crippled in the same way that a blackout cripples New York City. Nothing gets done. If you're like most business executives, you prefer to stay as far away as you can from the technical ministrations that keep the office LAN running. As with brain surgery, you prefer to leave it to people who know what they're doing.

If, however, you're among the growing legion of small business owners who have no choice but to pull out the Novell manuals on occasion and do everything you can to keep the office network humming, these products are for you. There are not a lot of shareware products available for the office network. Well, there are . . . sorta. They exist, but they're mostly for Unix (read: "the sacred language of the unmitigated egghead." Unix is to ordinary computer users what Chinese recipes scrawled in Chinese are to Americans who rarely venture beyond pot pies). There *are* a few worthy shareware items for the DOS network world, like ones that schedule the running of maintenance applications (such as backups on the network), send e-mail notes, maintain security, and even manage the network. These are our favorites.

Clocker

Windows

Clocker allows you to schedule tasks to be run any time of day or night on your office network. If you're familiar with the Unix cron scheduling utility and have been longing for something similar in Windows, this is your baby. Clocker gives you all the abilities of cron, plus much more.

With Clocker you can set up applications to run at a particular time and date, to run on a particular day of the week, and to repeat every day, week, or month, as you can see in Figure 25-1. The application can start at a specified time and repeat every few minutes until a specified time. You can add items to the private task schedule and they'll be executed on the host machine only. Or you can add tasks to the group schedule and they'll run on each machine running Clocker. When you're not entering tasks into the scheduler, Clocker minimizes into an icon that contains a little digital clock, just like the Windows Clock accessory.

The group scheduler is ideal for making network backups. You can also update files on each network machine by adding the copy procedure to the group schedule. And you can schedule the copy to run at night so that the procedure won't interrupt anyone's work during the day.

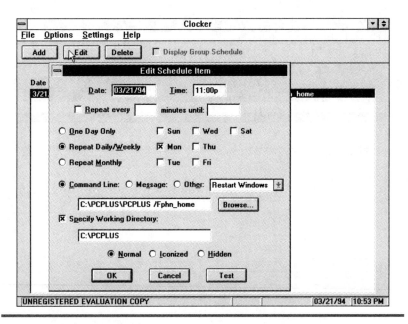

Figure 25-1   Clocker as set up to phone home via Procomm's
PCPlus at 11:00 p.m. each Monday

Winnovation
P.O. Box 271071
Ft. Collins, CO 80527
Phone: 303/226-8682
Fax: 303/226-8682
CompuServe ID: 71774,605
Price: $24.95
Online filename: CLOCKRxx.ZIP

Xpress Note

Windows

Xpress Note is a great messaging system for Windows users on a
network. Xpress Note works on any network as long as you can specify a
location for the message data on a network disk that all users have access
to. With Xpress Note you can send standard format memos; something
called Xpress Yellow notes which look something like 3M Post-It notes,
as shown in Figure 25-2; or phone message notes, as shown in Figure 25-3.

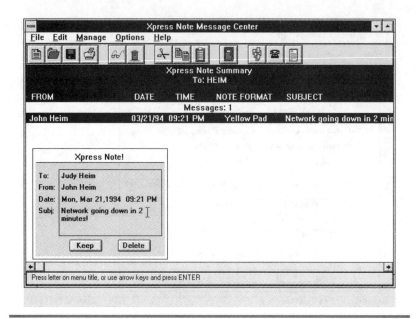

Figure 25-2   In Xpress Note you can send Yellow notes (something like 3M Post-Its)

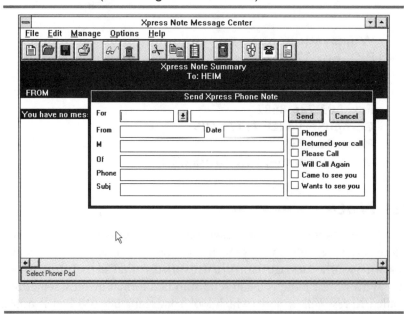

Figure 25-3   Xpress Notes lets you send phone messages to users on the network

You can print your messages and you can copy a text file into the body of the message you're sending.

Xpress Software
2130 Fillmore St., Suite 173
San Francisco, CA 94115
Phone: 415/677-7940 (voice)
Price: $29
Online filename: XPRESS.ZIP

NetBak

NetBak is a security tool to make your network backup procedure more secure. Usually, when you run an automated night-time backup of a network, the script that you use to run the procedure contains the network administrator's login name and his or her password. This is necessary so that the script can log in to the file server (where all your company's critical files are stored) and access the files to back them up. Otherwise, the employee running the backup must log in as the network administrator and set up the script to run later. Either way, these procedures allow anyone with access to the PC to get at everything on the network and have unlimited access to all files. This is not a good scenario.

With NetBak you don't have to include the network administrator's login ID and password in the backup script. And you don't have to leave the machine unattended and logged in to the network. NetBak will store the necessary login information in a secure way, then at the specified time log into the network and run the backup procedure. You can run NetBak from the scheduling software that comes with most tape backup devices or through any of the network scheduling utilities mentioned later in this chapter.

D & D Software Inc.
809 Jackson Ave.
Lindenhurst, NY 11757
Phone: 516/957-2448 (voice)
CompuServe ID: 70406,1163
Price: $40 single server edition; $100 multi-server edition
Online filename: NETBAK.ZIP

MarxMenu

MarxMenu is an absolutely wonderful scripting language for DOS-based office networks. No office LAN manager should be without it. It can automate any task that you need to do on a network, such as performing network backups, carrying out maintenance and security procedures like monitoring logins and file access, and running applications on the server, as you can see in Figure 25-4. You can also use it to design menus with which to run applications on the network server. You can do anything with MarxMenu that you can do in an AUTOEXEC.BAT file in DOS, plus a great deal more because it offers over 500 commands.

MarxMenu can be used on any office network, but its designers were especially kind to Novell network administrators. In the MarxMenu manual there is page after page of directions explaining how to automate network tasks on Novell LANs. The chapter on writing network login and logout scripts contains hints about using Novell that you may not find elsewhere, including an explanation of which commands belong in a user's AUTOEXEC.BAT file, which belong in the network login script, and which belong in the system login script on the network drive.

Another nice feature for Novell administrators is a utility that converts Novell menu scripts to MarxMenu scripts. Several functions in

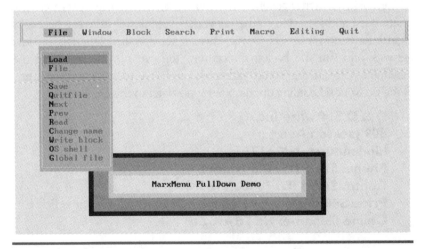

Figure 25-4　MarxMenu lets you automate tasks on networks

the scripting language support Novell semaphores. (*Semaphores* are a Novell feature related to its shared resources capabilities.) MarxMenu includes several date and time functions, such as a day-of-the-week function so that it can be used to run network backups at night. MarxMenu scripts are compiled to a machine-readable format that is executed by the MarxMenu loader. If the script is older than the compiled version it is automatically compiled by MarxMenu. You can distribute the compiled script to your users so they can't modify it.

Computer Tyme
411 N. Sherman, Suite 300
Springfield, MO 65802
Phone: 417/866-1222 or 800/548-5353 (orders only)
BBS: 417/866-1665
Price: $59.95 single user; $495 network (Each file server must be licensed separately.)
Online filename: MARXMENU.ZIP or MXMENU.EXE

DAYO Network Manager

TSJ Lab has some extremely impressive products for the office in its DAYO shareware series, and the DAYO Network Manager is no exception. It's a Novell network manager that offers two kinds of operation, either through the command line or interactively with graphical menus.

At the network command prompt you can kill—that is, log off—users who should not be on the network, you can list logged-in users, display network utilization statistics, and display network packets, as shown in Figure 25-5. You can do all the same things with DAYO Net's Windows-like menus, but face it, it's always more fun to stay as close to your techie roots as possible and type in as many commands as you can at an inscrutable prompt.

DAYO Net also lets you list all active network users and monitor the activities of a specific user. You can list active servers, change server date and time, get information about network disks, and shut down servers. DAYO Net's packet-monitoring allows you to view network traffic statistics. Finally, DAYO Net can give you information on network printers. DAYO Net gives you all the capabilities that commercial network managers need in order to perform all the duties of running a network.

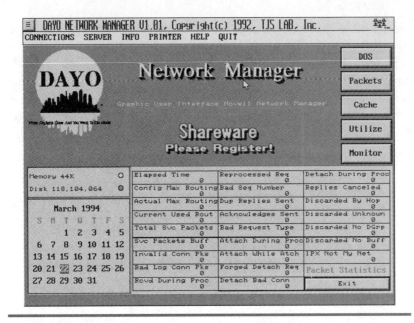

Figure 25-5   The packet monitor screen of DAYO Network
            Manager

TJS Lab, Inc.
5104 N. Orange Blossom Trail, Suite 200
Orlando, FL 32810
Phone: 407/291-3960
CompuServe ID: 76367,1401
Price: $149
Online filename: DAYONE.ZIP

SECURITY, ANTI-VIRUS, AND BACKUP TOOLS TO KEEP YOUR PC SAFE FROM INTRUDERS AND DISASTER

he threat of losing valuable data to a malicious computer virus, like the infamous Michelangelo virus, is every PC user's nightmare. So too is the prospect of losing data in a hard disk crash. And if you travel with a laptop computer, certainly the thought may have crossed your mind that one day you might leave a floppy disk in an airport lounge or on a plane and, without your knowing it, confidential information could wind up in the hands of a competitor.

Keeping your PC and data secure from these threats isn't hard. All it takes is a couple of precautions and a few good utilities to keep data safe from prying eyes, data-destroying viruses, or catastrophic computer accidents.

Let's talk about viruses first. A computer virus is malevolent computer code with the ability to infect hidden spots of your PC (like the hard disk boot sector or file allocation table). Once there, it self-replicates, copying itself onto floppy disks that you insert in the machine, or migrating over office computer networks to infect other machines. Like a time bomb, a virus may lie hidden for weeks or months, waiting until a set date to unleash its mischief. It could do something as innocuous as bouncing a ping-pong ball over the screens of all the PCs on the office network, or as harmful as selectively destroying program or data files. It may even reformat hard disks, thereby destroying all the data stored on them.

The most effective way to guard against this sort of disaster is to run a virus scan on all floppy disks from other users or PCs before you insert them in your own PC. The most popular virus scanner for this purpose is John McAfee's Viruscan. (In fact, next to the compression program PKZIP, Viruscan is the second most popular download from all online services and BBSs. We've put it on the disks included with this book for your convenience.) Viruscan scans files for characteristic code signatures of hundreds of known viruses and alerts you when it finds something suspicious. Some Fortune 500 companies have set up virus control departments that routinely scan *any* floppy disks that are brought in the door. These include demo disks carried by computer salespeople, diagnostic disks of computer repair technicians, and shrink-wrapped commercial software. They'll also scan the hard disks of any purchased PCs, which are among the most common transmitters of viruses.

Your chances of contracting a virus by downloading files from online services or BBSs are relatively slim in comparison to contracting a virus through the passing of a floppy disk from one machine to another. See Chapter 2 for more advice on how to avoid viruses when downloading shareware. Still, you'd be wise to download shareware to a floppy disk and scan all files with Viruscan before copying them to your hard disk and running them.

In addition to scanning disks for viruses, it's also a good idea to run a memory-resident virus scanner that will monitor all program activity on your PC. Virus monitors watch for suspicious activity, like a program bypassing DOS to write directly to disk or writing to the boot sector of your hard disk. When they spot a program doing something it should not, they halt the activity and in some cases purge the offensive software from the system. The shareware program VShield is a popular virus monitor, but you should also check out some of the commercial monitors like Norton/Symantec's Norton Anti-Virus and Certus International's Certus for additional virus-nabbing capabilities.

No virus monitor can prevent everything that a virus might do to infect your PC. To be absolutely foolproof, a virus monitor would end up preventing legitimate software from running. Nor will every virus scanner detect every known virus. But these products do provide a large degree of protection and they should be used conscientiously by anyone concerned about viruses.

Your second line of defense against viruses is to keep regular backups of your hard disk. There are a number of shareware backup programs on the market. Our favorite is MegaBack, which is described below.

Finally, a good encryption utility will help you keep your valuable data safe from people who should not see it—whether you transport it on floppy disks between customer sites, or send it off via electronic mail to coworkers or clients. An *encryption program* transforms files, such as those making up a word processing document or spreadsheet, into secret code. The secret code is based mathematically upon the password that you give the encryption program. When a document is encrypted using good encryption software, no one, not even someone with a super-computer and hundreds of hours of processing time, will be able to crack the code and read your file. For some reason, all the most secure encryption programs are shareware ones. Maybe it's because shareware authors are hackers at heart.

Viruscan

They bear names like Atomic, Civil War, Demolition, Invisible Man, Iraqi Warrior, and Jerusalem. And Viruscan scans for them all. There are over two thousand known viruses—new ones crop up every week. Viruscan scans floppy disks and hard drives for the trademark program code signatures of these malicious invaders.

You should use Viruscan to regularly scan your hard disk, as well as any shareware you download or any floppy disks from other PCs. Viruscan is a simple program. You can tell it to scan all the files on a specific disk, all the files in a particular subdirectory, or a single file. It works on all the common office computer networks, including Novell, 3Com, Lantastic, and DEC Pathworks, so you can use it to scan network drives too.

When Viruscan discovers a virus hidden in data, it warns you, then lets you store recovery information about the file. Another McAfee Associates shareware product, Clean-Up (detailed below), can use this recovery information to restore the file and purge it of the virus. Viruscan can also add validation codes to the end of program files so that its other shareware companion program, VShield, can check to see if the file has been modified. Viruscan will work with VShield in this way to detect previously unknown viruses.

You'll find Viruscan on the disks included with this book. Viruscan is updated regularly, to keep up with the growing number of computer viruses. You should make sure you always have a version with up-to-date viral "signatures." You can get one from McAfee Associates' BBS. The program will display a warning if it's more than seven months old.

note

As this book was going to press McAfee Associates, Inc. was getting ready to release a new version of Viruscan with a more user-friendly interface than its existing command line interface plus Clean-Up built in. Figure 26-1 shows how the new Viruscan will indicate that it has detected a virus.

McAfee Associates, Inc.
2710 Walsh Avenue, Suite 200
Santa Clara, CA 95051
Phone: 408/988-3832
Fax: 408/970-9727
BBS: 408/988-4004
CompuServe: type GO MCAFEE at any prompt
Internet: support@mcafee.com
Price: $25
Online filename: SCANV114.ZIP

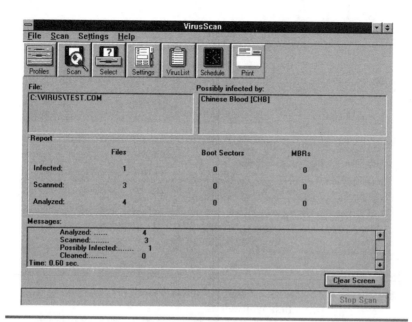

Figure 26-1   Viruscan scans files and sectors of your disk for signs of infection by viruses like the Chinese Blood virus

Clean-Up

Clean-Up, the companion program to Viruscan, scans program and data files on your floppy or hard disks for a particular virus and disinfects and repairs the file if a virus is found. Use Viruscan to scan your data or disks for any known viruses; then, if it finds one, tell Clean-Up to make a thorough search for copies of it in your system and eradicate them. Clean-Up can find and remove hundreds of viruses, including the common Michelangelo and Jerusalem viruses that have infected so many corporate computer networks. See Figure 26-2 for the results of Clean-Up's scan for the Michelangelo virus.

You can tell Clean-Up to fix all the files on a specific disk, all the ones in a specific directory, or just a single file. After it's done, Clean-Up will generate a report on what actions it took to disinfect your data. It also gives you the option of approving each action before Clean-Up actually performs the file recovery. Clean-Up can remove viruses other than just previously known ones if you're also using the McAfee Associates product Viruscan.

```
C:\BOOK\SBU\VIRUSCAN>clean a: [Mich]
CLEAN 9.15 V104 Copyright 1989-93 by McAfee Associates. (408) 988-3832
Cleaning [Mich]

Scanning memory for critical viruses.
Scanning 640K RAM
Scanning Volume: DEFAULT.FUL


No viruses found.


CLEAN 9.15 V104 Copyright 1989-93 by McAfee Associates. (408) 988-3832

     This McAFEE(TM) software  may  not be used by a business, government
     agency or institution without  payment of  a negotiated license fee.
     To negotiate a license fee contact McAfee Associates (408) 988-3832.
     All use of  this software  is  conditioned upon  compliance with the
     license terms set forth in the LICENSE.DOC file.


     Copyright (c) McAfee Associates 1989-1993. All Rights Reserved.


C:\BOOK\SBU\VIRUSCAN>
```

Figure 26-2   Clean-Up has just finished scanning for the
                    Michelangelo virus

McAfee Associates, Inc.
2710 Walsh Avenue, Suite 200
Santa Clara, CA 95051
Phone: 408/988-3832
Fax: 408/970-9727
BBS: 408/988-4004
CompuServe: type GO MCAFEE at any prompt
Internet: support@mcafee.com
Price: $35
Online filename: CLEAN114.ZIP

VShield

DOS

VShield is another popular product from McAfee Associates. It's a
memory-resident monitor that scans the programs you run for viruses. It
scans for a distinctive virus signature, or string of characters that viruses
are known to have. If it finds a virus, the infected software is prevented
from running, and a warning appears on the screen.

Use VShield in conjunction with Viruscan to detect viruses that may not have been previously known. VShield comes packed with a Windows version that lets VShield display messages in Windows, and a utility that can be used in network login scripts.

McAfee Associates, Inc.
2710 Walsh Avenue, Suite 200
Santa Clara, CA 95051
Phone: 408/988-3832
Fax: 408/970-9727
BBS: 408/988-4004
CompuServe: type GO MCAFEE at any prompt
Internet: support@mcafee.com
Price: $25
Online filename: VSHLD114.ZIP

MegaBack

Backing up programs and files on your hard disks can be an onerous chore. You can make it a snap with MegaBack. You use MegaBack's menus to create a selective list of the files you want to back up. MegaBack displays directory listings of all the contents of your hard disk, and you can move through these directories, marking which files you want to back up. Once you're done, MegaBack gives you an estimate of the number of floppy disks you'll need to back up all those files. This is an especially nice feature since few things are more frustrating than backing up for hours, just to run out of disks. Once you've assembled the floppy disks, it starts backing up, as shown in Figure 26-3.

It's just as easy to restore files to your hard disk from the floppies. Give MegaBack the name of the file to restore, or ask it for a list of the files in the archive directory, as shown in Figure 26-4. MegaBack lets you scroll through the list, marking the files you want to restore. You can have it restore individual files, entire directories, or all the files from a particular drive.

MegaBack's compression isn't as fast or tight as that of PKZIP, but its ease of use and many other advantages make it an excellent backup utility.

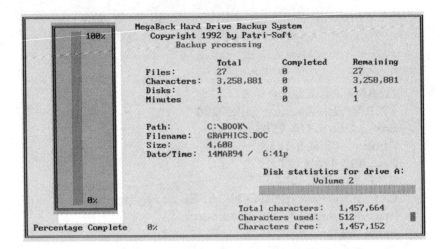

Figure 26-3   MegaBack is ready to begin backing up data

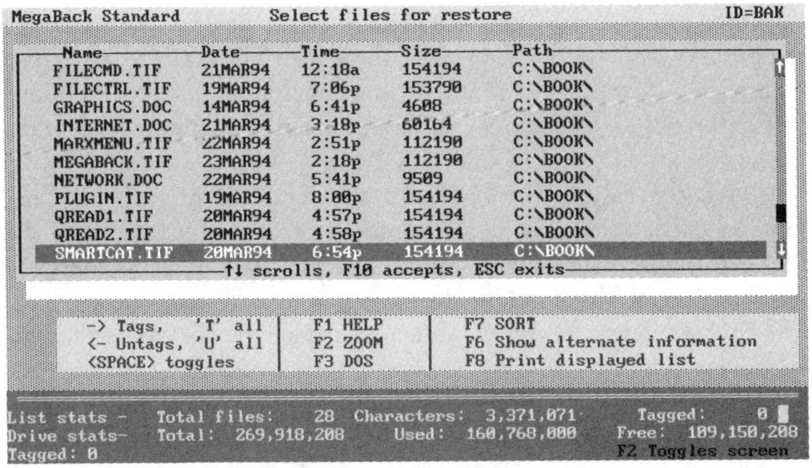

Figure 26-4   MegaBack's restore file list

For more information on PKZIP, see Chapter 11, "Tools and Toys."

Patri-Soft
5225 Canyon Crest Dr., Suite 71-358
Riverside, CA 92507
Phone: 909/352-2820
Fax: 909/352-1527
BBS: 909/352-2825
CompuServe ID: 76347,2477
Price: $39
Online filename: MBACK220.ZIP

WinLock

WinLock locks up your PC keyboard, preventing anyone from accessing your PC, if you leave it unattended for a certain period of time. In order to unlock it, you must enter the correct password in the login password dialog box, shown here:

Should someone try to guess your password, the first time the erroneous password is entered, a message appears saying that the password is case-sensitive. If a second wrong password is entered, the screen flashes different colors and an alarm sounds. WinLock displays a log file of password attempts, as shown in Figure 26-5, and allows access to the PC when the correct password is finally entered.

You can vary the length of inactivity that will trigger WinLock. You can also activate it yourself automatically if you know that you're going to be away from your PC for a while.

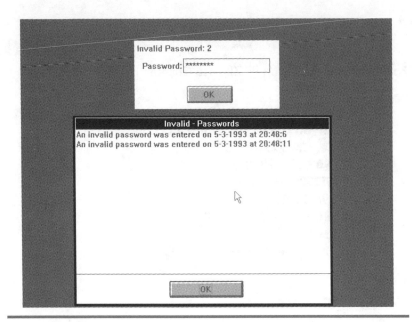

Figure 26-5 WinLock's response to two unsuccessful login tries

TeraVision, Inc.
785 Virginia Ave., MS:12E
Campbell, CA 95008
Phone: 408/378-9328
Fax: 408/378-9374
Price: $19 plus $2 shipping and handling
Online filename: AWLOCK.ZIP

Encrypt-It

Windows

You need never worry again about diskettes full of confidential information falling into the wrong hands. Encrypt-It can encode your confidential files, making them virtually impenetrable to prying eyes. It's also ideal to use on electronic mail. Everyone knows that electronic mail is never completely safe from snooping, whether it's sent on an office network or a commercial information service.

Encrypt-It is easy to use. In a Windows-style dialog box, you select the files that you want to encrypt. Then you select Encrypt from Encrypt-It's main menu and a dialog box appears, as shown in Figure 26-6. Enter a password when prompted and you're done. When anyone tries to read your files without the password, all they'll see is gibberish. Encrypt-It takes your password and builds a unique code from it. It then gives you the option of wiping your original file from the disk. When you delete a file from your PC, it's not really deleted. Only its name is deleted from the disk's file table. Anyone can search the disk with common disk utilities like Norton Utilities and read the deleted file. Encrypt-It will overwrite the file with zeros and ones so that it cannot be read. Be careful, though. Once a file is overwritten, it's gone for good.

You decrypt files in pretty much the same fashion as you encrypt them: you select the file, then enter the password. Keep in mind that if you send an encrypted file to a friend, he or she will need a copy of Encrypt-It and the password to decode your file. You can run Encrypt-It

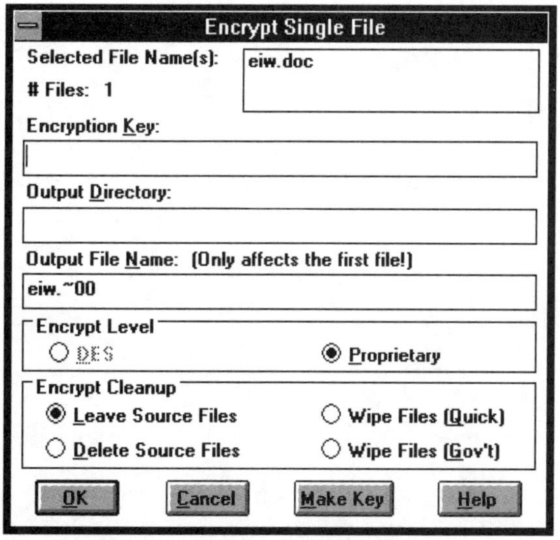

Figure 26-6   Encrypt-It displays this dialog box during coding and decoding of files

on a single file or group of files. Encrypt-It encodes files with its own proprietary encryption algorithm. If you register the program, you also get the National Bureau of Standards' Data Encryption Standard (or DES), which is the encryption algorithm that government agencies and contractors are required to use (that's because the government can read any files encrypted with it). The proprietary algorithm used in Encrypt-It is much more secure than DES.

MaeDae Enterprises
5430 Murr Rd.
Peyton, CO 80831
Phone: 719/683-3860
CompuServe ID: 72571,3245
GEnie ID: MAEDAE
Price: $59
Online filename: EIW212.ZIP

CHAPTER 27

PC HELP TOOLS FOR WHEN THE GOING GETS ROUGH

t's 2:00 a.m. and you're furiously tapping out the last paragraphs of a marketing report, due first thing in the morning. Suddenly, your PC reports some flaky error message: "Disk error: unable to write to Drive C: Abort? Retry? Fail?" Your palms sweat. You want to scream. "We're losing power on the warp engine, Captain," keeps playing through your mind. It's too late to call a PC repairman. And you haven't a bit of software on your shelves to help you figure out what's going wrong—much less to help you figure out how to fix it! If only you had listened to reason and bought a copy of Norton Utilities at the office supply store last week.

What do you do? Try dialing an information service like CompuServe or America Online and downloading one of these shareware PC diagnostic tools. They'll help you figure out what's going wrong, and may even get you back up and running in time to finish your report by morning.

PC-Glossary

Ever wonder what bubble memory is? Or ask yourself what the heck is Boolean logic? Are you responsible for buying your company a computer and the salesperson is spilling gibberish around you? If you need to get up to speed on all the latest techno-babble, PC-Glossary is for you. Just pop this cunning computer glossary up on your screen, as shown in Figure 27-1, and get the low-down on Zulu time, WYSIWYG, and the difference between a 386SX computer chip and a 386DX one. Its entries give you the information you need to use computer terms correctly, rather than the stuffy, inscrutable definitions you find in most computer dictionaries.

The glossary's slick "See Also" feature, shown in Figure 27-2, lets you quickly jump to related PC terms for further edification. For instance,

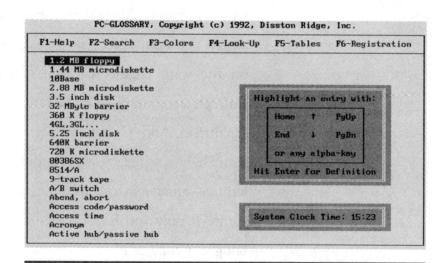

Figure 27-1 PC-Glossary lists computer terms with easy-to-understand definitions

```
            PC-GLOSSARY, Copyright (c) 1992, Disston Ridge, Inc.

   See Also: ▓User-supported software▓ ASP  Copyright  Computer program
   Use the Arrow Keys to Select a Cross-Reference, then Hit Enter

    ▓Shareware▓

    Shareware is a distribution method for software programs developed
    by independent programmers or authors.  It is a marketing technique
    rather than a type of software.  It allows the author to market the
    program with minimal start-up expenses while encouraging feedback
    from the users.

    Programs acquired through the Shareware method may be freely copied
    and passed on to others, but each user is expected to register with
    the author and pay a usage fee.  The fee may include some or all of
    the following:  printed documentation, the latest version of the
    program on disk, telephone support, free updates, and commissions,
    but most importantly a legal license to continue using the software.


              ▓Hit Escape Key to Return to Top Level.▓
```

Figure 27-2   PC-Glossary provides illumination into the
definition of "shareware" and other terms

look up "baud rate" and PC-Glossary will point you to "Zmodem,"
"protocol," and "bps rate" with the touch of a couple keys.

PC-Glossary includes a set of appendix-like tables—information that
doesn't fit easily under any one category—including lists of the most
common computer viruses and explanations of the most common filename extensions, like .EXE and .ZIP. Think of it: you'll never again be at
a loss when the subject of "worm drives" comes up at the water cooler.

> **Disston Ridge, Inc.**
> **4915 22nd Ave., North**
> **St. Petersburg, FL 33710**
> **Phone: 813/323-0961**
> **Price: $29**
> **Online filename: GLOS52.ZIP**

HDTEST

If you've never encountered a chilling DOS read/write error message,
count your blessings. Chances are, though, that you've faced more than
one. What are they? Occasionally a cluster on your hard disk—a *cluster*

is a small segment of the disk that DOS reads and writes to all at once—can go bad. The magnetic media on a patch of the disk surface wears out and can't be used any more. When this happens you get a DOS read/write error message. Messages like this do not signal an imminent catastrophe, but if they become common it may be a sign that your disk is in danger of failing.

You can use HDTEST to repair occasional bad clusters on your hard disk. HDTEST tests each cluster on the disk for errors, as you can see in Figure 27-3. It writes 20 different test patterns to each cluster, and checks that it can read back each pattern correctly. If a cluster contains your data, HDTEST restores it at the end of the test. If it can't read back any of the patterns it writes to each cluster, it marks the cluster as bad so that DOS will no longer use it. It then takes the data that was stored in that cluster and remaps it to another cluster that tested good. Usually this lets you recover any data stored in bad clusters and banish those nasty read/write errors. Norton/Symantec's Disk Doctor in Norton Utilities and Gibson Research's SpinRite do the same thing, but at a higher price.

HDTEST can also fix intermittent disk problems—the kind that occur when clusters are written to the disk in a fashion that's slightly out of alignment. As HDTEST exercises the disk, it realigns any askew clusters. The whole process requires two to five hours, depending upon

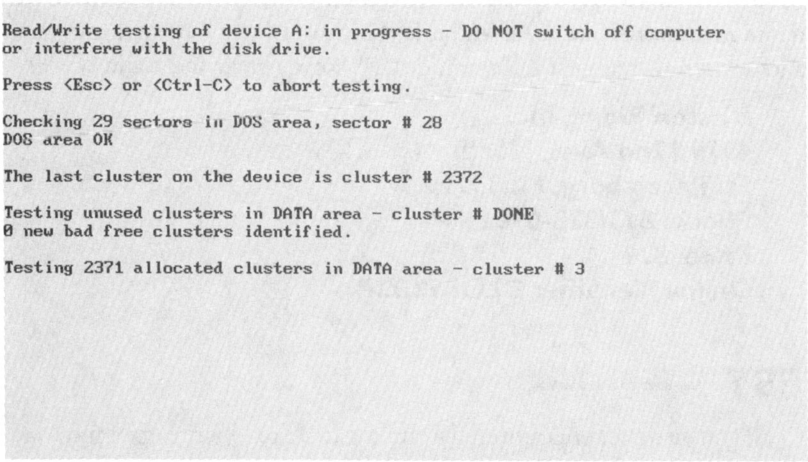

```
Read/Write testing of device A: in progress - DO NOT switch off computer
or interfere with the disk drive.

Press <Esc> or <Ctrl-C> to abort testing.

Checking 29 sectors in DOS area, sector # 28
DOS area OK

The last cluster on the device is cluster # 2372

Testing unused clusters in DATA area - cluster # DONE
0 new bad free clusters identified.

Testing 2371 allocated clusters in DATA area - cluster # 3
```

Figure 27-3   HDTEST is exercising the A: drive, looking for bad data clusters the speed and size of your disk. If all this sounds very technical, rest assured that all you need to do to test your drive with HDTEST is type **HDTEST** and the drive letter at a DOS prompt. Remember, diagnosing and fixing hard disk problems is serious stuff. Always be sure to back up your hard disk before you attempt to run disk tests.

Computer Counselors, Inc.
1515 W. Montgomery Ave.
Rosemont, PA 19010
Price: $35
Online filename: HDTEST.ZIP

VSUM

Although the virus scan programs we mentioned in Chapter 26 are extremely useful and most often solve any virus problems your company might have, there may be times when your company's PCs exhibit strange behavior that is the consequence of a viral infection unrecognized by your scan program. Or, your scanning software may identify the virus but not tell you exactly how to get rid of it. That's where VSUM comes in.

VSUM is an invaluable interactive database of information and guide to a wide variety of computer viruses. It lists all the viruses known to the Anti-Viral Product Developers consortium of the National Computer Security Association. It is compiled and kept up to date by the consortium's librarian, Patricia M. Hoffman. VSUM is invaluable in diagnosing and purging viruses from PCs and networks. If you run into a virus that you can't figure out, look it up in VSUM and you'll find out what it is, how to clean it up, and how much damage it can do if you don't clean it up.

You can search for information by the name of the virus or by its relationship to other viruses. The program allows searching of the virus listing on the basis of the date of activation and size of the virus (or the number of bytes by which a file's size is increased when it is infected). As shown in Figure 27-4, entries contain a great deal of useful information on each virus, including its name, any aliases it might have, symptoms of infection, detection and removal instructions, plus the McAfee Scan I.D. for use with Clean-Up. (See Chapter 26 for more information on Clean-Up.) The removal instructions consist of a list of the anti-virus programs that can recognize and remove the particular virus.

VSUM is *very* useful to businesses. Sometimes, people will experience the symptoms of a computer virus for a long time before they realize what it is. For instance, someone told us that he was in a bank and noticed that there were little ping-pong balls bouncing over the screens of all the PCs in the bank. He asked a teller about them and was told that it was some weird quirk of their computers that had slowly infested all of the machines. Well, it wasn't some weird computer quirk. It was the Ping-Pong Virus. All the PCs in the bank were infected with it and no one knew.

Patricia M. Hoffman
3333 Bowers Ave., Suite 130
Santa Clara, CA 95054
Phone: 408/988-3773
Fax: 408/988-2438
BBS: 408/244-0813
CompuServe ID: 75300,3005
Price: $30 for home use; sliding price scale for multiple PCs
Online filename: VSUM.ZIP

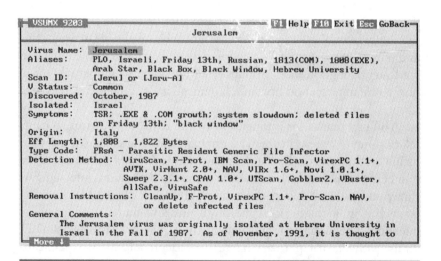

Figure 27-4   VSUM will tell you all about nasties like the Jerusalem virus

SYSCHK

DOS

If you've ever needed to bring a computer repair specialist into your office, you know how expensive his or her time can be. Just diagnosing the problem may cost your company hundreds of dollars. Well, even if you still need to call in the tech support forces, you can at least know what the problem is ahead of time with SYSCHK. SYSCHK won't fix your problems, but it can certainly help save you the expense of paying a repair person to figure it out.

SYSCHK is diagnostic software that can tell you things about your PC you might not know otherwise—things like how your communications ports are set up and what memory-resident programs are running. This information can be retrieved by selecting categories from a menu, shown in Figure 27-5, along with the Input /Output Information screen. You use the program when something like your fax-modem, for example, isn't working right, or when some software package won't load properly into memory. It will give you incredibly detailed information about what's going on. Although this information isn't for the computer illiterate, you don't need to be a rocket scientist to understand most diagnoses.

The memory resident map will show you where in memory terminate-and-stay-resident (TSR) software (software that you load into the

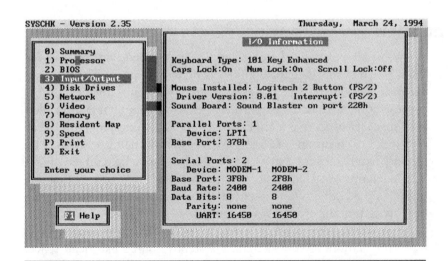

Figure 27-5   SYSCHK is invaluable for diagnosing
communications problems

background and it stays hidden, appearing only when you initiate a certain set of keystrokes) is loaded and what memory-interrupts the packages are using, which you need to know to get conflicting TSRs working together. If your communications software isn't dialing out, SYSCHK will tell you if your internal modem is configured to use the same areas of memory that your communications software is talking to. If it isn't downloading high-speed files properly, it helps to know if you have a high-speed 16550A UART chip or not.

SYSCHK will also tell you what kind of hard disk you have, the brand of your video card, and how your PC's memory is configured. This is the kind of stuff you really need to know in order to keep your PC running properly and diagnose problems, but often your PC's manual forgets to tell you these things.

Advanced Personal Systems
Attn: Paul Griffith
105 Serra Way, Suite 418
Milpitas, CA 95035
Phone: 408/298-3703
Fax: 408/945-0242
Price: $20
Online filename: SYSCHK.ZIP

WindSock

Windows

We've all experienced something like it. You open up Excel under Windows and your Word for Windows window disappears. The response to mouse clicks slows. These are symptoms of Windows growing unstable due to excessive demands on a particular kind of computer memory called heap space. *Heap space* is a critical area in memory that programs use as workspace to "heap up" or store variables during their operation. The memory usage statistics that Windows displays on its help screen are no help in figuring out what's going on because they often indicate that lots of memory and other system resources are available when in actuality the heap space is running dangerously low.

Run WindSock and you'll be able to tell if a Windows application is especially gluttonous of a particular system resource like heap space. You're not going to want to keep WindSock active all the time, but you will want to load it before running Windows software that you're having trouble running.

WindSock will graphically display memory usage statistics including the percentage of the system heap that particular applications are using, how much GDI heap is being used for graphic resources by devices like light pens, how much user heap is being used by Windows objects like windows and classes, and so on, as shown here:

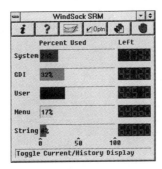

If you put WindSock into "history mode," as shown in the following illustration, it will display a line graph of how system resources are used over time, and how the usage changes with the applications that are loaded.

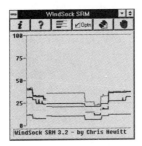

note

Do not confuse this WindSock with the very popular commercial Windows e-mail reader of the same name that's used on company networks.

Chris Hewitt
Technical Pixies
25 Coleman St.
North Fitzroy, VIC 3068
Australia
CompuServe ID: 100036,133
Price: $10
Online filename: WINSOC.ZIP

APPENDIX

COMPUTER BULLETIN BOARDS AND ONLINE SERVICES

omputer bulletin boards, or BBSs, are a great place to hunt for shareware. There are tens of thousands of BBSs throughout the country. For a list of the ones in your city, visit a local computer store or ask at your local computer user group for recommendations. In fact, most computer user groups run their own BBS for the purpose of making their extensive shareware collections available to members—and you usually don't even have to be a member to download software from the BBS.

The Association of Shareware Professionals certifies select BBSs as repositories of members' shareware products. The Association maintains a database of roughly 500 certified BBSs around the country (a list too long to include in this book). For more information on ASP-certified BBSs, contact the ASP by writing to 545 Grover Rd., Muskegon, MI 49442-9427, by phoning 616/788-5131, or by faxing 616/788-2765. You can also reach the ASP forum on CompuServe by typing **GO ASP-FORUM** and pressing ENTER at any prompt.

The following list of BBSs was derived from *Boardwatch Magazine's* annual Reader's Choice BBS contest—with a few of our own favorites thrown in. *Boardwatch Magazine* is another excellent source of information on BBSs around the country, as well as around the world. You can write Boardwatch at 8500 W. Bowles Ave., Suite 210, Littleton, CO 80123, or call 800/933-6038, or fax 303/973-3731. You can also call its BBS at 303/973-4222.

When you call BBSs, remember that most are run as hobbies by computer fans. If you call a particular BBS regularly, pay the subscription fee if one is requested. BBSs are very expensive to run. Whenever you download software, always upload some in return—that's one of the rules of the BBS world. And don't forget to deport yourself in a polite manner, whether you're exchanging e-mail with the BBS operator (or *sysop*) or another user. BBSs are hard to run and they're a lot of work; there's nothing that sysops dread more than uncouth guests.

Computer Bulletin Boards

Albuquerque ROS
Albuquerque, NM
505/299-5974
Tons of shareware

Blue Ridge Express
Richmond, VA
804/790-1675
Lots of shareware

Cajun Clickers
Baton Rouge, LA
504/756-9658
Online games

Canada Remote Systems
Mississauga, Ontario
416/213-6002
Canada's biggest BBS

Channel 1
Cambridge, MA
617/354-8873
A huge BBS with Internet access

Chrysalis
Plano, TX
214/690-9295
Internet access

Deep Cove
White Rock, British Columbia
604/536-5885
Internet access

deltaComm
Cary, NC
919/481-9399
Support center for Telix shareware communications software

Eagle's Nest
Littleton, CO
303/933 0701
Tiny system but free

Exec-PC
Elm Grove, WI
414/789-4210
*World's biggest BBS: offers every shareware program in existence, plus
    Internet access*

Executive Network
Mt. Vernon, NY
914/667-4567
Internet access and lots of international traffic

H H Infonet
New Hartford, CT
203/738-0342
Professional, technical, and business-oriented

Microfone Infoservice
Metuchen, NJ
908/494-8666
Online games

Mercury Opus
St. Petersburg, FL
813/321-0734
Internet access, lots of Windows shareware

Micro Message Service
Raleigh, NC
919/779-6674
Family oriented

Mog-UR's EMS
Granada Hills, CA
818/366-1238
Internet access

Nashville Exchange
Nashville, TN
615/383-0727
Software, support, plus Internet's Usenet conferences

One Stop PCBoard
Richland, WA
509/943-0211
Lots of active conversations

OS/2 Shareware
Fairfax, VA
703/385-4325
First stop for OS/2 shareware

PC-OHIO
Cleveland, OH
216/381-3320
Internet access, support center for using office networks

Plains Bulletin
Fargo, ND
701/281-3390
Software support

Planet BMUG
Berkeley, CA
510/849-2684
Gateways to other BBSs

Prostar
Auburn, WA
206/941-0317
Lots of games

Radio Daze
Mishawaka, IN
219/256-2255
International access, lots of shareware

Seaside
Santa Barbara, CA
805/964-4766
ASP-certified BBS

Software Creations
Clinton, MA
508/368-7139
Home for hot computer maker Apogee

Sound of Music
Oceanside, NY
516/536-8723
Lots of shareware product support and international traffic

Space BBS
Menlo Park, CA
415/323-4193
Internet, Usenet, many BBS echoes

Totem Pole
Flint, MI
313/238-1178
Large file collection

24th Street Exchange
Sacramento, CA
916/448-2483
ASP-certified BBS

U.S.A. BBS
Little Rock, AR
501/753-8575
Internet access

Westside
Los Angeles, CA
213/933-4050
Lots of shareware

Windows On Line
Danville, CA
510/736-8343
First stop for Windows shareware

Wizard's Gate BBS
Columbus, OH
614/224-1635
ASP-certified board

Online Services

Major Online Services Where You'll Find Shareware

America Online
8619 Westwood Center Drive
Vienna, VA 22182-2285
800/827-6364 (voice)

CompuServe Information Service
5000 Arlington Centre Blvd.
Columbus, OH 43220
614/457-8600 (voice)

Delphi Internet Services Corp.
1030 Massachusetts Ave.
Cambridge, MA 02138
800/695-4005 (voice)

General Electric Information Service (GEnie)
401 N. Washington St.
Rockville, MD 20850
800/638-9636 (voice)

Prodigy Services Co.
445 Hamilton Ave.
White Plains, NY 10601
800/776-3449 (voice)

Online Services that Offer Internet Access

a2i Communications
1211 Park Ave., Suite 202
San Jose, CA 95126
408/293-9010 or 408/293-9020, both modem;
type **GUEST** when you log on

Delphi Internet Services Corp.
1030 Massachusetts Ave.
Cambridge, MA 02138
800-695-4005 (voice)

HoloNet
Information Access Technologies
46 Shattuck Square, Suite 11
Berkeley, CA 94704
510/704-0160 (voice)
510/704-8019 (fax)
510/704-1058 (modem)

Internet address: info@holonet.net (automated);
support@holonet.net (human)

Performance Systems International, Inc.
510 Huntmar Park Dr.
Herndon, PA 22070
800/827-7482 (voice)
703/904-1207 (fax)

Portal
20863 Stevens Creek Blvd., Suite 200
Cupertino, CA 95014
408/973-9111 (voice)
408/725-1580 (fax)

Long-Distance Calling Services that Offer Cheap Ways to Call Out-of-Town BBSs

Global Access
G-A Technologies, Inc.
P.O. Box 31474
Charlotte, NC 28231
800/377-3282 (voice)
704/334-9030 (bbs)

PC-Pursuit
SprintNet
12490 Sunrise Valley Dr.
Reston, VA 22096
800/736-1130 (voice)

Index

J

K

L

X

To Install the Programs

The programs that accompany this book are contained on two disks in compressed self-extracting format. A hard disk is required for installation. Disk #1 has the Windows-based programs and the Windows-based installation program, INSTALL. (Disk #2 also has a few Windows-based programs.) INSTALL will prompt you when to switch disks.

To install the Windows-based programs, do the following:

1. Insert Disk #1 into the appropriate drive.

2. From the Windows Program Manager run **B:INSTALL** (substitute the appropriate drive letter for B:).

3. Follow the prompts on the screen. Be sure to use the default subdirectory name of \SWBUS so the DOS-based programs installed later will work correctly.

4. When prompted, place Disk #2 in the appropriate drive to complete the installation process.

5. At your option, INSTALL will now execute "DOSINS," the installation program for the DOS-based software. These files must also be installed for all the the Windows-based program to work.

Note: If you bypass DOSINS now, you can still run it later.

To install the DOS-based programs, do the following:

1. Insert Disk #2 into the appropriate drive.

2. From the DOS prompt type **B:DOSINS** (substitute the appropriate drive letter on your system for B:).

3. Follow the prompts on the screen. Be sure to specify the correct SOURCE and TARGET disk. The SOURCE disk is the drive letter you are installing FROM and the TARGET is the drive letter you are installing TO.

4. After you have made your selection, press F10 to continue.

5. When the installation procedure is complete press ESC to return to the DOS prompt.

6. Now type **SWBMENU** for a customized DOS menu.

Note: Some of the software may require additional configuration.

Caution: Some of the programs on the disks, like TickleX, require large amounts of memory to run. If you encounter a problem running any of the programs, reboot your computer using a boot disk (which can be created by inserting a blank disk in drive A and typing **SYS A:**). *Once you've freed up enough memory, the programs should run fine.*

Documentation

Instructions for using the software are contained in documentation files that accompany some of the programs. These instruction files have different names. They're often named DOC.TXT or

INFO.DOC or MANUAL.DOC. After you unZip and/or install these programs, look for the files that end with .DOC to locate the documentation.

You can view and print the documentation from a selection in SWBMENU or from icons in the Windows Program Manager Group, Business Shareware.

Note: These programs are the work of individual shareware authors not associated with Osborne/McGraw-Hill. If you decide to continue using these programs beyond a trial period, you are obligated to pay the author the requested software registration fee. These programs are not free. And since many of these authors make their living via shareware channels, please be considerate and reimburse them for their work!

You will find information on contacting the software authors in the files accompanying their respective programs. Look in the documentation file or in an accompanying file called REGISTER.TXT, VENDOR.DOC, or some variation of those names. These files will contain the name of the author, his or her address and other contact information, as well as details on registering the software. Once you mail in your payment for the software, you will receive verification of registration and technical support for the product.

Note: Tech support for these programs is provided solely by the programs' authors. Contact names and registration information for the software can be found in the VENDOR.DOC and REGISTER.TXT files that accompany the program, or else in the software's documentation file. Please do not contact either Osborne/McGraw-Hill or the authors of this book for technical support for any program contained on the disks. Pay the program's authors, and they'll support you. If you have problems with the installation of the programs or with the disk media, call Osborne/McGraw-Hill at (800) 227-0900 for a replacement disk.

Limited Warranty

Osborne/McGraw-Hill warrants the physical disks enclosed herein to be free of defects in materials and workmanship for a period of sixty days from the purchase date. If Osborne/McGraw-Hill receives written notification within the warranty period of defects in materials or workmanship, and such notification is determined by Osborne/McGraw-Hill to be correct, Osborne/McGraw-Hill will replace the defective disks.

The entire and exclusive liability and remedy for breach of this Limited Warranty shall be limited to replacement of defective disks and shall not include or extend to any claim for or right to cover any other damages, including but not limited to, loss of profit, data, or use of the software, or special, incidental, or consequential damages or other similar claims, even if Osborne/McGraw-Hill has been specifically advised of the possibility of such damages. In no event will Osborne/McGraw-Hill's liability for any damages to you or any other person ever exceed the lower of the suggested list price or actual price paid for the license to use the software, regardless of any form of the claim.

OSBORNE, A DIVISION OF McGRAW-HILL, INC., SPECIFICALLY DISCLAIMS ALL OTHER WARRANTIES, EXPRESS OR IMPLIED, INCLUDING, BUT NOT LIMITED TO, ANY IMPLIED WARRANTY OF MERCHANTABILITY OR FITNESS FOR A PARTICULAR PURPOSE. Specifically, Osborne/McGraw-Hill makes no representation or warranty that the software is fit for any particular purpose, and any implied warranty of merchantability is limited to the sixty-day duration of the Limited Warranty covering the physical disks only (and not the software), and is otherwise expressly and specifically disclaimed.

This limited warranty gives you specific legal rights; you may have others which may vary from state to state. Some states do not allow the exclusion of incidental or consequential damages, or the limitation on how long an implied warranty lasts, so some of the above may not apply to you.

About the Software That Accompanies This Book

We've included a collection of shareware programs on the disks that accompany this book. These are some of the best and most useful shareware programs around. We think you'll enjoy trying them out—and will find them beneficial. In fact, some of these are the most frequently downloaded Windows and DOS programs from computer bulletin boards and online services. On the disks you'll find the following Windows programs:

▶ Above & Beyond (ABV30.EXE)—A spiffy personal information manager that runs under Windows. Schedules your appointments, keeps your notes and phone book, and much more.

▶ WizManager (WIZMGR15.EXE)—An ultra-cool Windows utility that will add a button bar to your Program Manager to let you perform file maintenance tasks like directory sorts and file moving from within the Program Manager.

▶ Drag and Zip (DRGZIP40.EXE)—A Windows utility to help Zip and Unzip downloaded files. All you have to do is point and click.

▶ PKZIP & PKUNZIP (PKZ204G.EXE & PKUNZIP.EXE)—The world's most popular shareware download. The indispensable file compression and archive utilities that all online services and BBSs use.

▶ Reminder (RM-13F.EXE)—This program will help you stick yellow reminder notes that are like electronic versions of 3M Post-It notes on your Windows application screens. Remind yourself to call the dentist, make your lunch appointments on time, and return phone calls.

▶ WinUpD8R (UPD8R-21.EXE)—A Windows utility that helps you keep hard disk directories and files updated and in sync when there are two or more PCs in your life (like your laptop, office PC, and home PC).

▶ A Project/Event Planner (APLANR24.EXE)—This popular Windows project planner will assist you in organizing projects no matter how complex. Schedule jobs, meetings, employee assignments and everything else needed to get the project done.

You'll also find the following DOS programs:

▶ TickleX (TICK-X.EXE)—A DOS-based personal information manager and scheduler that includes a full-screen calendar with weekly and monthly views, and reminders. Run it as a regular application or as a memory-resident one.

▶ Viruscan (SCN200.EXE)—McAfee's popular virus scanner. Run it on your hard disk regularly and on shareware after you download it to ensure it's virus-free. This version of SCAN also includes the "clean" command for removing viruses.

▶ Telix (TLX322-1.EXE, TLX322-2.EXE, TLX322-3.EXE, TLX322-4.EXE)—A popular communications program for calling BBSs and online services. Telix will probably work better than the program that came with your modem when you bought it.

Technical Support
No Longer Available